Regionalism and Party Politics in Canada

Edited by

Lisa Young and Keith Archer

OXFORD

UNIVERSITY PRESS

OXFORD

UNIVERSITY PRESS

70 Wynford Drive, Don Mills, Ontario M3C 1J9
www.oup.com/ca.

Oxford University Press is a department of the University of Oxford.
It furthers the University's objective of excellence in research, scholarship,
and education by publishing worldwide in

Oxford New York

Athens Auckland Bangkok Bogotá Buenos Aires Cape Town
Chennai Dar es Salaam Delhi Florence Hong Kong Istanbul Karachi
Kolkata Kuala Lumpur Madrid Melbourne Mexico City Mumbai Nairobi
Paris São Paulo Shanghai Singapore Taipei Tokyo Toronto Warsaw

with associated companies in Berlin Ibadan

Oxford is a trade mark of Oxford University Press
in the UK and in certain other countries

Published in Canada
by Oxford University Press

National Library of Canada Cataloguing in Publication Data
Main entry under title:
Regionalism and party politics in Canada

Includes bibliographical references and index.
ISBN 0–19–541599–X

1. Political parties—Canada. 2. Regionalism—Canada.
I. Young, Lisa II. Archer, Keith, 1955–

JL195.R43 2001   324.271   C2001–901437–6

Cover Design: Peter Barata
Cover Image: Pal Hermansen/Stone

1 2 3 4 - 05 04 03 02
This book is printed on permanent (acid-free) paper ∞.
Printed in Canada

Contents

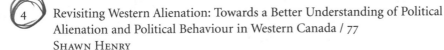

Acknowledgements

This book benefited from the assistance of many individuals and organizations. It originated from a conference organized by Lisa Young, Keith Archer, and Tom Langford at the University of Calgary in the Spring of 1999. The conference invited papers that explored the changing character of party competition and party alignment in Canada from a variety of theoretical and methodological perspectives, all of which centred to a greater or lesser degree on the character of regionalism. The conference was supported by the University Research Grants Committee and the Special Projects Fund of the University of Calgary. Additional financial support was provided by the Faculty of Social Sciences, the Department of Political Science, and the Department of Sociology at the University of Calgary. We also received support from the office of the United States Consulate in Calgary, with particular support from then-US Consul General Lisa Bobbie Schreiber Hughes, and from Betty Rive of the United States Information Service. The conference proved both lively and enjoyable, for which we are grateful to our sponsors.

The conference itself was organized in honour of Dr Mildred Schwartz, and provided an opportunity to reflect on her remarkable career, which began with an appointment in Sociology at the University of Calgary at a time when the university was still a branch of the University of Alberta. A number of colleagues participated in the conference in a variety of ways, and we would like to acknowledge their contribution. They include Rainer Knopff, Roger Gibbins, and Ted Morton of the University of Calgary; Lynda Erickson of Simon Fraser University; Ken Carty of the University of British Columbia; Fred Engelmann of the University of Alberta; and Richard Vengroff of the University of Connecticut.

We received administrative and editorial assistance from a variety of individuals, including Jennifer Stewart, Kari Roberts, Andrea Lynch, Reagan Petrie, Judi Powell, and Tracey Rancy, all of the University of Calgary. In addition, it was a pleasure to work with Laura Macleod and Len Husband of Oxford University Press in the final preparation of the manuscript.

We also wish to acknowledge the efforts of the authors of the various chapters. The conference papers were written to a tight time frame, in the context of significant changes occurring in the Canadian party system. In addition, we requested a number of revisions that the authors invariably handled with care, speed, and good humour.

Finally, we are indebted to Mildred Schwartz, both for her pioneering research on regionalism and party politics in Canada, and also for allowing us to hold the conference in her honour. At the time of the conference, Mildred held a Fulbright visiting fellowship at the University of Calgary. What might have been a time of relatively quiet reflection and writing in fact turned out to be an opportunity to revisit her work *Politics and Territory: The Sociology of Regional Persistence in Canada*, which had been published a quarter century previously, amidst the swirl of activity that invariably accompanies such a conference. The demands we placed on Mildred during this time far exceeded what one might reasonably expect from a host. Nonetheless, Mildred responded with exceptional patience, and considerable hard work, to ensure that the conference and subsequently the book were completed to high standards. Like many scholarly leaders, Mildred showed herself to be selfless and accommodating of the needs of others. Her presence on our campus, albeit briefly, was a wonderful reminder that scholary excellence is built upon hard work, rigorous critical scrutiny, attention to detail, and an attitude of collegial respect. For all that, we shall remain in her debt.

Foreword: Revisiting Regionalism and Political Parties

Mildred A. Schwartz

To be named the first Thomas O. Enders Fellow, to spend the fellowship period at the University of Calgary, and to have a conference organized in recognition of my work on regionalism and party politics were truly an overwhelming combination. These events of 1999 provided an unusual opportunity to bring together my interests in social and political issues affecting Canada and the United States in the setting where those interests germinated. But the ways in which the two honours touch my personal and professional life were far beyond anything you could imagine.

I came to Calgary for the first time thirty-nine years ago. I had been working in Toronto after finishing course work at Columbia and had only recently decided to complete the Ph.D. Hired, sight unseen, as an assistant professor in sociology, I experienced all the terrors of a totally untried teacher, facing students in introductory sociology, social psychology, social stratification, and political sociology. I learned how to put together a new course, stand before classes of mystified undergraduates, write exams, and grade essays.

To me, Alberta was an unknown territory. Of course, I knew that Alberta was home to the United Farmers and Social Credit. What I had no way of knowing was how quickly being in Alberta would determine career-long interests in regionalism and political parties. Even now, the United Farmers and Social Credit are part of my ongoing research in protest parties and movements. There may be some who arrive in Alberta and see it as no different from other parts of Canada. But it did not take long for me to realize, Dorothy-like, that, 'Toto, I have a feeling we're not in Ontario anymore.'

I wrote my dissertation during my two years in Calgary. I would go home every evening, prepare a quick dinner, and immediately turn to it. Fortunately, I was able to draw on many resources. Shortly after arriving, I had met Fred Engelmann, who had suggested that we collaborate on a book about Canadian political parties, the first of two we would write together.[1] Fred was always available to teach me about politics and to be a sounding board for my ideas about political science. His wife, Mary Engelmann, helped me by putting together the countless tables that went into the appendix of the dissertation.

The university library, perhaps more modest then than many of our own personal libraries today, was housed in the basement of what is now the administration building. (At that time, it was one of only two buildings on campus.) Luckily, Lois Carrier (who also became my good friend) was the reference librarian. She helped me immeasurably by obtaining all the books on which I depended through the wonders of inter-library loan. Gene Oetting, then in the psychology department, advised me on data analysis. Computations were done, free of charge, at the computer centre. Perhaps even more startling to recall in today's age of personal computers, when I cannot tell you the last time I had any secretarial help, the university provided typed drafts of the dissertation, including its final version. I will always have fond memories of Elise Wittig, who supervised typing services.

The final product, which some of you know as *Public Opinion and Canadian Identity*,[2] examined how Canadians viewed their nation from the 1940s into the 1960s. I found region and ethnicity to be the two critical factors shaping those views. Regionalism as a unique outlook had its basis, I wrote, in 'the settlement of distinct social or ethnic groups, the development of regional subcultures through isolation, or the economic conditions peculiar to an area'.[3] I then turned to the role of political parties because, I argued, 'It is political parties in a heterogeneous society which may overcome the critical cleavages and help build a sense of national identity.'[4] In fact, my findings reflected the political and partisan difficulties of developing any broad-based sense of nationhood.

Calgary was at that time a place in flux. The university had recently changed its status from a teacher's college to a branch campus of the University of Alberta, and already, there were signs that the move to greater autonomy could not be held back. Change is always exciting, but it is also disturbing. There were a number of people trying to carve out their turf who were easily threatened, even by a relatively naïve assistant professor without a Ph.D. I was subject to unexpected harassment from people much my senior, who told to me to my face that I was a pushy Jew and, behind my back, told students that girls know nothing about politics. As a result, and like many other junior faculty at the time, I wanted to leave Calgary as soon as I could. The only way I could do that, I recognized, was to write my way out. So, even negative experiences produced benefits. I completed my dissertation, began work with Fred on our first book, wrote two articles, and, as Tom Langford pointed out to me recently, established a productive style that has helped throughout my career.

After moving to Chicago, I did not forget my concerns with Canadian regionalism nor lose my sense that *Public Opinion and Canadian Identity* did not give regionalism the full attention it warranted. I then welcomed the opportunity to begin a new project, originally undertaken as a study of the 1965 election, with John Meisel, Philip Converse, Maurice Pinard, and Peter Regenstreif. Although I was not completely successful in convincing my collaborators of the merit of what I wanted to study, the compromises we made still allowed me to return to the theme of regionalism. One final product, and my sole responsibility, became *Politics and Territory*,[5] an empirical examination of the forces of regionalism and the ways in which they are mediated by partisan attachments. I began with great confidence by stating that 'the spatial makeup of Canada compounds every critical social and political problem the country faces'.[6] Regionalism was defined as the 'manifestation of politically mobilized territorial cleavages'.[7] I found the role of political parties to be complex, often constrained in the ways it could hold in check regional cleavages and sometimes even enhancing those cleavages.

The book had a difficult journey to publication and then received a fairly critical reading from Canadian social scientists. It appeared at a time when class divisions, whether from a classical economic or a Marxist perspective, were the favoured analytical concept and regionalism was trivialized.[8] But a class-centred interpretation ran counter to my own findings. Regardless of predictions to the contrary, regionalism was not a declining force.

It was not until the 1990s that I came, once again, to seriously address issues of regionalism. I did this now in the context of constitution building and drew on the work of my dissertation adviser, Juan J. Linz.[9] For the first time I was prepared to spell out in some detail my theoretical approach to regionalism and to address some of the issues raised by critics. For example, when I described how important life in Alberta was to my understanding of regionalism, that might suggest that regions were synonymous with provinces. While it is true that I often defined regions by their provincial boundaries, that was never the whole story. My point was always that regions are more than just political units.[10] One way to see the difference is to contrast regionalism with federalism. Here I quote from my own recent writing:

> As a system of government, federalism rests between the polarities of centralization and decentralization, depending on the powers and resources allocated to the central government compared to its constituent parts. . . . Regionalism is located along a different axis of organization: one that pulls regions between autonomy and dependence. Federalism determines the form by which a country is governed; regionalism determines how its interests are divided.[11]

Regionalism has its origins in three kinds of experiences. First, regions are opportunity structures, shaped by past experiences that lead to economic disparities. Out of these differences, regionalism emerges. It is reflected, for example, in the actions of Prairie farmers when they unite against policies of the central government.

Second, regions are systems of power, whose operation leads to differences among them. These power differentials can exist even when they are not formally institutionalized under a federal system of government. They become another source of regionalism, manifested, for example, in the way Premier Lucien Bouchard set up an 'us versus them' dichotomy between Quebec and the rest of Canada.

Third, regions are bounded cultures, 'in which traditions and values persist over time through the socialization of residents'.[12] Despite expectations that modernity has homogenizing effects, culture can have remarkable tenacity. Regionalism, then, has cultural roots. Even beer drinkers are cultural carriers, with taste buds favouring heavier brews in the East and lighter ones as they move west.

Culture is perhaps the most contentious element of regionalism because it is often viewed as the agent for turning region into regionalism. The issue becomes all the more troublesome when, for example, a Canadian government proposal for constitutional reform contains the statement that 'the reality of contemporary politics is that *provinces and territories, and not regions*, are basic to our sense of community and identity'.[13] This statement errs in confusing the political reality of provinces with the sociological complexity of regions, even when they have the same geographic boundaries, and then goes on to compound the error by basing identity on the former. Today, in fact, I would not place much weight on the importance of regional self-identification. As I wrote earlier, regional

> self-identifications remain a strong link with the concept of regional cultures, but their expression cannot be taken as a *sine qua non* of regionalism. . . . a culture exists in the behavioural manifestations of common norms and values; it does not require that they be consciously articulated.[14]

None of this is to say that I am completely satisfied with my past work on regionalism and politics. Nor is it likely that I will go further with it now. Yet I recognize areas where work is clearly needed. In general terms, they relate to the changing meanings of regionalism, since regionalism is no more likely than other social phenomena to remain fixed over time.

One critical area of study concerns the definition of regional boundaries, including the likelihood that definitions can vary depending on the interests involved and the time when regions are named. For example, Peter Trubowitz has argued that recent difficulties in establishing a bipartisan foreign policy in the United States are strongly tied to changes in regionalism.[15] One difficulty relates to partisan realignments, in which the Republican party has become strong in the Sun Belt. The second arises from conflicting regional interests, in which the Sun Belt is more likely to favour military spending and free trade. All of this is associated with an underlying shift in regional definitions. Previously, it was the Deep South that was distinctive, made up of states shaped by their experiences in the Civil War and its aftermath. Today, it is the Sun Belt that has grown in importance, formed by new patterns of migration and new kinds of economic developments.

Trubowitz's example illustrates the way regionalism can be affected by the changing demographic, economic, and political status of regions. Alberta provides a particularly striking example of an area that has undergone such changes. The question that remains is how Alberta's new status is reflected in current developments in regionalism.

Another area that I feel deserves further study is the processes through which regional cultures develop and change. Seymour Martin Lipset,[16] for example, now emphasizes culture as the attribute that best explains differences between Canada and the United States. When he revisited his definitive work on the CCF in Saskatchewan, *Agrarian Society*,[17] he explained the presence of a viable social democratic party in Canada and its absence in the United States by the impact of a counter-revolutionary versus a revolutionary tradition. But, if culture is truly important, we need to know much more, not only of its origins, but also of its adaptations and its transmission through time and space.

Although I have suggested that it is unlikely I will return to the serious study of regionalism, I have great satisfaction in knowing that the topic remains of interest to others, including Harry Hiller[18] and Janine Brodie.[19]

My subsequent research has given much less overt attention to regionalism and more to political parties, especially from the perspective of organizational theory. Yet regional concerns are still present. My research on the Republican party of Illinois began out of curiosity about connections between national and state parties of the same name. Although the literature suggested that there was little connection between, for example, state legislatures and congressmen from the same party and district, that did not seem plausible to a student of Canadian politics. I was not surprised, therefore, to find many kinds of contacts among seemingly autonomous elements of the party, which led me to entitle the study, *The Party Network*.[20]

For the last several years, my major project has considered protest parties and movements. My principal focus is how these political organizations, facing hostile environments, base their continuity on strategies for changing themselves. And where would I begin to look for such parties and movements, if not in the four western Canadian provinces as well as four comparable western and midwestern American states? In this case, my research is not a comparison among regions but a way of using known regional variations to select areas prone to political protest. In addition, I am in the early stages of research on the formation of cross-border ties associated with NAFTA. Here again, I pay close attention to regional interests as they define interests and affect transnational ties. In summary, then, the interests that were first formed here in Calgary many years ago continue to generate new research problems and new themes about which to write.

My life has been a reminder of the old Yiddish expression, 'as man lebt, delebt man'—to live is to live through (experiences). The saying has many connotations. It is, for one thing, future-oriented. It implies some sense of reward out of living itself. Yet there are also negative connotations, involving an expectation that one will have to live through bad experiences as well as good ones. But that's the point of survival—living through what life brings to arrive at a greater appreciation of one's humanity and mortality.

Four years ago I was diagnosed with multiple myeloma and, after being put into remission, treated with an autologous stem cell transplant. The procedure involved the removal of stem cells, the most elemental component of the blood system. Then I was hospitalized and given high doses of chemotherapy to kill my bone marrow, so that I was technically close to death. Finally, my stem cells were reinfused into my blood stream with the expectation that they would begin reconstructing my marrow along with other blood cells. Fortunately, everything went as expected and I am now clear of any sign of disease.

The transplant has had profound effects on me. Although I had no stigmata to indicate how drastically my body had been treated, I experienced something akin to rebirth. At times I would look in the mirror and not quite recognize myself. When I first had requests for participation in meetings (and as a sign of my own hopefulness, I always said yes), I responded with secret amusement. Who was being asked, I wondered, some ghostly figure who wasn't quite of this world? As I write, it is three years since the transplant and, along with renewed energy, the residue of my medical experience remains. It gives a new sense of urgency to everything I do, a new appreciation as I awake each day, and a new desire to connect with others. The opportunity to come back to Calgary as an Enders Fellow and to participate in the wonderful conference that yielded the papers in this book was an incredibly moving experience. I accepted these honours not only as a recognition of past work but as a sign of confidence that the best is still to come. You understand now what I meant when I said, '*as man lebt, delebt man*'.

NOTES

1. Frederick C. Engelmann and Mildred A. Schwartz, *Political Parties and the Canadian Social Structure* (Scarborough, Ont.: Prentice Hall, 1967); Frederick C. Engelmann and Mildred A. Schwartz, *Canadian Political Parties: Origin, Character, Impact* (Scarborough, Ont.: Prentice Hall, 1975).

2. Mildred A. Schwartz, *Public Opinion and Canadian Identity* (Berkeley: University of California Press, 1967).

3. Ibid., 146.

4. Ibid., 127.

5. Mildred A. Schwartz, *Politics and Territory: The Sociology of Regional Persistence in Canada* (Montreal: McGill-Queen's University Press, 1974).

6. Ibid., 1.

7. Ibid., 20.

8. As explained by Patricia Marshak, 'The Two Concepts of Canadian Regionalism', *Journal of Canadian Studies* 15 (Summer 1980) and Janine Brodie, 'The Concept of Region in Canadian Politics' in *Federalism and Political Community: Essays in Honour of Donald Smiley*, David P. Sugarman and Reg Whittaker, eds (Peterborough, Ont.: Broadview Press, 1989).

9. Juan J. Linz and Amando de Miguel, 'Within-Nation Differences and Comparisons: The Eight Spains' in *Comparing Nations: The Uses of Quantitative Data in Cross-National Research*, Richard L. Merritt and Stein Rokkan, eds (New Haven: Yale University Press, 1966).

10. Brodie, 'The Concept of Region', 36.

11. Mildred A. Schwartz, 'Regionalism and Canadian Constitution Building' in *Change and Impact: Essays in Canadian Social Sciences*, Sally Zerker, ed. (Jerusalem: The Magnes Press, 1994), 55–6.

12. Mildred A. Schwartz, 'Regions and Regionalism in Canada' in *Politics, Society and Democracy: Comparative Studies*, H.E. Chehabi and Alfred Stepan, eds (Boulder, Colo.: Westview Press, 1995), 155.

13. Government of Canada, *Shaping Canada's Future Together: Proposals* (Ottawa: Minister of Supply and Services, 1991), 18. (Emphasis in original.)

14. Schwartz, 'Regionalism and Canadian Constitution Building', 58–9.

15. Peter Trubowitz, *Defining the National Interest: Conflict and Change in American Higher Education* (Chicago: University of Chicago Press, 1998).

16. Seymour Martin Lipset, *Continental Divide* (New York: Routledge, 1990).

17. Seymour Martin Lipset, *Agrarian Socialism* (New York: Doubleday, 1968).

18. Harry H. Hiller, *Canadian Society: A Macro Analysis*, 2nd ed. (Scarborough, Ont.: Prentice Hall, 1991).

19. Janine Brodie, *The Political Economy of Canadian Regionalism* (Toronto: Harcourt Brace Jovanovich, 1990).

20. Mildred A. Schwartz, *The Party Network: The Robust Organization of Illinois Republicans* (Madison: University of Wisconsin Press, 1990).

Introduction

Lisa Young, Jennifer Stewart, and Keith Archer

Mildred Schwartz and the Study of Regionalism in Canada

Canada's party system lost its pan-Canadian veneer in the 1990s. The elections of 1993, 1997, and 2000 produced a distribution of seats in the House of Commons with stronger regional parties, and more distinctive regional blocks of MPs from hitherto national parties, than Canadians had seen for generations. The 2000 federal election resulted in an electoral map dominated by the Canadian Alliance from Winnipeg west, and by the Liberal party from Winnipeg east, with Quebec divided between the Liberals and the Bloc Québécois. On the surface, at least, Canadian politics has seldom been so regionalized.

The political divisions that have been laid bare through the party system in the 1990s have long formed a part of Canada's political character. The electoral system, which for generations acted to ameliorate these divisions, in the 1990s acted instead to reinforce them. The regional divisions and identities themselves have a long history.

The causes and consequences of regionalism's persistence in Canadian politics have long interested students of the Canadian party system. One notable contribution to that scholarship was a book, entitled *Politics and Territory: The Sociology of Regional Persistence in Canada*, written by Mildred Schwartz in 1974. On the twenty-fifth anniversary of the publication of that book, and in celebration of her appointment in 1999 as the Thomas O. Enders Fellow at the University of Calgary, a conference was held to reflect on the insights of Schwartz's analysis in the context of the changing party system, and particularly its increased regionalization. This book is a result of that conference.

When she published the classic work *Politics and Territory*, Mildred Schwartz challenged social scientists studying Canada to examine the influence of region and regionalism on Canadian social and political life. As the articles gathered together in this volume demonstrate, this challenge was taken up by sociologists, political scientists, and political geographers interested in Canada. *Politics and Territory* began a scholarly conversation in these disciplines that focused on making theoretical and empirical sense of region as a facet of Canadian social and political organization.

Politics and Territory argued that Canada has continued to experience significant regional divisions in its party system because of the sustained and systematic differences existing among the peoples of the different regions. Different settlement patterns, distinctive group memberships, and particularized regional cultures are all factors in the persistence of regionalism in Canada, according to this groundbreaking work. Schwartz's exploration of the roots of regionalized patterns in Canadian party politics remains relevant today. Certainly, the outcome of the three most recent Canadian federal elections appears to suggest that, if anything, regionalism is growing in importance in Canadian politics, as the party system appears to be growing ever more fragmented along regional lines. That said, many of the contributions to this volume suggest that, although regionalism remains important to Canadian political life, it is not as simple a structuring force as it appears on the surface.

Regionalism and the Contemporary Canadian Party System

In *Politics and Territory*, Mildred Schwartz argued that where regional differences in party systems exist, 'we may assume underlying differences in political traditions and in the social, economic, and political problems that parties are called upon to handle'.[1] The empirical evidence presented in *Politics and Territory* makes it abundantly clear that the Canadian party system in the 1960s was characterized by substantial territorial differentiation. Despite their claims to being national, neither the Liberal nor the Conservative party was able, in elections held between 1921 and 1965, to consistently win at least 30 per cent of the popular vote in every region. Neither party treated all regions equitably in forming cabinets when in government. Consistency in voting behaviour (voting for the same party federally and provincially) was relatively high in Atlantic Canada, but decreased as one moved westward. Although support for a national party encouraged some voters to think in national rather than regional terms, Schwartz found that this nationalizing effect of parties was subordinate to the effect of region on voters' attitudes.[2]

The outcomes of the federal elections in 1993, 1997, and 2000 offer a unique opportunity to revisit Mildred Schwartz's account of regional differentiation in the Canadian party system. If there was evidence of regional differences in the party system in 1965, then the pattern of regional differentiation between 1993 and 2000 is overwhelming. In 1965, two national parties (the Liberals and the Conservatives) held 86 per cent of the seats in the House of Commons; between 1993 and 2000, the figures ranged from 58 per cent to 61 per cent. In 1965, the regional challengers to the major parties were the predominantly Western-based New Democratic Party with twenty-one seats, the Quebec-based Ralliement des Creditistes with nine seats, and the Alberta-based Social Credit party with five seats. In the 1990s, two regional parties formed the official opposition: the sovereignist Bloc Québécois after the 1993 election, and the Western-based Reform party/Canadian Alliance after the 1997 and 2000 elections. After the governing Liberals, these were the largest parties in Parliament.

Moreover, as William Cross notes in his contribution to this volume, it is now possible to identify different party systems operating in each region. Atlantic Canada, long characterized by two-party competition between the Liberals and Conservatives, since 1993 has belatedly embraced the three-party competition among Liberals, Conservatives, and New Democrats that prevailed in the rest of English Canada before 1993. In Quebec, the pattern of competition between Liberals and Conservatives was supplanted by competition between the Liberals and the BQ. With the rise of the sovereignist Bloc before the 1993 election, the pattern of competition in federal politics in Quebec came to resemble very closely the pattern of competition in the province's provincial politics. Just as in provincial elections, the sovereignist/federalist cleavage now dominates federal elections in Quebec in an explicit manner. In Ontario, three-party competition was obliterated in the 1990s, when the province emerged as a Liberal stronghold. The Liberals won all but two seats in Ontario in 1997, and all but three in 2000. Manitoba, on the boundary between East and West, was the only province in which four-way competition took place. In Saskatchewan, where the New Democrats and Conservatives were once dominant, three parties were competitive through the 1990s and 2000: Reform/Canadian Alliance, the NDP, and the Liberals. In Alberta during the same period, the pattern of single-party dominance persisted, but Reform/Canadian Alliance supplanted the Conservatives to dominate politics in the province; in British Columbia, traditional three-party competition was replaced by a two-party contest between Reform/Canadian Alliance and the Liberals.

Can we attribute this increasingly differentiated pattern of regional political arrangement to growing social, economic, and political disparities between regions and a consequent rise of regional sentiment? To answer this, we can look to the two catalysts for change to the party system—the Bloc Québécois and the Western-based Reform party—and examine their roots in such disparities. Both appear, at least on the surface, to be products of growing regional impulses.

The Bloc Québécois manifests the most extreme variation of regionalism: the desire to secede. Since Confederation, Quebec has been the most distinctive region of Canada, with its distinctiveness rooted in the language, religion, and culture of its francophone majority. This distinctiveness, when coupled with the history of British conquest, has manifested itself in a Québécois nationalism. The modern variant of this nationalism emerged in the aftermath of the Quiet Revolution, and has taken the form of a political campaign to remove Quebec from the Canadian federation and launch an independent state. In 1976, the separatist Parti Québécois was first elected to govern Quebec. Nationalist sentiment in Quebec has increased since that time. In the first referendum on Quebec separation, in 1980, only 40 per cent of Quebeckers voted in favour; in the second referendum, in 1995, that figure rose to 49 per cent.

In part, the rise of the Bloc Québécois reflects growing support for sovereignty in Quebec. According to the Canadian Election Study team's account of the 1993 federal election, the Bloc attracted former Conservative voters who had defected from that party, but was also able to mobilize staunch sovereignist voters who had not participated in previous Canadian elections. Apparently, this group of committed sovereignists had refrained from participation in federal elections until a sovereignist party emerged as an alternative.

That said, it would be erroneous to attribute the emergence of the Bloc simply to a rise in sovereignist sentiment in Quebec. Rather, the party was formed and gained support in the aftermath of the failure of the Meech Lake Accord. The Accord, which was Prime Minister Brian Mulroney's attempt to bring Quebec back into the Canadian constitutional fold after the Constitution was patriated in 1982 without the approval of the government of Quebec, recognized Quebec as a 'distinct society'.[3] When Mulroney was unable to achieve the necessary ratification from all ten provincial legislatures and the Accord failed, several Conservative MPs from Quebec (including Lucien Bouchard, then a federal cabinet minister) left the Conservative caucus and went on to form the Bloc Québécois with the support of the provincial Parti Québécois.[4] In this sense, the party emerged in direct response to a political event, rather than as a grassroots manifestation of support for sovereignty. Nevertheless, the party would not have achieved the electoral support that it did had it not been for significant support for sovereignty among voters in Quebec.

When it first emerged in the late 1980s, the Reform party appeared to be a regional party. With support mainly from disaffected Conservatives disappointed by the Mulroney government, Reform rallied under the banner 'the West wants in' and constituted itself as an explicitly Western party. Like the Bloc, Reform catapulted to national prominence in the 1993 election, riding the wave of dissatisfaction with the Conservative government and the elite-driven constitutional politics of the Mulroney era.[5] After winning 52 seats in the 1993 election, the Reform party's leadership set its sights higher, seeking to expand the party's base of support sufficiently to allow it to form a government. This objective drove the campaign to disband Reform and replace it with the Canadian Alliance. We are left with the question of whether Reform, at least in its earlier incarnation, is best understood as a manifestation of growing regional sentiment in western Canada. In his contribution to this volume, David Laycock argues persuasively that Reform was more an ideological party than a regional one, even though its electoral success was limited by a suspicion outside the West that the party was essentially regional.

As Schwartz noted in 1974, the strength of regional attachments in Canada has meant that Canadian parties must struggle to win broad national support. Never in Canadian history has regional differentiation in the parties' support bases been so pronounced. Schwartz reminds us that even parties seeking to be national in scope can promote regionalism by acting as spokespersons for regional interests. This articulation of the interests of various regions may not be solely a matter of deliberate policy, she cautions, but may emerge from factors related to the party's supporters.[6] For example, the contemporary Liberal party may not deliberately set out to act as a party of Ontario, but its heavy reliance on Ontario voters will affect its actions so that it may become a party that defends Ontario interests.

This is the danger embedded in the highly regionalized contemporary party system. It is more relevant than ever to note Schwartz's observation that party politics not only reflects regionalism, but also perpetuates and feeds it. According to Schwartz, when parties are not evenly distributed across regions, 'then to the extent that they are avenues for channelling public demands, residents of different regions will have differential access to these means of influence. The results are another form of regional cleavage.[7] This observation is particularly apt in the aftermath of the 2000 federal election. In the days following the election, expressions of regional alienation and frustration were frequent in western Canada, as supporters of the Canadian Alliance saw their efforts to transform into a national party thwarted by the voters of Ontario (and, of course, the electoral system). With little representation in the national government, western Canadians' sense of alienation from and grievance with the federal government was likely to grow, while the federal government found itself without adequate grounding in the region to address these concerns.

Reading *Politics and Territory* now, we can see that Mildred Schwartz's analysis of the interplay of regionalism and party politics foreshadowed the contemporary situation. Regionalism has always been a significant force in Canada, and we have looked to national political parties to hold the country together despite its disintegrative tendencies. Over twenty years ago, Schwartz concluded that the strength of territorial claims and the weakness of partisan ties in Canada precluded a national politics in which region did not form the central cleavage. In subsequent years, our ties to parties have only grown weaker, with the possible exception of attachments to the regionally based Canadian Alliance and the Bloc Québécois. National parties have retreated to regional strongholds. If Schwartz's analysis continues to hold, the unprecedented regionalization of the current party system will strengthen regional attachments at the expense of national ones, and regionalism will once again be on the rise.

The Elusive Character of Canadian Regionalism

The essays gathered in this volume pay tribute to Mildred Schwartz's scholarly legacy by trying to come to terms with the current character of Canadian regionalism. Contemporary Canadian regionalism is elusive in the sense that it cannot be attributed to simple economic inequalities, but rather reflects complex processes of historical grievance and present social construction. It is elusive in the sense that the constructions of region, such as 'the West', exist in the popular discourse, but do not in fact constitute homogeneous regional entities. And regionalism is elusive in the sense that it structures Canadian party competition even at a time when regional economic disparities and attitudinal differences appear to be waning.

Part I of this book is a consideration of how scholars can approach the study of regions conceptually. Writing from the perspective of very different disciplines, political geographer Munroe Eagles and sociologist Harry Hiller agree that regions are social constructions, invented and reinvented by the actions of people who inhabit them. In Part II, we move on to consider the character of contemporary Canadian regionalism. Looking at measures of political cynicism and discontent, Harold Clarke, Jon Pammett, and Marianne Stewart find regional differentiation in such measures decreasing, but in Chapter 4, Shawn Henry finds that regional alienation remains alive and well, mainly in Alberta, but also in British Columbia, Saskatchewan, and Atlantic

Canada. Barry Cooper weighs in on the question of Western alienation with an examination of the myths that animate regional identities.

In Part III of the book, four authors examine the apparent regionalization of the Canadian party system. In Chapter 6, William Cross sets the stage by considering the patterns of regionalization in the federal election campaigns of 1993 and 1997. In their studies of the Reform party, the Liberal party, and the NDP, David Laycock, Joseph Wearing, and David Stewart argue that these political parties are not regional parties, in the sense of parties acting primarily as agents for a particular region. Rather, the logic of political competition and the electoral system have forced parties to develop regional strongholds for the purpose of electoral success.

Finally, Part IV of the volume compares the Canadian experience with those of other countries, and considers the potential implications of globalization for Canadian regionalism. In Chapter 10, Hudson Meadwell provides an analysis of secessionist movements in modern democracies, noting that the Quebec secessionist movement is the strongest in this category. Meadwell attributes the success of this movement to the federal design of the Canadian state. In Chapter 11, Anthony Sayers presents a comparison of the impact of regionalism on political parties in Canada and Australia, arguing that Canadian institutions have channelled regional impulses in a way that encourages political parties to develop regional bases of support. In Chapter 12, Livianna Tossutti considers the implications of trends toward globalization for regional movements, focusing on Quebec and Northern Italy. She concludes that there is some evidence suggesting that trends toward globalization strengthen such regionalist movements but cautions that, particularly in the case of Quebec, there is also considerable evidence of traditional nationalism.

The chapters gathered in this volume are not a comprehensive overview of the study of regionalism in Canada, but they do demonstrate the diversity of intellectual perspectives being brought to bear on this persistent issue. The continuing salience of the study of regionalism for political scientists and sociologists in Canada is indicative of the scholarly legacy of Mildred Schwartz in both disciplines.

NOTES

1. Mildred A. Schwartz, *Politics and Territory: The Sociology of Regional Persistence in Canada* (Montreal: McGill-Queen's University Press, 1974), 16.

2. Schwartz, *Politics and Territory*, 289–97.

3. The Accord also fulfilled Quebec Premier Robert Bourassa's four other conditions: a constitutional veto for Quebec, limits to federal spending power, some control over immigration policy, and a formal voice for Quebec in Supreme Court appointments.

4. For a complete account of the rise of the Bloc, see R.K. Carty, William Cross, and Lisa Young, *Rebuilding Canadian Party Politics* (Vancouver: University of British Columbia Press, 2000), ch. 3.

5. For an account of the rise of Reform, see Carty et al., ch. 3.

6. Schwartz, *Politics and Territory*, 108–9.

7. Ibid., 16.

Part 1

Approaches to the Study of Regionalism

Introduction

The two chapters in this section focus on the question of how we should approach the study of regionalism. The authors are writing from the perspective of different disciplines: Munroe Eagles is a political geographer and Harry Hiller a sociologist. Despite their distinct disciplinary backgrounds and the different intellectual traditions on which they draw, both Eagles and Hiller argue that regions are social constructions and should be studied as such.

In his chapter, Eagles rejects the tradition of geographic determinism, which holds that Canada's regional cleavages stem inevitably from its large physical size and proximity to the United States. Instead, he argues that geography provides only the raw materials for regionalist mobilization. Region matters, in this view, only to the extent that it is a source of social and political mobilization. In this respect, Eagles' political ecology approach relies on understanding the local geographic context as a means of explaining the kinds of political movements that emerge from regions. Density of urbanization, industrialization, linguistic or ethnic minorities, or religious groups in a given locale will, he argues, influence the politicization of region. Eagles' ecological understanding of regionalist impulses also emphasizes the importance of governments and political actors in heightening the political and social importance of boundaries and borders.

In a similar vein, Harry Hiller argues that region is best understood as a social construction. He argues that within the discipline of sociology, region has tended to be under-theorized. Hiller notes that the publication of Mildred Schwartz's *Politics and Territory* 'threw the gauntlet down to Canadian sociologists to rediscover the role of region . . . and the response was mostly to use region as one variable among many in explaining behaviour.' Sociologists have often had difficulty dealing with region, Hiller suggests, because space was viewed simply as a setting for events rather than as something with its own explanatory value.

Drawing on the work of sociological theorists Anthony Giddens and Henri Lefebvre, Hiller describes regionalism as a product of social interaction in a geographic locale. This social interaction creates a local culture which, in turn, fosters a common view of region. According to Hiller, 'sharing a territory provides a basis for communality that potentially could be as powerful as class, gender, or race under the right conditions (the severest of which would be some kind of collective threat).' For Hiller, then, regionalism is an entirely social construction resulting from interaction among people sharing a common space.

Both of these accounts remind us that the regions and regionalisms that play such a crucial role in Canadian political life are not inevitable products of Canadian geography, nor is their character carved in stone. Rather, these regions and the regionalist sentiments that animate them have been constructed through a long process involving competing political élites, economic forces, and social interactions within the region.

Chapter 1

Political Geography and the Study of Regionalism

MUNROE EAGLES

If some countries have too much history, we have too much geography.
William Lyon Mackenzie King, June 1936

After a relatively long period of neglect and intellectual devaluation, in recent decades the perspective of political geography has enjoyed a renaissance. Resurgent academic interest is based on several intellectual and empirical factors, not the least of which has been the surprising and enduring strength of regional identities and regionalist politics, which have threatened to disrupt and even dismember many liberal democracies since the 1970s. The very existence of minority nationalist movements in those countries thought to have experienced modernization and social mobilization most thoroughly offered a challenge to the view that geography had been trumped by modernity. At the outset, therefore, it should be noted that political geography as an academic specialization has benefited from the persistence and even resurgence of regionalism in contemporary politics.

This chapter, however, explores the specific contribution of a political geographic approach to our understanding of regionalism. I will not attempt to be even-handed in this treatment; other chapters in this book will develop different, and valuable, theoretical perspectives that focus on factors other than geography. It is clear, however, that each of the 'competing' factors, such as culture and economics, has its own associated geographic dimension, and this makes it somewhat difficult to tease out political geographic perspectives from rival ones. Rather than attempt to 'claim' all of these as components of a geographic perspective (something that is tempting for geographers who emphasize the integrative nature of their discipline) this chapter instead concentrates on the value added by attending to some of the specifically geographic dimensions of regions and regionalism.[1]

First, however, it is important to review some issues concerning the conceptualization of regions and regionalism. This will establish the necessary but insufficient role of geography in the definition of regions. Geographic factors become raw materials that influence human settlement, interaction, identity, and ultimately politics. In the second section of the chapter, it will be argued that regionalism is a form of political mobilization best understood as a specific expression of the relationship between human beings and their environment. A case is advanced for a political ecological approach to regionalism that focuses on the relationship between politics and features of the larger geographic context. A number of concepts and tools from traditional political geographic/ecological analysis are introduced for analytical purposes. The primary focus is on the concepts of context and political mobilization, boundaries, the coexistence of multiple geographic scales, and the 'sense of place'. While these concepts can be employed in any political ecological analysis, arguably they have special applicability to the analysis of regionalism.

Conceptualizing Region and Regionalism: The Role of Geography

From a geographer's point of view, at least, regions are first and foremost spatial entities.[2] Acknowledging that regions are geographically defined territories does not take us very far, however, for any given space is divisible into an infinite number of possible regions. Partitioning space into regions is a human activity, reflecting the analytic interests of the investigator or the political interests of the individuals claiming to speak or act on behalf of the region concerned. For these reasons, even the simple identification of regions and the fixing of regional boundaries is far from a straightforward process. For many, 'region' connotes a territorial unit that is smaller than a state or province but larger than a single 'locality'. For others, 'region' denotes a specific level of government (as in the province of Ontario, for example). Still others use the term 'region' to refer to groups of countries (or parts of countries) sharing some attribute(s). Given the plethora of uses, it is not surprising that there is considerable confusion in the literature on Canadian regions and regionalism. As Garth Stevenson has put it, 'the term "region" is commonly used in a number of different ways, most of which seem quite irrelevant to the phenomenon which Canadian scholars are attempting to explain when they invoke the concept of "regionalism".[3]

Reduced to its minimum, a region is a unit that is definable on the basis of geographic difference, or variation, in something (anything). For various purposes geographers might define regions in terms of the incidence of disease, consumption of some commodity, average daily temperatures, soil types, or party support. A region is simply an area that is internally homogeneous according to some measure or measures. Understood this way, regions can be identified arithmetically, by using a number of statistical techniques and a set of small geographic building blocks from which larger regions can be built.[4] A set of regional boundaries that maximizes variation between units and minimizes variation within units, or that clusters units similar on a number of dimensions, will be the result. Many of the regions that result from such procedures will be geographically 'ugly' (non-compact, non-symmetrical, and so forth). Furthermore, these regions will be 'analytic' as opposed to 'real' categories, since the rationale for their existence is only in the mind of the cartographer who identified the boundaries. They need not, in other words, be perceptible or meaningful to their residents.

Many regions identified through such analytical practices will not be politically salient or significant. For regionalism to be considered important politically, under-lying geographic differences should regularly give rise to distinctive patterns of political behaviour or demands and expressions of discontent. As Mildred Schwartz has argued, 'We associate "regionalism" with situations of politically relevant divi-siveness and territorial cleavages, often accompanied by some consciousness on the part of residents that they have distinctive, regionally based interests.'[5] Regionalism, then, is defined as a political movement based on a defined geographic area that, on the basis of some sense of shared identity and/or shared political interests, regularly generates political demands (often for increased political autonomy or even politi-cal independence).

According to this conceptualization, regions are defined by their political distinc-tiveness, established inductively by looking for spatial variations in some political orientation or behaviour. This process is different in that it does not start with regional units defined by geography, demography, sociology, or any other feature and then seek to identify political consequences associated with these regions. The precise geography of regional units in this approach is derived from analyses of political life. A simplifying variation of this that has been popular in Canada has been to equate regions with provinces, or aggregations of provinces (as in 'the Maritimes', for exam-ple). A strong justification for this simplification is that provincial political élites are primarily responsible for the politicization of geographically based demands and for articulating underlying sentiments of regional discontent. As a result, according to Carl Hodge, regionalism has become 'provincialized' in this country.[6] However conve-nient the acceptance of provincial jurisdictions might be for analytic purposes, few are prepared to argue that these units are equally equipped to serve as all-purpose regions (that is, as internally homogeneous on all politically significant measures). As will be argued in the second section of this chapter, while provincial élites and the intergov-ernmental process may be central to the articulation of regional demands, it is nonetheless important to examine geographic variations in regionalist sentiment *within* provinces.

Regionalism depends in some measure on the activities and interests of the politi-cal actors who act in the name of a region's residents. The resources and capabilities that these actors can draw upon depends on the geographic endowments of the area, the characteristics and attitudinal orientations of the region's populace, and the insti-tutional structure within which these actors must operate. Endogenous geographic attributes are, therefore, only part of the equation of regional politics. Over time, the activities of political leaders, along with the effects of the institutional structures both within and beyond the region itself, will shape the nature of the region as a meaning-ful political unit. These processes have become the centrepiece of a revisionist politi-cal geography, sometimes called the 'new regional geography'. In this school of thought, the distinction between 'region' as a geographically bounded unit and the politics of regionalism becomes blurred. That is, the region is interpreted or defined largely as a product of human action and interaction. Regions are not conceptualized as containers to be statistically defined by spatial analysts and regional scientists in terms of their homogeneity on some measure. Rather, regions are thought of as evolving projects, the creation of human actors working with other residents and using the elements available in their geographically, historically, and institutionally defined environment.[7] According to Kevin Cox, in contrast to the traditional static approach to defining regions that is characteristic of spatial analysis and regional science, the new regional geography emphasizes the importance of context in shaping social life, territorial identities, and politics:

> Social life, including the economic, the cultural, and the political, always is situated, and the strategies people and organizations engage in, and the new structures of social relations they form and which serve to encapsulate their activities in the future, can be understood only in terms of the particular resources and rules, respectively available and operative, in particular contexts. These contexts can, of course, exist at a variety of geographic scales and are in a constant state of formation, transformation, and dissolution.[8]

Regions form, or do not form, according to human decisions and actions within a particular context, and geographic variations in the process of region-formation are of profound interest to political geographers.[9]

Before turning to a discussion of the various geographic factors that may influence the pattern of region formation, some brief reflections on the role of geography in regional politics are in order. The foregoing discussion implies that there are a number of possible roles for geography in conceptualizing region and understanding regionalism. In principle, the role of geographic factors can range from complete determinism, in which a particular political outcome is simply derived from a particular geographic foundation, to the other extreme, in which geographic factors are merely a minor influence on some political outcome. A range of alternative strategies is identifiable in between these two extremes.[10] A cautionary note about the inadequacies of geographic determinism is in order, for although few would defend geographical determinism in the abstract, its language occasionally creeps into the discussion of regionalism in Canada. Hints of it are to be found in Mackenzie King's lament about Canada having too much geography that opens this paper.

Probably the most familiar of such geographically determinist arguments come from geographers like André Siegfried, who contend that Canada's lack of centralization, weak national identity, and chronically fractious regional politics are the inevitable product of its physical location and regional diversity. According to Siegfried, 'the Canadian problem' stemmed from two features of its geography: 'From a geographical point of view, Canada is merely the northern extension of the United States. There is no natural boundary between the two countries, but merely a political frontier along the parallel of latitude. The very straightness of the boundary betrays its artificiality.'[11] The first aspect of Canada's geographic problem, then, was whether the nation could maintain its independence on a continent it cohabited with a culturally similar demographic giant. The second aspect of Canada's problem 'arises from its geological structure, and from the position in relation to one another, of its various regions'.[12] This diversity made the cultivation of a single 'centre of gravity' within the country difficult and, Siegfried argued, Canada's future was cast in doubt by its geography. Similarly, William Westfall has argued, 'The rigidity of Canada's physical features and the relative constancy of her climate mean that the regional structure of Canada is also rigid and constant. . . . Consequently, we have strong regional identities within a relatively weak nation-state.'[13]

Because the view that Canada's problem with regionalism is inevitable has an inherent plausibility and popularity, it is worth noting that others have seen an underlying unity in Canadian history that results from other aspects of its geography. In one of the most influential interpretations of Canadian economic history, for example, Harold Innis argued that Canada's development was profoundly influenced by the beaver and the country's geography. According to Innis, demand for beaver pelts in Europe, along with the animal's non-migratory nature and Aboriginal Canadians' interest in European manufactured goods, combined to shape the early commercial, transportation, and communication infrastructure of the country:

Canada emerged as a political entity with boundaries largely determined by the fur trade. These boundaries included a vast north temperate land area extending from the Atlantic to the Pacific and dominated by the Canadian Shield. *The present Dominion emerged not in spite of geography but because of it*. The significance of the fur trade consisted in its determination of the geographic framework. Later economic developments were profoundly influenced by this background.[14]

As trappers depleted the supply of beavers, the frontier was pushed westward. The high costs of opening up the West for the fur trade made the development of commercial monopolies attractive, and these centralized economic organizations in turn paved the way for equally centralized political institutions after 1867. Of course, Innis acknowledged that the development of capitalism in Canada altered the staples-based economic imperatives and that subsequent political patterns were more complicated and less geographically determined than his staples theory allowed. Indeed much of the history of Canadian federalism entailed a dismantling of the federal pre-eminence guaranteed in the British North American Act, 1867. Yet, according to Innis, the cast of Canadian development was set early on, reflecting the imperatives of a succession of staples commodities and their exploitation.

The cautionary point to be made here is not that geography is unimportant in explaining Canadian history and politics, but rather that geography cannot be seen to determine any particular political or historical outcome. Nor does geography (nor can geographic analysis) provide any simplistic or objective set of regional containers that can be defined cartographically and then be assumed to have political consequences. However, geographic factors will influence virtually any political process or institution by providing individuals and political élites with the incentives and resources (the raw materials) for political mobilization. What is necessary is a perspective that appreciates the importance of geography in shaping human activities but does not construct this relationship deterministically. The next section will introduce the perspective of political ecology, a particular political-geographic approach that focuses on the interdependence of human beings and their geographic and socio-political settings.

The Political Ecology of Regionalism

Ecology, according to the *Oxford English Dictionary*, is defined as 'that branch of biology which deals with the relations of living organisms to their surroundings, habits, and modes of life, etc.'. By extension, political ecology is an approach to understanding any political phenomenon (attitudes, behaviours, organizations, institutions, and the like) by seeking to understand how that phenomenon is shaped by features of its geographic environment. While the interdependence of geography and politics has long been recognized, among the first scholars to explicate systematically an ecological perspective on politics (and on international relations in particular) were Margaret and Harold Sprout. Geography was at the core of their conception of political ecology:

> Geographic quality is central to the ecological perspective and to any scheme for analysis of ecological relationships. This is so because systematic analysis confirms the common-sense observation that the distribution and arrangement of phenomena upon the earth's surface are always, or nearly always, related significantly to what people undertake and to what they accomplish. The ecological perspective and ecological theories bring the dimensions of location, distance, space, distribution, and configuration sharply into focus in many social contexts, not least in the context of politics in general. . . .[15]

While the Sprouts were interested primarily in the political ecology of international relations, the case for a political ecology of regionalism ought to be even more readily and easily made, given the centrality of geography to the constitution of regions. In addition to the list of geographic attributes mentioned by the Sprouts (including distance, location, and space), there are other qualities inherently related to the underlying geography of a region that influence its political life. This section will focus on four such factors: the importance of geographic contexts for political mobilization, a region's boundaries, questions of scale with respect to region, and the 'sense of place' that often forms in a region. A brief discussion of each of these will serve to illustrate the specific value added by a political-geographic perspective on regionalism.

1. Geographic Contexts and Political Mobilization

Perhaps the most important contributions that political geographers or political ecologists can make to the understanding of regionalism as a political movement comes as a result of the perspective's insistence on the importance for any type of political mobilization of features of the local context. An elementary assumption of this perspective is that any human behaviour, whether or not it is territorial in nature, will be influenced by features of the geographic context in which it occurs. John Agnew identifies three elements of 'place'—locale, location, and sense of place—that combine to explain its distinctive political life.[16] 'Locale' refers to the ways in which social relations—patterns of sociability and social interaction, and the like—are organized in the geographic setting. 'Location' refers to the kinds of social, economic, and political processes that organize life in the region and integrate it with processes operating at larger spatial scales. 'Sense of place' refers to the structure of feeling that results from the other two forms of place-specific norms and practices; it provides the 'glue' for place-based politics. According to Agnew's provocative argument, explanation in political science can only arise when the specific combination of these elements is understood. Abstract social categories such as class, status groups, and ethnic minorities are not in themselves responsible for political action. Instead, these factors become politically salient only as a result of political activity within particular contexts or places. As Agnew expresses it:

> Place is defined as the geographic context or locality in which agency interpellates social structure. Consequently, political behavior is viewed as the product of agency as structured by the historically constituted social contexts in which people live their lives—in a word, places.[17]

Place and contexts matter since they represent unique combinations of historically constituted relations and processes. To understand the political orientations and behaviours of individuals, including regionalism, political ecologists require information not only about the personal characteristics of residents but also about their neighbours, as well as the communication, economic and social environments within which individuals live, and data on traditions and institutions of the political setting.[18] Though Agnew illustrated his ecological perspective by using the example of Scottish nationalism, the general perspective is intended to be useful for understanding a wide variety of political phenomena. Place influences more than politics and can even affect phenomena that we might hypothesize to be entirely personal or at least spatially invariant. For example, Durkheim's classic *Suicide* demonstrated that there were social patterns related to the religious composition of the local community that helped to explain the incidence of this most profoundly personal action.[19] By the same token, one might expect women in Catholic Italy to confront similar social and political challenges and hence to adopt relatively uniform organizational and political responses. However, Judith Hellman's *Journeys Among Women* revels the deep contextual differences in the form and character of the women's movement in different regions of Italy.[20] Regardless of the nature of the issue, then, political ecologists believe that local contexts matter, and that geography should be brought back into political inquiry.

Regionalism is defined as a political movement based on the embeddedness of individuals in a particular geographic environment, and in this respect, a political-geographic/ecological perspective on regionalism is a logical intellectual development. Geographic variations in regionalism and its associated political behaviour will reflect the influence of numerous factors. Modernization theory, for example, suggests that regionalist and other territorially based political appeals will be less successful in heavily industrialized and/or urbanized areas. One related hypothesis might be that support for regionalist political mobilization would be strongest in those parts of a region least exposed to industrialization and urbanism.[21] Since social interaction continues to be shaped by geography, political discussion and opinion formation will depend upon individuals' density and proximity, as well as their political preferences and orientations. The residential density of language or cultural minorities is one obvious factor that contributes to (or militates against) the politicization of linguistic or religious cleavages.[22] For example, Richard Johnston has argued that the variable density of Catholics across Canadian provinces accounts for variations in the politicization of class in Canadian electoral politics.[23] Where Catholics are present in sufficient number, the (regionally differentiated) religious cleavage in Canadian politics overpowers the class cleavage, according to his provocative analysis. Similarly, regions that are socially homogeneous and communally cohesive enjoy advantages in terms of mobilization potential.[24] Clearly, the politicization of region will be influenced by a wide variety of contextual factors.

2. Boundaries

One of the mainstays of traditional political geography has been the study of boundaries, borders, and frontiers. Scholarship on boundaries has focused on their evolution over time, their relation to topography and other 'natural' markers, their conflict potential, and their effects on the political evolution of different areas. Several aspects of the study of boundaries are likely to be relevant to an understanding of regionalism: most obviously, the extent to which topological, cultural, economic, social, and jurisdictional boundaries are congruent. Strong regions, associated with segmented societies, will have boundaries whose demarcation is based on a geographic fault line separating groups across a relatively large number of such dimensions. It is unfortunate that little effort has yet been made to seek to identify Canadian regions in terms of the distribution of opinion or sentiment. Instead, most scholars have tended simply to rely on provincial (or aggregates of provincial) boundaries in their geographic characterization of Canadian regionalist sentiment.

Jurisdictional or political boundaries have a special utility to nation-building politicians, since these boundaries can either institutionalize sociologically, economically, or geographically meaningful regions, or they can fragment such regional uniformities by dividing them across a number of sub-national jurisdictions. Napoleon's extensive reforms to the administrative infrastructure of the French state in the early nineteenth century, for example, epitomize the latter strategy of centralizing nation building, in that the boundaries of sub-national *départements* were deliberately drawn to break up the provinces of the *ancien régime*.[25] The Napoleonic state, then, systematically aimed to break down sub-national regionalisms and mobilize the French behind the national goals of *liberté, égalité, et fraternité*. While ultimately unsuccessful in this respect (witness the regional reforms that established elected regional assemblies in the 1980s), the centralizing reforms did serve to cultivate at least some sense of 'Frenchness' in opposition to the national identities of France's neighbours.[26]

Borders and boundaries are instruments of political control. Among other things, they enable political élites to protect or promote an existing culture or territorial identity, as events in Quebec since the 1970s exemplify. Jean Laponce takes this even further, in advocating a kind of 'ethnic federalism' for Canada in which the province of Quebec would be given greater powers over language and cultural policy within its borders as a necessary means for preserving its cultural distinctiveness.[27] The existence of provincial borders, and the cumulative impact of the activities of provincial politicians, undoubtedly have consequences for the cultivation of regionalist sentiments. Mildred Schwartz has outlined the logic for such influences on regionalist sentiment:

> The effects of these provincial boundaries on the continuity of regionalism are inestimable. Provinces are the arenas for mobilizing and expressing contending interests. Through their jurisdictions, the lives of citizens are regularly touched in ways distinct from any other level of government. A federal system of government makes routine both the existence of distinctive regional interests and the means for coping with these. Province as region and regions as combinations of provinces daily manifest one of the critical barriers to a lessening of regional ties.[28]

Similarly, Roger Gibbins has attributed the greater significance of region in Canadian as opposed to American politics to underlying differences in the federal systems and political institutions of these two countries.[29] An interesting attempt to isolate the long-term cultural effects of a provincial border can be found in Ian Stewart's study of residents of the Nova Scotia-New Brunswick provincial border region. His survey of opinion in the areas on either side of the boundary led him to 'conclude that the existence of the boundary between New Brunswick and Nova Scotia has independently had a divisive impact on the political culture of the border zone'.[30] When we discuss the 'sense of place', we shall examine additional evidence that the activities of *provincial* political and cultural élites have played an important role in the shaping of regional consciousness in Canada.

The study of boundaries has been thrust to the forefront of Canada's current debate about regionalism by the results of the 1995 referendum on separation in the province of Quebec. Since then, the question of what boundaries should apply to the newly independent state of Quebec in the event of a 'yes' majority has become something of a political issue. The separatist provincial government insists on the territorial integrity of the province as currently constituted, while opponents of separatism advocate adjusting the province's boundaries according to voting results in the referendum. The Canadian government has been deliberately vague on this question, but it has not ruled out the possibility that the new boundaries ought to reflect the geographic distribution of the 'yes' vote at the sub-provincial level. This would mean that the new state of Quebec would likely lose much of its current territory, including a large portion of the Island of Montreal.[31] Regional boundaries, then, not only are important in shaping regionalist sentiment but also, in their geographical delineation, can become politically contentious through regionalist political mobilization.

3. Geographic Scale

A closely related aspect of regionalism, one to which political geographers are especially sensitive, is the coexistence of regions and regionalism at various spatial scales. It is a truism that individuals' sense of identity with places exists at a variety of scales, from the micro-neighbourhood to the country as a whole. For example, I might consider myself a Cape Bretoner, a Nova Scotian, a Maritimer, an 'Eastern Canadian', a Canadian, and/or an ex-patriate Canadian, with different sentiments of regional identity being invoked or evoked according to different circumstances. Understanding the complex nesting of identities held by residents of a region, identifying the geographic boundaries of an individual's various spatial identities, and understanding when identities associated with a particular spatial scale become politically salient, is of great interest to a political geographer.

Recent work on scale by political geographers has suggested that just as regions as units of political significance are constructed, so too are more general forms of mobilization and resistance at various spatial scales the product of human political construction.[32] The decision to mobilize at a particular spatial scale is a strategic and political decision that can be revisited and changed as conditions develop. While I am disposed to locate regionalism at a spatial scale somewhat larger than that of a local community, territorially based differences emerge from time to time at much smaller spatial scales. The strength and salience of these sub-regional identities must be acknowledged if regionalism is to be fully understood.

Unfortunately, many studies of regionalism in Canada and elsewhere are insensitive to the issues of variable scale, and this frequently leads them to 'anthropomorphize' regions; that is, to see regions as behaving like individual human beings, with a unity of purpose and uniformity of opinion. The literature on minority nationalism, for example, is particularly susceptible to this criticism. Little attention is paid to the geographic variations in support for the nationalist cause within the region itself. Therefore, popular theoretical explanations for the rise of minority nationalism are often tested at only one level of analysis—that of the boundaries associated with the observed nationalist activity—using what is commonly known as a 'most similar systems' comparative design.[33] By the same token, studies of regionalism in Canada that use provinces as their analytic building blocks gloss over a variety of potentially significant sub-provincial cleavages. Ontario, with its deep north-south geographic division, and the associated differences in the party systems in these two large regions, provides only one of the more obvious examples of this difficulty.[34] A province's geography and topography and the relative isolation of its communities can also create distinctive 'small worlds' within a province's borders by insulating some areas from the diffusion of political movements.[35] Even within relatively small units, such as parliamentary constituencies, that are drawn in part to reflect communities of interest, there can be considerable diversity. An example of this can be found in densely populated urban Canada, in the constituency of Toronto Centre-Rosedale, which is geographically and socio-economically divided by Bloor Street into an affluent northern section and a much poorer southern section containing several large public housing projects. A political-geographic perspective is likely to be much more attentive to the sub-regional geographies of minority nationalist or regionalist mobilization.

4. The Sense of Place
A fourth contribution that political geographers can make to the study of regionalism relates to their interest in the human tendency to identify closely with one's territory of residence (defined, as noted earlier, at a variety of scales). This identification with a 'homeland' is, as Yi-Fu Tuan notes, virtually universal among human beings:

> This profound attachment to the homeland appears to be a worldwide phenomenon. It is not limited to any particular culture and economy; it is known to literate and non-literate peoples, hunter-gatherers, and sedentary farmers, as well as city dwellers. The city or land is viewed as mother, and it nourishes; place is an archive of fond memories and splendid achievements that inspire the present; place is permanent and hence reassuring to man, who sees frailty in himself and chance and flux everywhere.[36]

Such sentiments are, of course, the root of the romantic conception of nationalism that emerged in the eighteenth and nineteenth centuries to become one of the most potent and deadly ideologies of all time. Geographic features often provide evocative and powerful anchors for group identity and symbols of group unity. In many cases, the geographic feature in question may not be in any sense remarkable or unique. Instead, it may serve as nothing more than a metaphor for the common features, shared history, or ways of life that define the region. For example, the rhetoric of regionalism and minority nationalism is replete with references to the land or the soil, as in the preamble of the 12 June 1995 multi-party agreement referred to in the wording of Quebec's most recent referendum question on sovereignty:

WE, THE MEN AND WOMEN OF THIS PLACE,
Because we inhabit the territories delimited by our own ancestors, from Abitibi to the Iles-de-la-Madeleine, from Ungava to the American border, because for four hundred years we have cleared, ploughed, paced, surveyed, dug, fished, built, started anew, discussed, protected and loved this land that is cut across and watered by the St. Lawrence River. Because it is this land alone that represents our pride and the source of our strength, our sole opportunity to express ourselves in the entirety

of our individual natures and our collective heart. . . . We, the people of Quebec, declare that we are free to choose our future. . . .[37]

Such evocative and almost primordial appeals to territorially defined group solidarities were unanticipated by most post-World War II social and political theorists. Popular modernization theories had posited the eventual displacement of local and regional identities and political alignments by national (or even international) cleavages and alignments. Political geographers, however, have long pointed to the persistence and importance of these sentiments of place at more intimate spatial scales. While many of these territorial identifications may be quite small, we have seen earlier in this chapter that the language of regionalism has been so prominent a part of intergovernmental relations in Canada that frequently Canadians associate region with province or with groups of provinces.

David Elkins has explored the sense of place held by Canadians by examining their responses to a request to identify the regions of Canada as they perceived them. The 2,562 respondents to the 1974 Canadian National Election Survey came up with 700 different geographic combinations of regions. Despite these differences, Elkins argues that 'the impression one forms by reading these varying answers is quite distinct: people were thinking of Canada as currently defined in political and territorial terms, not something larger and only rarely something smaller.'[38] Questions of the spatial identities of Canadians are far from settled by research, however, and political geographers have an important contribution to make in this area of research on regionalism.

Conclusion

What, then, is distinctive about a political geographic perspective on regionalism? It is clear that despite the obvious salience of territory for this political phenomenon, geography does not determine anything. Regions, no matter how distinctive, internally homogeneous, or geographically endowed, need not give rise to any particular pattern of political mobilization. Geography provides only the raw materials for regionalist mobilization. The conditions under which residents will be available for mobilization, and which prompt political leaders to advance regionalist claims, have to be specified by reference to factors other than a region's geographic foundations. Mildred Schwartz's scholarship has considerably advanced our appreciation of this dynamic. She has demonstrated that the Canadian landscape provides a rich set of opportunities for regionalist mobilization and has documented persistent regional inequalities and differences that are the grist for Canada's political mills.

Political geography adds more value to our understanding of regionalism than this, however. Political geographers have a long tradition of appreciating the persistence of territorial identities and the 'sense of place' in contemporary societies. Political geographers are more likely than other scholars to be sensitive to any geographic variations in regional identity and support for regionalist politics *within* the regions concerned. Emphasizing the importance of regional boundaries (and perhaps formal borders) in shaping regionalist politics is also one of the distinctive contributions that political geographers can make. Political ecologists interested in the interrelationships between political life and various features of the broader geographic context will focus on aspects of this phenomenon that other perspectives may either ignore or attend to only in passing.

This chapter has argued that the distribution of different kinds of people and resources, or the development of communications and transportation systems, or the emergence of networks of political institutions across a region's landscape, can have an important conditioning role for any form of collective action that arises in the territory (including support for and involvement in regionalist politics). In sum, the study of regionalism constitutes one of the distinctive, indeed defining, activities of political geographers. What remains is for future research to exploit fully the perspective's potential to contribute to our understanding of this important phenomenon in Canadian political life.

NOTES

1. Of obvious relevance here is the work on 'regional political cultures' and on the political economy of uneven development within capitalist states. For a discussion of these two approaches to the understanding of a particularly virulent form of regionalist politics, that of minority nationalism, see Anthony H. Birch, 'Minority Nationalism and Theories of Political Integration', *World Politics* 30 (1978): 325–44. *New* institutionalists, who focus on how institutions can shape behaviour, might emphasize the effects of federalism on exacerbating and politicizing regionalist sentiments and grievances. See Carl Hodge, 'Canada in Abstract: The Provincialization of Regional Politics' in *Canadian Politics: An Introduction to the Discipline*, Alain-G. Gagnon and James P. Bickerton, eds (Peterborough, Ont.: Broadview Press, 1990).

2. Some scholars have attempted to define 'functional regions' by grouping together territorial units that share a number of characteristics but are non-contiguous. For an interesting application of this to Ontario, see R.H. MacDermid, 'Regionalism in Ontario' in *Canadian Politics*. These non-geographic regional analyses are beyond the scope of this paper.

3. Garth Stevenson. 'Canadian Regionalism in Continental Perspective', *Journal of Canadian Studies* 15, 2–3 (Summer 1980): 16.

4. For examples of different region-building techniques, see Elizabeth Gidengil, 'Centres and Peripheries: The Political Culture of Dependency', *Canadian Review of Sociology and Anthropology* 27, 1 (1990): 23–48; B.N. Boots and A. Hecht, 'Spatial Perspectives on Canadian Provincialism and Regionalism', *Canadian Journal of Regional Science* 12, 2 (Summer 1989): 187–206.

5. Mildred A. Schwartz, *Politics and Territory: The Sociology of Regional Persistence in Canada* (Montreal: McGill-Queen's University Press, 1974), 5. Regionalism is, therefore, related to but distinct from what has been termed 'ethnic nationalism' or 'minority nationalism'. All these phenomena deal with entities within, or possibly between in some diasporic minority groups, a nation-state (or, in the case of some diasporic minority groups,

across nation-state boundaries). However, regionalism does not necessarily involve demands on the part of the region for autonomy or independence, whereas the other concepts imply this.

6. Hodge, 'Canada in Abstract'.

7. Annsi Paasi, 'Deconstructing Regions: Notes on the Scales of Spatial Life' *Environment and Planning* 23 (1991): 239–56.

8. Kevin R. Cox, 'Concepts of Space, Understanding in Human Geography, and Spatial Analysis', *Urban Geography* 16, 4 (1995): 309.

9. The discussion here echoes an earlier one in social theory pertaining to class formation. In much the same way that class analysts refer to the process of class formation as involving the transformation of class from an analytic category into a political actor (as Marx put it, of moving from being 'a class in itself' to become a 'class for itself'), so too might a region be similarly transformed.

10. Margaret and Harold Sprout, for example, distinguish five general 'postures' regarding the human-milieu (environment) relation: environmental determinism, free-will environmentalism, possibilism, probabilistic behaviouralism, and cognitive behaviouralism. Harold Sprout and Margaret Sprout, *The Ecological Perspective on Human Affairs, With Special Reference to International Politics* (Princeton: Princeton University Press, 1965), 47.

11. André Siegfried, *Tableau politique de la France de l'Ouest sous la Troisième République* (Paris: Armand Colin, 1913), 25–6.

12. Students of political geography will note the similarity in Siegfried's interpretation of Canada to his earlier argument about the relationship among soil types, land tenure, and political conservatism in the West of France. In his classic *Tableau politique de la France de l'Ouest sous la Troisième République*, Siegfried argued that the type of soil and vegetation, the degree of population concentration, the form of land holdings, and the mix of farms of different sizes all affected the dependence of the peasantry on the conservative clergy. Areas with low population density, a mixture of small with a few large farms, and sharecropping would have a peasantry heavily dependent on the clergy, and thus likely to be conservative.

13. William Westfall, 'On the Concept of Region in Canadian History and Literature', *Journal of Canadian Studies* 15, 2–3 (Summer 1980): 4.

14. Harold Innis, *The Fur Trade in Canada: An Introduction to Canadian Economic History* (Toronto: University of Toronto Press, 1930), 393. Emphasis added.

15. Sprout and Sprout, *The Ecological Perspective*, 14.

16. John Agnew, *Place and Politics: On the Geographical Mediation of State and Society* (Boston: Allen & Unwin, 1997), 28.

17. Ibid., 43.

18. See Sten Berglund and Soren Risbjerg Thomsen, eds, *Modern Political Ecology Analysis* (Abo: Abo Akademis Forlag, 1990); Munroe Eagles 'Political Ecology: Local Influences on the Behaviour of Canadians' in *Canadian Politics*; Svante Ersson, Kenneth Janda, and Jan-Erik Lane, 'The Logic of Political Ecology Analysis' in *Partier, Ideologier, Valjare: En Antologi*, Dag Anckar, Erik Damgaard and Henry Valen, eds (Abo: Abo Akademi, 1982).

19. Emile Durkheim, *Suicide: A Study in Sociology* (New York: Free Press, 1895, 1957).

20. Judith Hellman, *Journeys Among Women: Feminism in Five Italian Cities* (Toronto: Oxford University Press, 1987).

21. Munroe Eagles, 'The Neglected Regional Dimension of Scottish Ethnic Nationalism', *Canadian Review of Studies in Nationalism* 12, 1 (Spring 1985): 81–98.

22. Jean Laponce, 'Assessing the Neighbour Effect on the Vote of Francophone Minorities in Canada', *Political Geography Quarterly* 6, 1 (January 1987): 77–87.

23. Richard Johnston, 'The Geography of Class and Religion in Canadian Elections' in *The Ballot and the Message: Voting in Canada*, Joseph Wearing, ed. (Toronto: Copp Clark Pitman, 1991).

24. Munroe Eagles and Stephen Erfle, 'Community Cohesion and Voter Turnout in English Parliamentary Constituencies: Research Note', *British Journal of Political Science* 19, 1 (January 1989): 115–25.

25. Peter Gourevitch, *Paris and the Provinces: The Politics of Local Government Reform in France* (Berkeley: University of California Press, 1980).

26. Peter Sahlins, *Boundaries: The Making of France and Spain in the Pyrenees* (Berkeley: University of California Press, 1989).

27. Jean Laponce, 'The Case for Ethnic Federalism in Multilingual Societies: Canada's Regional Imperative', *Regional Politics and Policy* 3, 1 (Spring 1993): 23–43.

28. Mildred Schwartz, *Politics and Territory*, 324.

29. Roger Gibbins, *Regionalism: Territorial Politics in Canada and the United States* (Toronto: Butterworths, 1982), 191.

30. Ian Stewart, 'More than Just a Line on a Map: The Political Culture of the Nova Scotia-New Brunswick Boundary' *Publius* 20, 1 (Winter 1990): 99–111.

31. See Linda Gerber, 'Referendum Results: Defining New Boundaries for an Independent Quebec', *Canadian Ethnic Studies* 24, 2 (1992): 22–34.

32. See David Delaney and Helga Leitner, 'Introduction: The Political Construction of Scale', *Political Geography* 16, 2 (February 1997): 93–7.

33. See Eagles, 'The Neglected Regional Dimension'.

34. Geoffrey R. Weller, 'Hinterland Politics: The Case of Northwestern Ontario', *Canadian Journal of Political Science* 10, 4 (1977): 727–54. See also R.H. MacDermid, 'Regionalism in Ontario' in *Canadian Politics*.

35. Jeremy Wilson, 'Geography, Politics, and Culture: Electoral Insularity in British Columbia', *Canadian Journal of Political Science* 13, 4 (1980): 751–83.

36. Yi-Fu Tuan, *Space and Place: The Perspectives of Experience* (Minneapolis: University of Minnesota Press, 1977), 154.

37. Preamble to the Question Presented in the Quebec National Assembly, September 16, 1995.

38. David J. Elkins, 'A Sense of Place' in *Small Worlds: Provinces and Parties in Canadian Political Life*, David J. Elkins and Richard Simeon, eds (Toronto: Methuen, 1980).

Chapter 2

Region as a Social Construction

Harry H. Hiller

In her landmark study *Politics and Territory: The Sociology of Regional Persistence in Canada*, Mildred Schwartz[1] confessed that she was inclined to see regionalism as 'an essentially political phenomenon'. Because Schwartz identifies herself as a political sociologist, it is to be expected that she would approach regionalism primarily in terms of its political manifestations. While I am prepared to admit that political expressions of regionalism are its most visible expressions, I would like to offer a more broadly based sociological approach.

Sociologists have often had difficulty dealing with region because space has usually been viewed as a matter of setting rather than as something with explanatory value. The more important variables were considered to be class, race, and more recently, gender. Within American sociology, region did take on some significance with attempts to understand the unique dynamics of the American South, particularly in the work of Howard Odum and Rupert Vance in the 1930s. That tradition was sustained at the University of North Carolina by John Shelton Reed, who focused on Southern regional identification and regional subcultural persistence.[2] However, sociologists have generally left region to geographers and the political aspects of regionalism to political scientists.

In Canada, macrosociologists attempting to understand the dynamics of Canadian society were keenly interested in regionalist movements and less interested in region. The work of S.D. Clark,[3] for example, focused on the expressions of social disorganization and marginality on economic frontiers of settlement. The motivation behind the *Backgrounds to Social Credit in Alberta* series was a metropolitan fascination with radical agrarianism and political innovation on the frontier. In much the same manner, Lipset[4] sought to explain why Saskatchewan produced the first socialist government in North America. Two sociological studies[5] in the 1950s did attempt to describe limited aspects of regional culture but, again, primarily as a means to explain political innovation using frontiers of settlement and marginality as the underlying explanatory themes. In short, the focus was on regional political mobilization rather than on region as a unit of analysis.

Schwartz's work in 1974 threw the gauntlet down to Canadian sociologists to redis-cover the role of region in the analysis of Canadian society; however, the response was mostly to use region as one variable among many in explaining behaviour. This can be called the regional differences approach. Most quantitative sociological analysis of large data sets routinely came to use region as an independent variable, typically as 'place of residence'. However, virtually none of this research contributed to a study of region and regionalism because the focus was primarily on other substantive issues. The major exception was the attempt to understand Quebec sentiments, but in the context of ethnic nationalism rather than regionalism, as autonomy, self-determina-tion, and ultimately independence became the bywords for understanding the mood of that province. While region implies some form of participation in a larger whole, self-determination and independence have a very different meaning.

It is noteworthy that the best sociological contribution to the analysis of regional-ism in the late 1970s and early 1980s began with the study of Newfoundland society, seeking to interpret the relationship of the Atlantic region to the larger Canadian soci-ety.[6] Using a modified world systems perspective (but also moving beyond this perspective, as we shall see), Ralph Matthews[7] conceptualized the meaning of Atlantic regional differences not so much as disparities or deficiencies measured against some national norm, but as the result of processes of underdevelopment caused by external forces exploitative of the region. This produced what he called regional dependency. While most studies of Quebec focused on changes within the province as the expla-nation for Quebec nationalism, Matthews' studies of Atlantic regionalism stressed the role of factors external to the region. This emphasis on the relational aspects of regionalism, whereby some regions were dominant and others subordinate, suggested that regions were the product of power relationships within the national society. Understanding regionalism as a phenomenon of inter-regional relations was a theme picked up by other sociologists through the 1980s, but since that time very little has been written by Canadian sociologists on the topic of regionalism from a fresh perspective.[8]

One of the criticisms of studies of regionalism is that they are not rooted in socio-logical theory.[9] The goal of this chapter is to review the primary themes that sociol-ogists use in the study of Canadian regionalism. Then, in view of the fact that many sociologists have lost sight of region as an object of study, an attempt will be made to examine the work of two European sociologists who have rediscovered territory and space as an important aspect of sociological analysis. Building on their work, an attempt will be made to present a different way of conceptualizing region that is rooted not only in territoriality but in interaction occurring within that space.

The Sociological Use of Political Economy in Understanding Regions

A major debate among sociologists is whether regionalism is natural or created.[10] Studies that emphasize regional culture or compare characteristics across regions usually assume that regionalism is natural: the result of different environmental,

demographic, and economic characteristics. Yet the dominant view in Canadian sociological discussions on regionalism since Schwartz's work is that regionalism is
created, which is to say, it is the result of human action. Using dependency, core-
periphery, and development-underdevelopment theories,[11] various studies have
examined regions in relation to one another as an expression of power differentials
and in relation to decision-makers in the national and international economy. From
this political economy perspective, regions are the product of a dynamic inter-regional
relationship with a special focus on uneven economic development, so that cultural
or geographic factors are minimized. What are the contours of this perspective?

Uneven development reflects the inability of regions to compete equally because
some have advantages over others. Contrary to popular opinion, these advantages
are not so much natural as created through the decisions of economic élites, large
corporations (particularly multinationals), and those who possess political power
and influence. For example, the National Policy of 1879, frequently identified as *the*
blueprint for Canadian nation building, is interpreted as a policy that reaffirmed the
dominance of central Canadian capital.[12] Freight rate structures, the protective
tariff, and population settlement policies ensured that both Atlantic Canada and the
West would be a captive hinterland for central Canadian industrial development,
and furthermore ensured that the hinterlands would be forever caught in a 'staples
trap' of resource production. Thus, regionalism can be viewed as a consequence of
the victory of central Canadian capital because it strengthened the objective of
capital accumulation.[13]

In its strongest form, this perspective on regionalism views it as the product of
élitist control and even class exploitation.[14] According to this perspective, élites establish and sustain regional patterns that enhance their profit making and encourage
national economic policies that strengthen their position. Peripheral regions possess
a reserve labour pool that can migrate to core regions when work is available and
return to the periphery when it is not there to be supported by federal transfer
payments. The federal government thus contributes to regionalism by supporting the
profit-making objectives of central Canadian capitalists. Furthermore, the periphery
is highly dependent for its economic strength on resource-based industries (as
opposed to value-added industries), which are subject to considerable fluctuations in
marketability and value, so that employment in these industries is unpredictable.
Furthermore, since most of the capital for these resource-based industries is provided
from outside the region, profits are removed from the region, so that little further
development occurs there. To the extent that élites within peripheral regions benefit
from these arrangements, they are content to preserve the status quo, which perpetuates regional underdevelopment.

Another variant of the political economy approach factors foreign capital into this
pattern of uneven regional development.[15] Foreign capital may reinforce existing
regional inequality by providing venture capital in resource exploitation when
domestic capital is unwilling to do so, but in a manner complementary to the
power of Canadian capital. Foreign capital may also contribute to uneven regional

development by establishing subsidiaries in the region adjacent to their own industry (for example, Ontario subsidiaries or Michigan- or New York-based industries), or by contributing to regional hyper-growth by selecting locations at the core of existing Canadian industry and finance control.

Regionalism then, from this perspective, is a response to capitalist forces. For example, if Ontario grows rapidly by attracting population because of the opportunities it offers, it does so because national policies advocated by economic élites, and implemented by the state, enhance capital accumulation that is regionally biased.[16] This conceptualization of regionalism understands it as the result of inequalities where dominance and resistance are the motors of human action. The fact that the working class in the core region may also benefit is sometimes ignored, though an overheated regional economy may also be problematic for workers.

No better illustration can be found of the regional tensions that may result than in the western Canadian response to the National Energy Policy of 1980.[17] What the federal government proposed as being in the national interest was viewed in the West as an attempt to cut off the regional economic boom. Whereas central Canadian industry demanded cheap, guaranteed supplies of energy to enhance profitability, Western energy interests argued for higher prices for a non-renewable resource, as well as pressing for incentives to encourage non-conventional resource extraction, in order to strengthen their regional economy and increase profits. The political economy approach uses terms such as 'concentration' and 'centralization' to emphasize the ways capitalist power exploits differences and divisions within a society to maximize accumulation objectives. Disputes between regions must largely be understood as either a class rebellion against élite control or as the mobilization of the grassroots by competing class fractions between regions. Indeed, Richards and Pratt argued that it was a nascent or arriviste bourgeoisie in the 'new' West that mobilized regional feeling.[18]

Political economy models of regionalism, then, focus on regionalism as uneven economic development, and socio-cultural differences are either minimized or explained as derivative from unequal class relations. The strong suit of this approach is that it provides an explanation of how regions are related to one another, rather than merely visualizing a region as a subcultural artifact of the whole.

Political economy is interdisciplinary, and contributions to this perspective have come from economists and political scientists as well as sociologists. But it is relevant to point out that, to the extent that sociologists have discussed regionalism as a phenomenon, the political economy perspective was their dominant approach in the latter decades of the twentieth century.

The Political Structural Perspective on Regions

Schwartz's definition of regionalism as 'politically relevant divisiveness'[19] uses eight sets of conditions as the basis of regionalism. Five of the eight conditions are socio-political systemic factors and an additional condition is the outcome that produces regionalized political behaviour. At the end of her study, she concludes that economy, demography, and polity are the most important factors producing regionalism but regionalism is still understood as a political phenomenon.[20]

It is not surprising that political scientists have tended to view regionalism as a consequence of political structures.[21] The party discipline required in the federal parliamentary system, the lack of an effective region-based federal house of debate, the principle of representation by population that allows the more populous central Canadian provinces to dominate,[22] the increasing importance of provincial governments in competitive economic developments that are frequently labelled 'province-building'[23] or economic provincialism, the increasing federal-provincial confrontations whereby provincial governments attempt to weld their populations into a 'governmentalized society'[24] in opposition to federal interests—all these factors have been understood as contributing to regionalism. Expressing this sentiment, McCormick has chided, 'If regionalism did not already exist, provincial governments would find it useful to invent it.'[25] In fact, Gibbins argued in the early 1980s that underlying socio-regional differences appeared to be waning within Canadian society at the same time that regionalism within the political system appeared to be growing. He concluded that the primary cause of regionalism is found in the political system and that regionalism is essentially a matter of 'political cause and effect'.[26]

Brodie has taken this argument one step further and has combined it with a political economy perspective by arguing that regions are political creations of state development strategies. These strategies support regionally based class interests and therefore are not spatially neutral.[27] She understands regionalism as a relational concept in which regions have interdependencies that are made dynamic by changing historical circumstances. While most Canadian sociologists have not focused on the political structural elements producing regionalism, they have accepted the logic of this work done by others.

An Evaluation

The common theme in both the political economy and the political structural perspectives is that while regionalism is real, it is more readily explainable by appealing to other factors. Regionalism, initially, may have been conceptualized as an independent variable, but increasingly regionalism has been viewed as effect rather than cause. Nowhere is this point made more strongly than in the statement by Richard Simeon that regions are simply containers and that regionalism by itself does not explain anything.[28] Some studies of regional variations in individual attitudes (that is, political values and ideologies), for example, have demonstrated that region is not a significant explanatory variable for whatever differences may exist[29] and that social class explains more of the variance.[30] The point is that class structural differences between regions may be more fundamental than region as a geographic unit. Furthermore, differences within regions have often been ignored in the search for differences between regions. For this reason Cuneo[31] and Clement[32] argued that regionalism is a misplaced focus, for it is not a spatial issue that is in question as much as an expression of class struggle. Though Clement in particular asserted that his was not an economic determinist position, it is clear that the essence of regionalism is its materialist basis in conflict between classes or class fractions, for 'regions per se are not exploitative, classes are'.[33]

The search for causes of regionalism, then, has led to conclusions that province or region of residence is not as important as non-spatial factors such as social class or ethnicity. The danger of this conclusion is that it minimizes territory to the point where either regionalism is reduced to something else or, more seriously, when spatially specific movements arise, the territorial aspect of regionalism has no place in the explanatory model. Marchak,[34] for one, rejected the notion that regionalism is 'a simple manifestation of class relations' and argued for the importance of a shared territorial base and culture that emerges from a shared experience. In spite of this acknowledgement, there has been no attempt to develop the significance of this observation or to incorporate both territory and culture within an explanatory frame-work. Repeatedly, other analysts have made similar acknowledgements about regional culture but go no further.

One vocal advocate for the rediscovery of regionalism in sociological analysis has been sociologist Ralph Matthews.[35] Matthews has taken what he calls a volun-taristic perspective, in which he focuses on the actions of individuals in sustaining regional feeling. Region, for Matthews, is not so much a territorial fact as it is a social psychological condition. He argues that it cannot be measured by compar-ing social structural characteristics across regions or by measuring differences in values, but only by ascertaining to what extent region is a part of personal identity and to what extent people are committed to a region. For a region to exist as a distinct entity, fundamental differences in the social organization of the region must be shown to exist. When these objective characteristics are combined with a subjective sense of belonging together (and conversely, a sense of difference from other parts of the society), regionalism as a consciousness of kind emerges. Regionalism, then, is socio-psychological in nature (though Matthews places his approach within a dependency framework), and he demonstrates empirically at the individual level that province of residence is a significant predictor in matters of federal/provincial relations when differences in class, status, and ethnicity are controlled, and level of commitment to and satisfaction with the region is part of the analysis. This gives Matthews confidence that region of residence can be a significant independent variable.

Matthews' work is important, even though he does not develop his voluntaristic perspective theoretically, because it focuses on the individual rather than the groups or institutions more typical of other models, and because he suggests that regional differences between individuals are more likely to occur when matters of regional substance, as opposed to general values,[36] are part of the analysis. His work also suggests that long-time residence in a region and/or commitment to it may produce a more localized consciousness that must be included in the analysis of issues affecting that region. How we move from the individual to the collectivity, however, is unclear in Matthews' model.

There is no doubt that political and economic factors play a major role in producing regionalism. But is there something missing?[37] Can a sociologist bring an additional perspective to bear in understanding how territory is related to social action? The argument here is that regionalism must be understood not just as an outcome of political factors or economic variables but as a social construction.

Space and Contemporary Sociological Thinking

While space and territory, in North America, have been largely left to geographers, many of whom have also linked with political economy to understand social action and territory,[38] it is noteworthy that in Europe, sociologists have rediscovered space.[39] Ironically, this rediscovery is occurring precisely at the time that space is being obliterated and made irrelevant by the internet and other new technologies. Of specific interest is the work of Giddens and Lefebvre, who have had a significant impact on what is called the new urban sociology.[40] Without going into the details of their work, it is possible to distill some significant points that may have relevance to an analysis of regions.

Anthony Giddens[41] criticizes sociologists who are, in essence, 'space-blind' and argues against the view that space is merely a setting for social interaction or a passive environment.[42] He observes that elements of space become part of interaction through what he calls 'time-space distanciation'. The concept of distanciation refers to the continuity, or stretching, of societies in both time and space. Not only is a society constructed on face-to-face interaction (what he calls 'co-presence') but it is now also possible for social relations to be maintained between actors not co-present, in conditions of high space-time distanciation. He envisages the nation-state as the crucial power-container of class societies by extending its control over time and space.

Giddens has played an important role in drawing attention away from structural interpretations or structural determinism toward the role of human agency in what he calls structuration theory. By emphasizing the reflexivity or recursiveness of human action, Giddens wants to show how social structures both are constituted by human agency and yet at the same time are the very medium of this constitution. For Giddens, the structures of society are its resources, rules, and ideas (not organizations as in structural functionalism) which are not only constraints to social interaction but also enabling tools by which human agents act to reconstitute the structure of society. In other words, there is a reciprocity between human agency and social structures so that society structures the individual at the same time that the individual structures society. Sociologists who focus on how society structures the individual overemphasize its constraining nature, for in fact the key point is that social structure is not just external to the actor. Structural practices of social systems are both the medium and the outcome of practices they recursively organize. However, in emphasizing the role of human agency, it is acknowledged that intentional acts often have unintended consequences. The result of this approach is that it turns our attention away from world systems theories and dependency to the local level, where people of all social classes face choices (though admittedly some may be more constrained than others) and through these choices, both as individuals and collectively, reconstitute society.

The notion of regionalization of locales was proposed by Giddens as a counterbalance to assumptions that societies are homogeneous and unified. He noted that temporal and spatial differentiation occurs in a whole range of settings from large to small. 'If the world economy has its centres, and cities have their centres, so too do the daily trajectories of individual actors.'[43] For example, some rooms in a house have a more peripheral role (for example, the spare bedroom) than others that are central (for example, the kitchen). 'Centre-periphery distinctions tend frequently to be associated with endurance over time. Those who occupy centres establish themselves as having control over resources that allow them to maintain differentiation between themselves and those in peripheral regions. The established may employ a variety of forms of social closure to sustain distance from others who are effectively treated as inferiors or outsiders.'[44] In other words, the arrangement of social action in space is related to different roles that space is assigned, but this assignment of space is the result of human action that attempts to control resources and create barriers to those considered outsiders. For example, the class distribution of urban populations is both an intended effect and an unintended consequence of the sifting that produces regionalized cultures in urban space. People make choices that are constrained by structural options but, in making those choices, produce regionalized cultures that reflect their own agency.

Giddens thought he was putting time and space at the heart of social theory by showing how both time and space are stretched (distanciation) through authoritative and allocative resources even when people are absent in time (through history) and space (that they cannot personally always occupy). Whether indeed Giddens has presented these ideas in a convincing way or whether he has raised more questions than he has answered is a major issue.[45] In fact, one of his critics who argues that space is indeed simply a backdrop and plays only a passive role in human interaction does, nevertheless, concede that Giddens is right about interaction being constituted and reproduced differently in different places.[46] It could indeed be argued that in the end Giddens does not deal at all well with how space is produced by human action, but as a sociologist he at least helps draw our attention to the fact that social processes are related to space.

The French sociologist-philosopher Henri Lefebvre (1902-1991) wrote a book entitled *The Production of Space* in 1974. It was not translated into English until 1991, which somewhat muted its impact on the North American sociological community. Lefebvre's Marxist background had made him aware that space must be understood as rooted in capitalism—a social system in which spatial arrangements must be understood as symptomatic of powerful economic forces. He also acknowledged the role of the state in shaping behaviour. But where LeFebvre broke with Marxists was in stating that ideas and meanings were not perfectly subject to dominant material conditions, for people can take back space and rename it and give it new meaning. He acknowledged that there was a contradiction between the consumption of space that produces surplus value and space that produces enjoyment.[47] The former he identified as abstract or representational space, which was the way investors, business, and government understood space, and the latter he called social space, which emphasized its livability.[48] Lefebvre saw this conflict in the use of space as being as important as class conflict itself, and in his view it serves as the basis of spatio-analysis, in which the production of space implies a shift from domination to appropriation (that is, 'personalizing' the space and making it one's own).[49]

Lefebvre's willingness to accommodate independent action in a form of anti-structuralism provided a more balanced view of space: he saw it as reflecting the intentional acts of capital and the state, but he also accepted that spatial patterns arise from the outcomes of human activity. These conflicting forces then lead to political struggles over the meaning of space, but the materialization of social organization is understood to result in spatial configurations that give space causal power.[50] Lefebvre's work has been enormously influential in urban sociology and has served as a foundation of John R. Logan and Harvey L. Molotch's[51] analysis of the key role played by the conflicts between 'exchange value' (the monetary value of space) and 'use value' (the everyday living value of space) and the interests which stand behind them.

Contributions to Sociological Theorizing about Region

Without in any way attempting to bring the work of these two theorists together or to synthesize them, what insights can be gained from these perspectives that impact our analysis of regions? Since many sociologists do not take space or territory seriously, how might these analysts contribute to our theorizing about region as a social construct? Six points can be distilled:

1. Between the analysis of individual interaction (the micro) and statewide collectivities (the macro) stands an intermediate grouping of local collectivities. There needs to be a renewed emphasis on the role of local communities in framing human action. Region, then, is an important interstitial site for understanding interaction.
2. Local activities sharing space develop their own culture and social organization in that space, partially as an adaptation to the received structure of that space (the constraining aspect), but also partially as a creative response by inhabitants who wish to make that space their own (its enabling character). Regionalism thus is the result of a blend of constraining factors and spontaneous creative activities.
3. There is a difference between an insider's and an outsider's view of space. An outsider may see space primarily for its exchange value, whereas an insider is much more conscious of the 'use value' of space. As Gottdeiner[52] has noted, the local community is a collective site of use values that have their basis in non-economic considerations. The way that an insider understands structured space

as a basis for regionalism may be different from the way the outsider sees it because for the insider it is a lived-in territory.

4. There is a need for balance in the analysis of space so that its structural dimensions do not minimize the role participants play in creating, constructing, and organizing their own space. Regionalism, then, is not just the result of operant external or structural forces but is also shaped by local human action.

5. Space is not just neutral or setting. As both built environment and natural environment, it comes to represent a people's understanding of themselves over time (a sense of history) with at least 'imagined' though murky boundaries (a sense of territoriality). Region does shape thinking and behaviour even if only in select or limited ways.

6. There is reflexivity or recursiveness in that people who share a space inhabit it and develop it at the same time that the structure of the space turns back and shapes its inhabitants. Thus regionalism must always be understood as a dynamic rather than static phenomenon.

In sum, and perhaps at the risk of oversimplification, a sociologist could make these points about regionalism as a social activity. Regionalization occurs because structural conditions exist that divide populations into geographic locales. In that sense, at least some aspects of regionalism are created. But regionalism is also created because local people are not passive: they not only respond to the restrictiveness of those structural conditions but also independently create their own culture and organization through social interaction.[53] Their understanding of their region will then become very different from the view of an outsider, whose rootedness in another region affects his or her perspective. This is not to say that regions themselves are socially homogeneous or without internal conflict. But it is to say that sharing a territory provides a basis for communality that potentially could be as powerful as class, gender, or race under the right conditions (the severest of which would be some kind of collective threat).

It has often been acknowledged that regions can be defined in a variety of different ways (geographically, ethnically) and that equating region with province as a political unit often occurs purely as a matter of convenience. In spite of these difficulties with boundaries, regions are frequently thought of as a particular matrix of characteristics that represent the sum of traits possessed by a region. This conception of region is passive, descriptive, and almost inert. Sociologists, not unlike other social scientists, need to begin with such territorial mappings. But a sociologist must also understand how and to what extent region is a social construction as the result not only of structural forces but also of social interaction and of collective struggles in dealing with territorial existence.[54]

From a sociological perspective, a region is produced by people who share a territory, creating and organizing themselves into their own local society. Regionalism (as opposed to region) is the politicization of these local traits into a consciousness of kind. It mobilizes selected elements of regional culture and attempts to translate them into a dominant world view. In that sense, regionalism appears hegemonic and represents an act of power. While élites may create regionalist definitions of the situation, regionalism can also emerge from grassroots sentiments. When regionalism emerges, it attempts to become an ideology, a way of seeing, a perceptual apparatus that may change over time or rise and wane depending on circumstances. But the key is that sharing a territory produces perceptions of collective interests.[55] Thus, regionalism is a dynamic and often emotional concept like other words ending in 'ism' (nationalism, socialism, capitalism) that contain assumptions and claim to have wide-ranging influence. From this perspective, then, regionalism as a vantage point from shared space is a natural outcome of the existence of regions. However, when it becomes the predominant (or perhaps exclusive) means of interpreting reality, regionalism becomes an ideology.

The argument presented here is a plea for sociologists not only to focus on the structural conditions creating and sustaining regionalism but also to examine how and what contributes to a regional world view as the result of interaction in a locale. In what ways does sharing a territory contribute to shared perceptions or interpretations that are less likely to be held by residents of other regions? How have residents organized themselves and economically supported themselves in ways that sustain these perceptions? In spite of other traits that may divide regional residents, what contributes to the search for commonalities that is part of sharing a territory? What interests do such attempts to forge regional unity represent?

Since regionalism involves a world view based on territoriality, it is partially natural and partially the result of framing;[56] that is, some person or group must sharply articulate and thus 'frame' the perspective. In that sense, regionalism becomes political and requires the mobilization of support. This means that while the regionalist perspective will be commonly known and available to residents of a territory, it may exist in a submerged state until it is triggered by changing conditions and circumstances. While many will be partial to the ideology because of its appeal to shared locality, it is not to be expected that all will embrace it; therefore, recruitment to action is primarily what makes regionalism both public and volatile. These dynamic expressions of regionalism are at their strongest in outbursts of collective behaviour and social movements. Nevertheless, the more latent and less volatile forms of regional perspectives that are part of everyday life should not be minimized. In short, regionalism as an interpretive apparatus does not exist only when newspapers and protesters tell us it does. And sociologists ought to play a key role in making us aware of the existence and nature of this pre-political behaviour.

In sum, I am arguing for a bottom-up understanding of regionalism—not to replace but to counterbalance the top-down theories. I believe that understanding regionalism as a response to structural conditions or external stimuli or as political action is to miss the origins of regionalism in local sentiment.[57] Schwartz understood this point by stating that perceptions, orientations, and states of mind were important (the remaining conditions prompting regionalism not noted earlier), but she admitted that she was unable to determine the extent to which these factors were important.[58] More recently, Schwartz[59] noted that giving primacy to regional self-identifications can be problematic if such identities cannot easily be verified through measurement: self-identifications can lead to rejecting the significance of regionalism just because they are not consciously articulated. What Schwartz is telling us, indirectly, is that regionalism must be understood as a consequence of localized interaction, which is consonant with the position taken in this paper.[60] Schwartz and others who make similar appeals to localized culture in theorizing regionalism are admitting that the sociology of collectivities sharing a territory must be included in the analysis. Nevertheless, this task is seldom embraced in detail. Sociologists can take a cue from Giddens and Lefebvre in developing more careful analyses of how space shapes behaviour and how humans shape space to create a distinct local organizational context.

The issue is not a choice between structural explanations and cultural explanations but a matter of showing how social action has a spatial referent. Lefebvre's concept of social space and the distinction between exchange value and use value reminds us that space becomes personalized by social groups because they live there and it is their home. The age-old tendency to identify with one's locale is a form of local patriotism that has always existed and that shows up in studies of the high levels of satisfaction and identification which people have with their place of residence.[61] For example, Newfoundlanders who come to Alberta to work look forward to the opportunity to return home to their own people where they feel they belong. Even sport teams (such as the Saskatchewan Roughriders, who claim the whole province as their territory) attempt to exploit these regional loyalties. Such loyalties emerge from the social organization that results when people share space.

A recent migrant to Calgary from an Eastern province remarked to me recently, 'You really get a very different view of Canada from living in the West and in Calgary.' This person went on to remark that whether it was the mountains, Calgary's unique Co-op, the Reform party, the Flames, or the predominant energy sector, there was a different feel to living in Calgary in terms of how people viewed the world and how social life was organized. All of this suggests that space or territory is important. It may not be the most important thing, nor is it the only important thing, but it is always present and affects behaviour even in its latent form. The fact that regional boundaries are fluid should not blind us to the fact that regional sentiments and regional identities exist. A sociologist is obligated to begin with how this sense of territoriality is socially constructed. Regions then are not necessarily political jurisdictions[62] but are socially constructed entities of organization belonging more or less uniquely to a group of people, and contributing to developing viewpoints on other regions and broader national realities.[63] This is not by any means to suggest that regions are homogeneous, but simply that regional interests can coalesce among people who share space.

Conclusion

A sociological theory of regionalism must begin, then, with how people sharing a territory construct their social life and how they understand themselves.[64] This is the

Figure 2.1: Levels of Regional Analysis

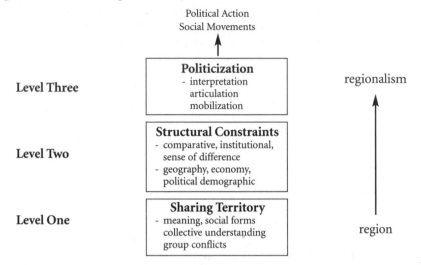

enabling aspect of social action.[65] Then we can add the structural constraints of polity and economy that provide additional explanatory power in understanding inter-regional relationships. The politicization of region that produces regionalism is the third step in the process of explaining how regional elements are mobilized and articulated to become a point of view, or an interpretive apparatus, or a perspective in understanding broader societal relationships. Regionalist movements are the end result of this third level of analysis, for they reflect both underlying social construction of space and the structural elements that shape it. Only after we have understood how region is created at the grassroots level, by structural forces, can we attempt to explain the forces and interests that stand behind the collective action of regionalist movements and understand how they exploit or manipulate the more latent forms of regional life.

NOTES

1. Mildred A. Schwartz, *Politics and Territory: The Sociology of Regional Persistence In Canada* (Montreal: McGill-Queen's University Press, 1974), 9.

2. John Shelton Reid, *The Enduring South: Subcultural Persistence in Mass Society* (Chapel Hill: University of North Carolina Press, 1972); John Shelton Reid, *One South: An Ethnic Approach to Regional Culture* (Baton Rouge: Louisiana State University Press, 1982); John Shelton Reid, *Southerners: The Social Psychology of Sectionalism* (Chapel Hill: University of North Carolina Press, 1983).

3. S.D. Clarke, *The Social Development of Canada* (Toronto: University of Toronto Press, 1942; S.D. Clarke, *Movements of Political Protest in Canada* (Toronto: University of Toronto Press, 1959).

4. Seymour Martin Lipset, *Agrarian Socialism* (New York: Doubleday, 1968).

5. Jean Burnet, *Next Year Country* (Toronto: University of Toronto Press, 1951); W.E. Mann, *Sect, Cult and Church in Alberta* (Toronto: University of Toronto Press, 1955).

6. For other studies from the Atlantic region, see Robert Brym and R. Sacouman, eds, *Underdevelopment and Social Movements in Atlantic Canada* (Toronto: New Hogtown Press, 1979); and Bryant Fairley, Colin Leys, and James Sacouman, eds, *Restructuring and Resistance: Perspectives from Atlantic Canada* (Toronto: Garamond, 1990).

7. Ralph Matthews, 'The Significance and Explanation of Regional Divisions in Canada: Toward a Canadian Sociology', *Journal of Canadian Studies* 15, 2 (1980): 43–61; Ralph Matthews, *The Creation of Regional Dependency* (Toronto: University of Toronto Press, 1983).

8. The last book on the topic was Robert J. Brym, ed., *Regionalism in Canada* (Toronto: Irwin, 1986). It might be possible to consider Harrison's (1995) study of the Reform party somewhat regionalist in nature given its Western roots. Yet, Harrison understands Reform more as political/ideological populism than as an expression of regional/inter-regionalist relations, and he certainly does not directly address the literature on regionalism.

9. Reid, *One South*, 34; Trevor Harrison, *Of Passionate Intensity: Right-Wing Populism and the Reform Party of Canada* (Toronto: University of Toronto Press, 1995).

10. Matthews, *Regional Dependency*; Brym, *Regionalism*.

11. Wallace Clement, *The Challenge of Class Analysis* (Ottawa: Carleton University Press, 1988), ch. 9; Carl Cuneo, 'The Class Dimension of Regionalism' in Lorne Tepperman and James Curtis, eds, *Readings in Sociology* (Toronto: McGraw Hill Ryerson, 1978); Brym and Sacouman, *Underdevelopment*; Patricia Marchak, 'A Contribution to the Class and Region Debate', *Canadian Issues* 5 (1980).

12. Janine Brodie, *The Political Economy of Canadian Regionalism* (Toronto: Harcourt Brace, 1990), 97–128.

13. J.F. Conway, *The West: The History of a Region in Confederation* (Toronto: James Lorimer, 1983); Gary Burrill and Ian McKay, eds, *People, Resources and Power: Critical Perspectives on Underdevelopment and Primary Industries in the Atlantic Region* (Fredericton: Gorsebrook Research Institute, 1987); Brym and Sacouman, *Underdevelopment*.

14. Cuneo, 'The Class Dimensions of Regionalism'; Clement, *Class Analysis*.

15. Garth Stevenson, 'Canadian Regionalism in Continental Perspective', *Journal of Canadian Studies* 15, 2 (1980): 16–28; Wallace Clement, 'A Political Economy of Regionalism in Canada' in D. Glenday, H. Guindon, and A. Turowetz, eds, *Modernization and the Canadian State* (Toronto: Macmillan, 1978).

16. Janine Brodie, 'The New Political Economy of Regions' in Wallace Clement, ed., *Understanding Canada: Building in the New Canadian Political Economy* (Montreal: McGill-Queen's University Press, 1997).

17. Larry Pratt and Garth Stevenson, eds, *Western Separation: The Myths, Realities, and Danger* (Edmonton, Alta.: Hurtig, 1981), especially the chapter by Peter Puxley.

18. John Richards and Larry Pratt, *Prairie Capitalism: Power and Influence in the New West* (Toronto: McClelland and Stewart, 1979).

19. Schwartz, *Politics and Territory*, ch. 5.

20. Ibid., 310.

21. David Bell, *The Roots of Disunity: A Study of Canadian Political Culture* (Toronto: Oxford University Press: 1992).

22. Roger Gibbins, *Regionalism: Territorial Politics in Canada and the United States* (Toronto: Butterworths, 1982).

23. Larry Pratt, 'The State and Province-Building: Alberta's Development Strategy' in Leo Pawitch, ed., *The Canadian State: Political Economy and Political Power* (Toronto: University of Toronto Press, 1977), 133–62.

24. Alan Cairns, 'The Governments and Societies of Canadian Federalism', *Canadian Journal of Political Science* 10 (1977).

25. Peter McCormick, 'Regionalism in Canada: Disentangling the Threads', *Journal of Canadian Studies* 24 (1989): 16.

26. Roger Gibbins, *Conflict and Unity: An Introduction to Canadian Political Life* (Toronto: Methuen, 1985), 82.

27. Brodie, 'New Political Economy'.

28. Richard Simeon, 'Regionalism and Canadian Political Interpretations' in Richard Schultz et al., eds, *The Canadian Political Process* (Toronto: Holt Rinehart and Winston, 1979), 293–301.

29. David J. Elkins and Richard Simeon, *Small Worlds: Provinces and Parties in Canadian Political Life* (Toronto: Methuen, 1980).

30. Michael D. Ornstein, 'Regionalism and Canadian Political Ideology' in Robert J. Brym, ed., *Regionalism in Canada* (Toronto: Irwin, 1986); Michael Ornstein, H. Michael Stevenson, and A. Paul Williams, 'Region, Class and Political Culture in Canada', *Canadian Journal of Political Science* 13 (1980): 227–71.

31. Cuneo, 'A Class Perspective on Regionalism' in D. Glenday, H. Guindon, and A. Turowetz, eds, *Modernization and the Canadian State* (Toronto: Macmillan, 1978), 132.

32. Clement, *Class Analysis*, 151.

33. Ibid., 152.

34. Marchak, 'Contribution', 81.

35. See also the work of J.D. House, another Newfoundland sociologist: J.D. House, *The Challenge of Oil* (St John's: Institute of Social and Economic Research, 1985); J.D. House, 'The Mouse That Roars: New Directions in Canadian Political Economy—the Case of Newfoundland' in Brym, ed., *Regionalism in Canada*.

36. For example, Ornstein argues against the existence of distinct political cultures between provinces by measuring attitudes to a wide range of issues from rent control to foreign investment to union power. Note that the goal is to understand political ideologies and really does not tap regional understanding. See Michael D. Ornstein, 'Regionalism and Canadian Political Ideology'.

37. It is interesting that political economy has very recently tried to re-specify the role that the spatial factor plays in their analysis. See Wallace Clement, *Understanding Canada: Building on the New Canadian Political Economy* (Montreal: McGill-Queen's University Press, 1997),

ch. 1; and Jane Jenson, Rianne Mahon, and Manfred Bienefeld, eds, *Production, Space and Identity: Political Economy Faces the 21st Century* (Toronto: Canadian Scholars' Press, 1993).

38. John Walton, 'Urban Sociology: The Contribution and Limits of Political Economy', *Annual Review of Sociology* 19 (1993): 301–20, 314.

39. Roger Friedland, 'Space, Place and Modernity: The Geographical Moment', *Contemporary Sociology* 21 (1992), 11–15.

40. In fact, the debate over whether regions are natural or created sounds much like the debate in urban sociology between the ecological perspective and the Marxist/political economy perspective. See M. Gottdeiner, *The New Urban Sociology* (New York: McGraw Hill, 1994).

41. A bibliography of Anthony Giddens can be found in Christopher Bryant and David Jary, eds, *Giddens' Theory of Structuration: A Critical Appreciation* (New York: Routledge, 1992). But perhaps the two most relevant pieces are *A Contemporary Critique of Historical Materialism* (1981) and *The Constitution of Society: Outline of the Theory of Structuration* (Cambridge: Polity Press, 1984).

42. Peter Saunders, 'Space, Urbanism and the Created Environment' in David Held and John B. Thompson, eds, *Social Theory of Modern Societies: Anthony Giddens and His Critics* (Cambridge: Cambridge University Press, 1989), 215–34.

43. Anthony Giddens, *The Constitution of Society: Outline of the Theory of Structuration*, 130–1.

44. Ibid., 131.

45. John Urry, 'Time and Space in Giddens' Social Theory' in Christopher Bryant and David Jary, eds, *Giddens' Theory of Structuration;* Saunders, 'Space'.

46. Saunders, 'Space', 231.

47. Henri Lefebvre, *The Production of Space* (Oxford: Blackwell, 1991), 359.

48. Ibid., 362.

49. Lefebvre also has a dialectical notion of space, acknowledging space as both a material object and a process involving social relations which acts back upon itself. See M. Gottdeiner, *The Social Production of Urban Space* (Austin: University of Texas Press), 1985.

50. Gottdeiner, *New Urban Sociology*.

51. John R. Logan and Harvey L. Molotch, *Urban Fortunes: The Political Economy of Place* (Berkeley: University of California Press, 1987).

52. Gottdeiner, *New Urban Sociology*, 170.

53. Compare this perspective with that of Brodie, who argues that regions are political creations in a top-down model of power. See Janine Brodie, *The Political Economy of Canadian Regionalism*, 17.

54. Gidengil demonstrates empirically that Canadians sharing a similar regional location in the centre-periphery system tend to share similar feelings of political efficacy. Again, however, the focus is on political elements. See Elisabeth Gidengil, 'Centres and Peripheries: The Political Culture of Dependency', *Canadian Review of Sociology and Anthropology* 27 (1990): 23–48.

55. While the argument developed here has much in common with the work of Matthews, my conceptualization of regionalism is quite different from his social/psychological definition

of regionalism as primarily attachment to the territory in which people live. See Ralph Matthews and J. Campbell Davis, 'The Comparative Influence of Region, Status, Class and Ethnicity on Canadian Attitudes and Values' in Brym, ed., *Regionalism in Canada*, 98–9.

56. The concept of framing has been applied to social movement mobilization, refering to the way individuals are able to locate, perceive, identify, and label events in the world through an interpretive framework, making the events meaningful, organizing experience, and guiding action. See David Snow, E. Burke Rochford, Steven K. Worden, and Robert Benford, 'Frame Alignment Processes, Micromobilization and Movement Participation', *American Sociological Review* 51 (1986): 464–81.

57. A tentative step in that regard was my attempt to distinguish between the negative aspect of regionalism that stressed alienation, resentment, and exploitation (typical of top-down explanatory models) and the more positive aspect of regionalism that stressed optimism, sense of power, and boosterish thinking (more typical of bottom-up thinking). See Harry H. Hiller, 'Western Separatism in Australia and Canada: The Regional Ideology Thesis' in *Australia-Canadian Studies* 5 (1987): 39–54. Another attempt was to explain Western separatism by focusing on disturbances to the symbolic order of regional societies. See Harry H. Hiller, 'The Foundation and Politics of Separatism: Canada in Comparative Perspective', *Research in Political Sociology* 3 (1987): 39–60.

58. Schwartz, *Politics and Territory*, 309–10.

59. Mildred A. Schwartz, 'Regionalism and Canadian Constitution-Building' in Sally F. Zerker, ed. *Change and Impact: Essays in Canadian Social Sciences* (Jerusalem: The Magnes Press, 1994), 58–9.

60. See also Schwartz's statement at the end of the same piece: 'regions are collective political actors and cultural systems, and hence sources of social action. This makes regions more than simply the political manifestations of federalism.' See Schwartz, 'Regionalism and Constitution-Building'.

61. John Goyder, 'Migration and Regional Differences in Life Satisfaction in the Anglophone Provinces', *Canadian Journal of Sociology* 20, 3 (1995): 287–307.

62. See Stevenson, 'Canadian Regionalism'. He also argues that regions can be independent of political and administrative boundaries.

63. Matthews argues that regions have replaced communities as the fundamental territorial social unit. See Matthews, *Creation of Regional Dependency*, 15.

64. A good base in that regard is demonstrated by the health of regional studies, as measured by regional journals and regional institutes. See Colin Howell and Martha McDonald, 'Diversity, National Unity and Self-Awareness: The Cameron Report on Canadian Studies', *Journal of Canadian Studies* 30, 4 (1995-96): 207–8.

65. Compare House's conception of 'social region' as a theoretical category in its own right analytically independent of social class. See House, 'The Mouse That Roars'.

Part 2

Understanding Contemporary Canadian Regionalism

Introduction

The most well-developed approach to understanding regionalism in Canada (with the possible exception of political economy) is that of political culture. There are two very different approaches to the study of political culture. The first is historical and literary, making broad observations about national or regional character from a study of literature, myths, and history. The work of Gad Horowitz on socialism in Canada and that of Seymour Martin Lipset on differences between the political cultures of Canada and the United States fall into this tradition. The second approach is behavioural, seeking to describe the characteristics of a national or regional culture by examining the political attitudes and behaviour of individuals. Mildred Schwartz's *Politics and Territory*, along with David Elkins and Richard Simeon's *Small Worlds,* were pioneering behavioural studies of regional differences in political culture. Both found substantial and significant patterns of regional differentiation in political attitudes.

In their contribution to this volume, Harold Clarke, Jon Pammett, and Marianne Stewart examine regional differences in Canadian political culture in the behavioural tradition pioneered by Mildred Schwartz. Recalling Schwartz's observation in *Politics and Territory* that 'distinct climates of opinion in each region' are 'an important barrier to consensus' in Canadian politics, Clarke et al. examine regional differences in political culture. This over-time analysis shows that some regional differences (most notably in political efficacy) have diminished over the period since Mildred Schwartz researched *Politics and Territory.* In fact, these authors conclude that many Canadians do not identify with their region of residence, and that region has little power in explaining Canadians' political attitudes and beliefs. More important than regional differences, they argue, is the Canadian electorate's overwhelmingly negative evaluation of the capacity of government. These unfavourable evaluations are not unique to Westerners or Quebeckers, but rather are elements of a pan-Canadian political culture of discontent.

Shaun Henry's findings diverge somewhat from this, suggesting that regional alienation remains somewhat salient in some parts of the country. The results of his study suggest that if alienation is what defines 'the West', then only Alberta genuinely qualifies as Western and Manitoba cannot even be considered part of the region. In the other regional periphery—Atlantic Canada—alienation lags behind that of Alberta, British Columbia, and Saskatchewan, but exceeds levels found in Manitoba. Henry's findings confirm that regional alienation in Canada is not simply political alienation independent of geographic locale: the most alienated, particularly in the West, tend to be politically active. Clearly, these are not the disenfranchised.

Barry Cooper's contribution to this volume employs the historical and literary approach to political culture. To understand Canadian regionalism, he argues, 'One must take into account not only voting data and economic interests but also texts and speeches that express regional imaginative consciousness.' Identity, including regional identity, grows from historical experience, and 'becomes articulate and finds a place in the world as myth or story that then is available to express political purposes and to justify political action.' Cooper locates Western regionalism in the context of what he calls the myth of Laurentian Canada, articulated by Harold Innis, Donald Creighton, Arthur Lower, and Northrop Frye. This myth, he argues, locates the heart of Canada in the St Lawrence River, eclipsing the Maritimes and largely ignoring the West. In the West, the spirit of new beginnings eliminates the theme of survival that is integral to the Laurentian myth of Canada. Cooper locates Western regionalism in the dissonance between the Laurentian and the Western myths. National public policies, he argues, 'have often simply given legislative expression to the Laurentian myth' and have been imposed by parties under the sway of this myth. These policies have 'harmed Western interests and have insulted Western pride', thereby spawning a multi-faceted strategy for Westerners to find a political vehicle that represents their interests and their vision in the national government. The most recent manifestation of this strategy is the Reform/Canadian Alliance party, which is struggling with the incompatibility of its populist leanings and the institutions of responsible government.

Taken together, these three chapters demonstrate the elusive character of Canadian regionalism. Looking at the phenomenon from a behavioural perspective, we find evidence that regionalism is in decline, and that 'the West' and 'the Atlantic region' are not the cohesive units they are often taken to be. Despite this, an examination of the myths that structure political identities leads to making a case for the persistence of regionalism because such myths are both enduring and pervasive.

Chapter 3

The Forest for the Trees: Regional (Dis)Similarities in Canadian Political Culture

HAROLD D. CLARKE, JON H. PAMMETT, MARIANNE C. STEWART

In recent years, rising discontent with political authorities, regimes, and communities has invigorated scholarly research on the sources, distribution, and consequences of political culture in emerging and established democracies. As is well known, the concept of political culture and its use in comparative inquiry owe much to Gabriel Almond and Sidney Verba's pioneering study, *The Civic Culture*.[1] Since its publication nearly four decades ago, *The Civic Culture* has motivated numerous investigations of political culture in countries that have markedly different forms of governance and social cleavage structures. In Canada, pressing problems of national integration have stimulated scholars to focus their inquiries on mapping public attitudes and beliefs that might sustain, or undermine, liberal-democratic political institutions and a national political community in a setting characterized by long-standing, regionally based economic and ethno-linguistic cleavages. As a result, the general analytic theme of regional and/or provincial differences has dominated research on Canadian political culture,[2] with some analysts[3] arguing that these differences are accompanied by regionally distinctive variations in orientations towards politics at the national and provincial levels of governance. The prevailing conventional wisdom is that Canada's public political psychology is a complex, multi-dimensional mirror of the regional diversity that characterizes its society.

In this chapter it is argued that, in important respects, the seemingly perennial quest for regional variations in political culture has missed the forest for the trees. We investigate a rival hypothesis of regional similarity, using data from the Canadian National Election Studies (CNES) and Political Support in Canada (PSC) surveys conducted over the 1965–90 period. We first document how Canadians think about regional divisions in their country and the extent to which their use of region corresponds to scholarly definitions of it. Next, we analyze regional distributions of such attitudes as political efficacy and trust, as well as core beliefs pertaining to the effectiveness and fairness of, and satisfaction with, government performance in several policy areas. We then document that political attitudes and beliefs integral to Canadian political culture during the 1965–90 period continued during the 1990s. This finding is important because the 1990s witnessed the occurrence of several 'polity-shaping' events: the collapse of a long-lived national party system, two failed attempts to resolve the country's long-standing constitutional impasse, and a Quebec sovereignty referendum that very nearly precipitated the dissolution of the national political community. Although subjects of high drama, these events were neither cause nor consequence of seismic shifts in public political psychology. In the conclusion, we reprise major findings and suggest that the pan-Canadian elements in political culture we have documented are not cause for celebration. They neither index an emergent national unity nor bode well for the quality of democratic political life.

Studying Civic Cultures

Political culture typically is defined as a set of attitudes, beliefs, and values that individuals hold about themselves as political actors, about other people in politics, and about government and political institutions. This definition has much to do with Almond and Verba's efforts in *The Civic Culture* to bring survey methodology to bear on important questions about the attitudinal and participatory underpinnings of liberal-democratic institutions in comparative perspective. In their conceptual inventory, Almond and Verba emphasized 'subjective political competence'—that is, a citizen's belief that he or she has the potential to participate effectively in the political process—and political trust—that is, a belief that political authorities behave honestly and govern effectively. Following the work of Talcott Parsons, and also evident in studies by David Easton,[4] Almond and Verba further distinguished among cognitive orientations (beliefs about 'political facts'), affective orientations (likes and dislikes grounded in emotional reactions), and evaluative orientations (judgments about 'outputs' of the political system, particularly government performance in various policy areas).

In Almond and Verba's theoretical framework, subjective competence or political efficacy is an important determinant of citizen political participation and the stability of a democratic political order. However, what they term a 'trust surplus' may be tantamount to tacit consent that produces an unwillingness to perform the activities necessary to hold public officials accountable, whereas a 'trust deficit' increases reception to mobilization efforts that foment protest for political change.[5] Moreover, persistent and widespread perceptions that government institutions fail to perform the tasks expected of them, or that the benefits and costs of government policies are distributed unfairly, are associated with a generalized cynicism and/or negativity about politics. Cynicism brings about withdrawal from public life, whereas negativity can stimulate engagement on behalf of sweeping reforms or revolution. By Almond and Verba's account, then, widespread citizen participation in the political arena is not necessarily 'a good thing' because it could have profoundly destabilizing consequences for a liberal-democratic regime.[6]

Given its status as a path-breaking study of the political psychology of democratic governance, it does not surprise that *The Civic Culture* has received both lavish praise and persistent criticism. Critics have focused on its failure to employ representative sampling procedures in several national surveys, the lack of appropriate definitional criteria involving both democracy and stability, and the characterization of Great

Britain and the United States as exemplary—that is, stable—democracies.[7] The thesis of democratic stability has attracted particular disapproval. Writing from a normative perspective, participatory democratic theorists have contended that *The Civic Culture*'s emphasis on securing stability, rather than maximizing democracy, neglected the contributions of civic engagement to the development of individual citizenship and public policy.[8] Other critics, judging *The Civic Culture* as an empirical theory of democracy, have argued that it was flawed by a failure to specify the behavioural mechanism that converts micro-level supportive citizen attitudes into macro-level regime stability.[9] Also, the strong associations between political efficacy and trust on the one hand and regime stability on the other have not materialized in the decades since the book appeared.[10] *The Civic Culture* thus is bedevilled by problems of cross-level inference, an absence of properly specified dependent variables, and lack of empirical support for key theoretical claims.[11]

Despite significant shortcomings, *The Civic Culture* was a highly innovative study, and its influence remains apparent in research on political culture in Canada and elsewhere.[12] An important case in point is Mildred Schwartz's *Politics and Territory: The Sociology of Regional Persistence in Canada*,[13] which did much to advance the study of Canadian political culture and heighten awareness of the significance and persistence of social divisions, particularly regional variations, in public political life.[14] As attention focused on the identification of regional variations in political culture and speculation on their dynamics over time, the distinction between 'citizen' and 'disaffected' regions emerged.[15] As for dynamics, Wilson argued that transitions from 'underdeveloped' to 'developed' political cultures would occur as political party and economic systems converged[16] across regions. Rejecting Wilson's tacit Marxist assumption that economics drives culture, Schwartz adopted a decidedly Weberian theoretical stance, arguing that regional variations in political culture would withstand the forces of economic growth and urbanization.[17] The political implications of her argument are significant because 'distinct climates of opinion in each region' are 'an important barrier to consensus'. By Schwartz's account, region was, and would continue to be, a central organizing principle in Canadian political life.

Arguments elevating the importance of region-specific forces in public political psychology did not lack credence. As is well known, in democratic federal systems, particularly in highly decentralized ones, the division of governmental responsibilities is associated with the expansion of the scope of government performance and the number of arenas of government responsiveness, public accountability, and citizen participation.[18] In Canada, the provinces are highly salient and important arenas of government authority and political action. A highly decentralized federal system and strong ethno-linguistic and regional cleavages have been reciprocally reinforcing,[19] and have influenced the evolution of federal and provincial party systems and patterns of party support at the two levels of government in various provinces. In turn, Canada's highly decentralized federalism and differentiated contexts of political action have been conducive to the development of regional disparities in public political attitudes and beliefs. As an extension of this argument, it might be expected that levels of political efficacy and trust, and evaluations of government performance, would rise and fall with the ebb and flow of salient events framed in regional terms. Over the past three decades, such events would include the October Crisis (1970), sovereignty-association referendums (May 1980; October 1995), the failure of the Meech Lake Accord (June 1990), and the national referendum on the Charlottetown Accord (October 1992). It also can be suggested that people who live in a region or province such as Ontario, where they traditionally have enjoyed varying combinations of economic, political, and social advantages, would report much higher levels of political efficacy and trust and more favourable evaluations of the effectiveness, equity, and fairness of government activities than those domiciled in less advantaged places such as the Atlantic provinces and the Prairies.

Does Canada consist of federal and provincial political worlds intertwined with divided loyalties? Is region a persistent source of significant variation in political culture? These questions are worth posing because, over the past several decades, expanding educational and employment opportunities have propelled a steep rise in geographic and socio-economic mobility that, in turn, has prompted a decline in enduring social relationships. These trends have been accompanied by a dramatic increase in the use of mass communications and computing technologies to acquire information about public affairs.[20] In turn, these developments have led to a loosening of the social anchors of political attitudes and, thus, have prompted some observers to inquire whether Seymour Lipset and Stein Rokkan's[21] famous 'frozen' social cleavages that defined the socio-political landscapes of mature democracies for much of the twentieth century have now 'gone stale'.[22] Although our focus is not on the social bases of partisan attitudes per se, our concern is similar, and we maintain that important (although not all) aspects of mass political culture in Canada are not strongly differentiated by spatial geographic distinctions.[23]

We further hypothesize that public political orientations in Canada have non-trivial short-term dynamics and respond to important public events. Periodic elections constitute one set of such events. In this regard, it is a plausible but seldom tested hypothesis that the occurrence of national elections in democratic polities is associated with temporarily heightened feelings of internal and external efficacy.[24] Elections are highly salient events when press and politicians alike repeatedly remind citizens that their ballots provide them with opportunities to determine who will govern. Elections also are times when competing parties, leaders, and local candidates work assiduously to convince voters that they are trustworthy and, if elected, will be responsive to public needs and demands.[25] If correct, the claim that elections affect political attitudes and beliefs implies that national election surveys cannot be relied upon to provide accurate portraits of significant aspects of political culture in democracies such as Canada. Data gathered in election surveys will overestimate levels of attitudes and beliefs such as political efficacy, interest, and trust, as these attitudes and beliefs exist in typical (that is, non-election) periods. We proceeded to test the conventional wisdom of regional variation in political-cultural attitudes against our rival hypothesis of regional similarity, together with the conjecture that elections influence the dynamics of these attitudes, using national survey data gathered in election and non-election years since 1965.

The Meaning of Region in the Public Mind

Although questions measuring political efficacy and trust were included in the first Canadian National Election Study (CNES), in 1965, and subsequent ones, the 1974 and 1979 CNES investigated the correspondence between individual Canadians' subjective sense of the country's regional nature and objective boundaries that usually are used in data analysis. Respondents were asked whether they thought of Canada as being divided into regions, and if so, to designate their region of residence. In 1974, fully 41 per cent said either that they did not think of the country as being divided into regions, or they did not know;[26] in 1979, the percentage of 'non-regional' Canadians was seven points higher, while the percentage of 'don't knows' remained the same (Table 3.1). Thus, only just over half of the eligible electorate demonstrated some sense of regional awareness.

Although people's definitions of their own regions were somewhat similar in the two years (Table 3.1), Canadians were less likely to designate their provinces as regions in 1979 than they were five years earlier. In both years, the West was the most cohesive regional unit and, in Quebec, the percentage identifying it as their region was the same (19 per cent) and equal to the percentage stating that they lived in a particular sub-region of the province. The finding that in 1974 fewer Canadians regarded their province as a region than in 1979 was especially noteworthy in two provinces— Ontario and British Columbia—typically categorized as separate regions for research purposes. Taken together, these data on the place of region in the public mind help to explain why the scholarly quest for regional variation in political culture has been a difficult one.

Regional Variations and Over-Time Trends

Political (In)Efficacy

Political efficacy, or as Almond and Verba called it, 'subjective political competence', is the attitude 'that individual political action does have, or can have, an impact on the political process'.[27] This definition was revised by Lane to distinguish between *external* political efficacy—the attitude that the political process will respond to efforts to influence it—and *internal* political efficacy—the attitude that one has the resources and skills needed to affect that process.[28]

Since 1965, several Canadian national surveys have included two 'agree/disagree' statements to capture external efficacy (Members of Parliament are unresponsive; government does not care what people think) and two others intended to measure internal efficacy (politics is too complicated to understand; people like me do not have a say in what government does).[29] Responses to these four statements in the CNES and other studies conducted in election and non-election years[30] consistently indicated that large percentages of the Canadian public lacked a sense of both external and internal efficacy (Figure 3.1). Indeed, in only two cases (government does not care,

Table 3.1: Definition of Own Region by Province, 1974, 1979

		NFLD %	PEI %	NS %	NB %	QUE %	ONT %	MAN %	SASK %	ALTA %	BC %	TOTAL %
Does not think regionally	(74)	28	25	26	40	31	33	23	19	21	28	30
	(79)	44	38	46	49	31	42	40	37	32	35	37
Does not know	(74)	38	20	15	13	16	8	4	5	12	3	11
	(79)	18	12	9	8	18	10	3	4	7	6	11
Own province	(74)	6	2	3	2	19	19	4	2	7	29	16
	(79)	5	1	1	1	19	13	2	1	5	15	12
Rest/West	(74)	10	4	6	16	7	3	36	33	43	35	14
	(79)	5	7	12	7	7	4	32	43	42	40	15
Atlantic, Maritime	(74)	14	45	46	23	–	–	–	–	–	–	3
	(79)	22	40	30	20	–	–	–	–	–	–	2
Central	(74)	–	1	–	–	2	13	12	2	1	1	6
	(79)	–	–	–	1	2	17	7	1	1	–	7
Prairies	(74)	–	–	–	–	–	–	15	30	10	–	3
	(79)	–	–	–	–	–	–	12	13	12	–	2
General area of own province	(74)	–	1	–	2	2	10	1	2	2	–	4
	(79)	–	–	1	1	1	6	1	–	–	1	3
Specific area of own province	(74)	–	–	1	2	20	4	–	–	–	–	7
	(79)	–	–	1	8	18	4	–	–	1	–	7
Economic, Linguistic	(74)	5	2	4	2	3	10	4	8	5	5	6
	(79)	5	2	1	5	2	4	3	1	1	3	4
N	(74)	102	97	180	134	702	702	113	101	179	252	2445
N	(79)	111	109	191	149	733	741	128	113	194	275	2672

measured in 1965 and 1968) did less than a majority of those interviewed fail to *agree* that MPs soon lose touch; government does not care about their opinions, politics is too complicated for them to understand, and people like them have no say in what government does.

Previous studies have attempted to demonstrate regional differences in political culture by demonstrating that Canadians' sense of political efficacy and their feelings of trust in government vary by region. In particular, pioneering analyses[31] used the CNES efficacy data as the principal empirical support for their general arguments that there are substantial regional differences in Canadian political culture. We do not question the choice of political efficacy as focal point for investigation; participatory democratic theorists[32] have made cogent cases for its importance. But the question remains, do politically efficacious attitudes vary *substantially* by region? To answer this question we employed responses to the four efficacy statements listed above in surveys conducted over the 1965–90 period and the conventional definition of five geographic regions (Atlantic provinces, Quebec, Ontario, the Prairies, British Columbia). Figures 3.2A and 3.2B show, with respect to the two external efficacy items (MPs lose touch; government does not care), that regional differences were evident in the 1960s, but have tended to collapse since then. Regional variations in the responses to an internal efficacy item (no say) also were apparent in the early surveys, but declined from the mid-1970s onward (Figure 3.2D).[33] Regional variation in the other internal item (politics too complicated) has remained quite modest, and no clear trends are evident (Figure 3.2C).

To calibrate the extent of regional variation in political efficacy more precisely, we performed multiple regression analyses of indices of external and internal efficacy,

Figure 3.1: Political Inefficacy, 1965–1990

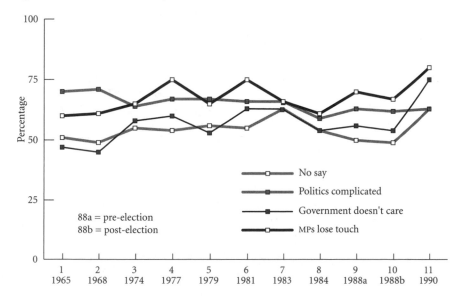

Figure 3.2

A. Percentages Agreeing MPs Lose Touch, 1965–1990

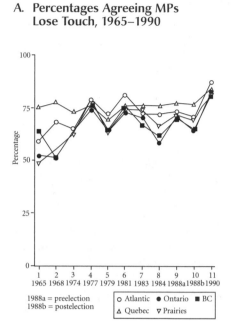

B. Percentages Agreeing Government Doesn't Care, 1965–1990

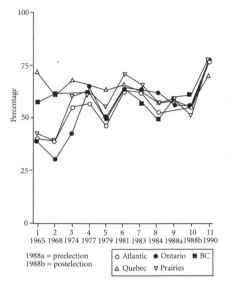

C. Percentages Agreeing Politics Complicated, 1965–1990

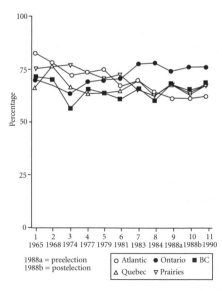

D. Percentages Agreeing They Have No Say, 1965–1990

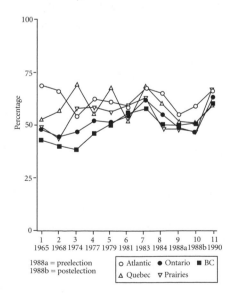

constructed using the four items described above.[34] Predictor variables include dummy variable measures of region/ethnicity (separating francophone and non-francophone groups in Quebec), as well as measures of age, annual family income, gender, and level of formal education.[35] The latter variables were included in the analyses as controls to ensure that any observed regional differences were not spurious artifacts of regionally correlated differences in socio-demographic variables that might influence politically efficacious feelings. To investigate possible over-time changes in group differences in efficacy, we performed the analyses using data gathered in surveys conducted in 1965 and 1988.

The regression analyses clearly showed that, even circa 1965, regional variation in external, and especially internal, political efficacy was not large. When only the regional/ethnic dummy variables were entered into the regressions, just 8 per cent of the variance in external efficacy and 1 per cent of the variance in internal efficacy were explained in 1965 (Table 3.2A).[36] Consistent with the impression conveyed by the graphic displays presented above, the former figure declined to 0 per cent and the latter remained at 1 per cent in 1988 (Table 3.2B). Regarding other predictor variables, persons having higher incomes and more extensive formal education had higher levels of both external and internal efficacy than did other Canadians. Gender differences in external efficacy were not significant; women, however, manifested lower levels of internal efficacy in both 1965 and 1988. Relationships involving age were similarly weak and inconsistent over time. Although inclusion of the several socio-demographic variables improved our ability to explain the two types of efficacy, the gains were far from impressive (Table 3.2). In sum, these analyses indicated that political *inefficacy* is widespread throughout Canadian society and that, previous claims notwithstanding, this has been the case at least since the mid-1960s when the first national election surveys were conducted.

Although instructive, the results just presented say little about possible long- and short-term changes in political efficacy. Data gathered over a quarter-century help us to study its long-term dynamics and, thereby, to determine if there have been national and regional trends in efficacy since the first election survey was carried out in 1965. Since surveys have been conducted in non-election as well as election years, we also can ascertain the extent to which (in)efficacious attitudes have exhibited short-term fluctuations in response to elections and related changes in political context.

We began by conducting aggregate-level regression analyses of time-series data composed of mean national and regional scores on the external and internal political inefficacy indices. Our time-series regression model included a linear trend term, a dummy variable to indicate whether the efficacy data were gathered in an election-year survey, and a 1990 period-effect dummy variable that enabled us to determine whether any apparent long-term trend was, in fact, an artifact of a precipitate decrease in efficacy in the post-1988 period.[37] The model was:

$$INEFF_t = B_0 + B_1ELECT_t + B_2TREND + B_3D90 + \varepsilon_t$$

Table 3.2: Regression Analyses, Political Inefficacy Indices, 1965 and 1988 Postelection Surveys

A. 1965 Predictor Variables	External Inefficacy			Internal Inefficacy		
	b	B	t	b	B	t
Age	0.00	.05	2.57b	0.00	.02	1.12
Education	−0.11	−.15	−7.20a	−0.18	−.27	−13.33a
Gender	0.01	.00	0.21	0.21	.13	7.28a
Income	−0.04	−.12	−5.35a	−0.04	−.14	−6.63a
Region/Ethnicity: Atlantic	0.12	.04	2.00c	0.19	.07	3.42a
Quebec: French	0.51	.27	12.59a	−0.00	.01	0.25
Quebec: Non-French	0.23	.06	2.92b	0.14	.04	2.02c
Prairies	−0.09	−.04	−1.85	0.01	.00	0.25
British Columbia	0.05	.02	0.84	0.02	.01	0.42
Constant	1.30	__	13.33a	1.51	__	17.08
R² =		.14			.16	
Region/Ethnicity Only R² =		.08			. 01	

B. 1988 Predictor Variables	External Inefficacy			Internal Inefficacy		
	b	B	t	b	B	t
Age	−0.00	−.01	−0.45	0.00	.06	2.94b
Education	−0.09	−.13	−5.04a	−0.15	−.22	−9.17a
Gender	0.08	.05	2.05c	0.14	.09	4.22a
Income	−0.05	−.11	−4.25a	−0.07	−.16	−6.92a
Region/Ethnicity: Atlantic	−0.02	−.01	−0.32	0.14	.05	2.18c
Quebec: French	0.07	.04	1.43	−0.02	−.01	−0.54
Quebec: Non-French	0.01	.00	0.10	0.14	.03	1.33
Prairies	−0.04	−.02	−0.76	−0.06	−.03	−1.14
British Columbia	0.03	.00	0.45	0.00	.00	0.04
Constant	1.61	__	14.19a	1.55	__	15.39a
R² =		.05			.14	
Region/Ethnicity Only R² =		.00			.01	

a: $p \le .001$; b: $p \le .01$; c: $p \le . 05$ (two-tailed test)

where: $INEFF_t$ = internal or external political *inefficacy* index score for survey conducted in year t; ELECT = election-year or non-election-year survey; TREND = trend (year of survey); D90 = 1990 period effect; ε_t = error term; B_0 = constant; B_{1-3} = regression coefficients.

We analyzed this model for Canada as a whole and then separately for each of the five regions. The external political inefficacy analyses are displayed in Table 3.3A, and the model fit for the country-wide analysis is presented in Figure 3.3. With respect to the latter, net of election-year and 1990 period effects, parameter estimates revealed that external *inefficacy* increased modestly over the quarter-century after 1965. As hypothesized, it also fluctuated with the occurrence of elections. Net of these effects, diminished external efficacy after 1988 (as shown by the significant 1990 period-effect coefficient) is apparent. Overall, the model fits the data very well, accounting for fully 88 per cent of the over-time variance in the external inefficacy index for the country as a whole.

The model also fits the data quite well in each of the regional analyses, but not all of the national effects just described are present. In each region, non-election years and the 1990 period effect were associated with decreased external efficacy. In most of English-speaking Canada (Ontario, the Prairies, British Columbia), people also became somewhat less efficacious over time. There was no significant trend in the Atlantic provinces, and external efficacy increased in Quebec over time. Taken together, these results are consistent with the response patterns displayed in Table 3.2, suggesting that levels of external efficacy in Quebec and other regions converged over time.

The internal inefficacy analyses are shown in Table 3.3B and Figure 3.4. For the country as a whole, election-year and 1990 period effects were similar to those just described, that is, internal efficacy increased in election years and decreased after 1988. However, there was a modest negative trend (a long-term decrease) in internal inefficacy over the 1965–90 period. Regional analyses showed that, in most cases,

Table 3.3: Regression Analyses of Political Inefficacy, Canada and Region, 1965-1990

A. External Inefficacy		b	b	b	b	b	b British Columbia
		Canada	Atlantic	Quebec	Ontario	Prairies	Columbia
Predictor Variables							
Trend		0.00d	0.00	−0.00c	0.01c	0.01c	0.01c
Election years		−0.15c	−0.09d	−0.07c	−0.19c	−0.22c	−0.23c
1990 Period Effect		0.21c	0.20c	0.21c	0.21c	0.21d	0.20d
Constant		1.01c	1.28c	1.85c	0.59d	0.57d	0.53d
	$R^2 =$	.88	.71	.92	.86	.84	.85
	D =	2.01	1.66	2.38	2.26	1.32	1.89

B. Internal Inefficacy		b	b	b	b	b	b British Columbia
		Canada	Atlantic	Quebec	Ontario	Prairies	Columbia
Predictor Variables							
Trend		−0.00d	−0.00	−0.00	−0.00	−0.01d	0.00
Election years		−0.05d	0.01	0.02	−0.10c	−0.07	−0.07
1990 Period Effect		0.10c	0.11	0.10	0.10d	0.12	0.05
Constant		1.49c	1.69c	1.49c	1.42c	1.73a	1.16a
	$R^2 =$	.50	.22	.17	.68	.38	.29
	D =	2.41	1.63	2.92	1.52	1.78	1.50

a: $p \le .001$; c: $p \le .05$; d: $p \le .10$

Figure 3.3: Actual and Predicted External Political Inefficacy Scores, Canada, 1965–1990

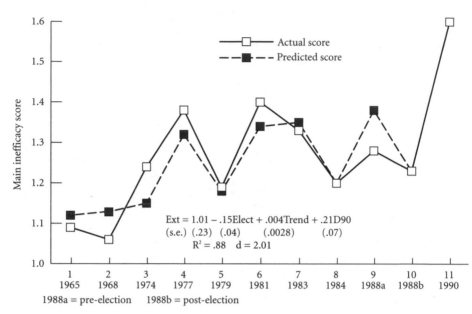

Ext = 1.01 − .15Elect + .004Trend + .21D90
(s.e.) (.23) (.04)   (.0028)   (.07)
R^2 = .88   d = 2.01

1988a = pre-election   1988b = post-election

Figure 3.4: Actual and Predicted Internal Political Inefficacy Scores, Canada, 1965–1990

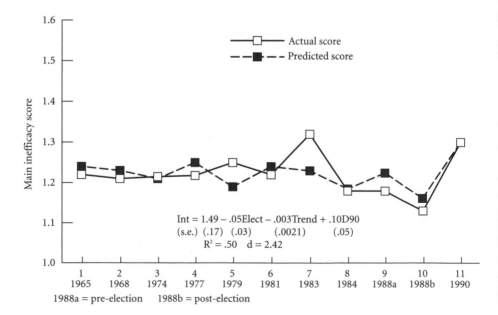

Int = 1.49 − .05Elect − .003Trend + .10D90
(s.e.) (.17) (.03)   (.0021)   (.05)
R^2 = .50   d = 2.42

1988a = pre-election   1988b = post-election

similar kinds of effects were at work in various parts of the country, but most were quite weak and statistically insignificant. For example, the trend term was signed negatively in every region except British Columbia but was significant only for Ontario. Similarly, although the election-year effect was negative in Ontario, the Prairies, and British Columbia, and the 1990 effect was positive in all regions, it was significant only for the former region. Overall, these findings are again consistent with the data in Figure 3.2, which suggest that, especially for the 'politics too complicated' item, internal political inefficacy was widespread, and quite stable in the aggregate, between 1965 and 1990.

Political (Dis)Trust

Political trust concerns judgments about the probity and wisdom of public officials and the efficient and effective operation of governmental institutions. Questions periodically have been asked in the Canadian surveys to ascertain whether respondents think that federal government officials are intelligent and trustworthy, and whether they believe such officials are dishonest and waste people's tax monies. Since the trust items have not been asked as frequently as the efficacy ones, a consistent set is available for only six surveys conducted over the 1979–90 period.[38]

Analyses of data generated by these questions indicated that substantial numbers of Canadians had low levels of political trust. Large minorities thought that federal governmental authorities were dishonest, lacked intelligence, and were untrustworthy, and overwhelming majorities agreed that these officials mismanaged the public purse. Nationally, this pattern of response did not vary much over time, although distrusting answers to all four questions were most frequent in 1990 (Figure 3.5). Contradicting the claim that trust in government varies widely across regions, regional differences in attitudes about the probity and wisdom of federal authorities were generally quite modest (Figure 3.6A–D). The most noteworthy pattern was that Quebeckers were less likely than other Canadians to believe that public officials were stupid and squandered citizens' tax dollars.

To determine the ability of region of residence to explain variations in political distrust, we used responses to the four items to construct an overall political distrust index.[39] We employed this index as the dependent variable in regression analyses similar to those for political efficacy discussed above. The results (Table 3.4) revealed that, in both 1979 and 1988, the regional dummy variables accounted for only 1 per cent of the variance in the index, and only one of these variables (British Columbia, 1988) has a statistically significant effect. Moreover, and unlike the efficacy analyses, all of the other predictors exerted very weak effects. Better educated persons were more trusting in both years, and higher income persons were more trusting in 1988. None of the other explanatory variables were statistically significant and, overall, the predictors accounted for only 2 per cent and 4 per cent of the variance in trust in 1979 and 1988, respectively.[40]

When we performed an aggregate time series analysis, similar to the one used for political efficacy, the results provided no evidence of long-term trends in trust. The

Figure 3.5: Distrust in Federal Political Authorities, 1979–1990

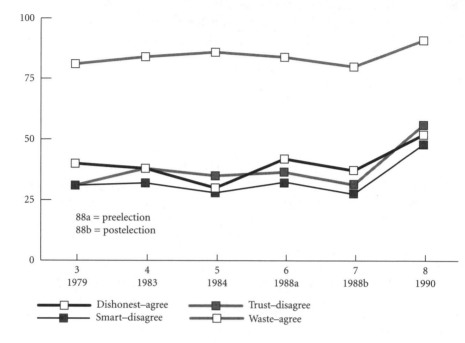

88a = preelection
88b = postelection

	Dishonest–agree		Trust–disagree
	Smart–disagree		Waste–agree

Table 3.4: Regression Analyses, Political Distrust Index, 1979 and 1988 Post-Election Surveys

Predictor Variables	1979 b	1979 B	1979 t	1988 b	1988 B	1988 t
Age	-0.00	-.06	-1.66	-0.00	-.02	-0.87
Education	-0.10	-.12	-3.37a	-0.10	-.09	-3.24a
Gender	0.06	.03	0.84	0.12	.05	1.94
Income	-0.00	-.00	-0.03	-0.06	-.10	-3.86a
Region/Ethnicity: Atlantic	0.10	.03	0.75	-0.13	.03	1.17
Quebec: French	-0.15	-.05	-1.50	-0.04	-.01	-0.43
Quebec: Non-French	0.36	.05	1.40	0.27	.04	1.48
Prairies	-0.05	-.01	-0.43	-0.16	-.05	-1.80
British Columbia	0.12	.03	1.00	0.23	.06	2.30c
Constant	2.22	__	10.03a	2.21	__	-3.86a
R² =		.02			.04	
Region/Ethnicity R² =		.01			.01	

a: p ≤ .001; b: p ≤ .01;   c: p ≤ . 05 (two-tailed test)

Figure 3.6

A. Percentages Disagreeing That People in the Federal Government Can Be Trusted To Do What is Right, 1979–1990

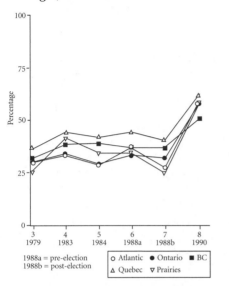

1988a = pre-election
1988b = post-election

○ Atlantic ● Ontario ■ BC
△ Quebec ▽ Prairies

B. Percentages Agreeing Many People in the Federal Government are Dishonest, 1979–1990

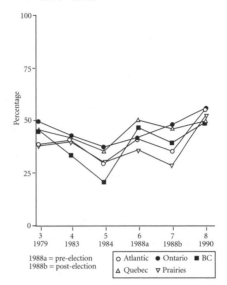

1988a = pre-election
1988b = post-election

○ Atlantic ● Ontario ■ BC
△ Quebec ▽ Prairies

C. Percentages Agreeing That People in the Federal Government Waste a Lot of Tax Money

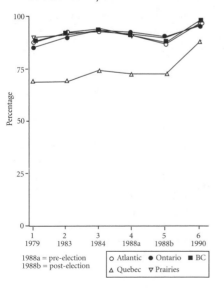

1988a = pre-election
1988b = post-election

○ Atlantic ● Ontario ■ BC
△ Quebec ▽ Prairies

D. Percentages Disagreeing That Most People in Federal Government are Smart

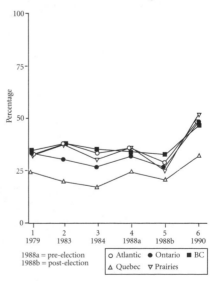

1988a = pre-election
1988b = post-election

○ Atlantic ● Ontario ■ BC
△ Quebec ▽ Prairies

only marginally significant trend term (p < .10) indicated a modest decrease in *distrust* in federal political authorities over the 1979–90 period in the Prairies (Table 3.5). However, as in the efficacy analyses, election-year effects were at work both nationally and in three regions (Ontario, the Prairies, and British Columbia). The finding that, in all cases, trust was higher in the election-year surveys was consistent with the proposition that, in a democracy, the occurrence of elections stimulates positive feelings about political authorities. Also, and similar to the efficacy analyses, the 1990 period effect operated nationally and in all regions but Quebec. Thus, although our analyses suggested that substantial distrust in federal political authorities has characterized public attitudes in every region since at least the mid-1960s, distrust increased further as the 1990s began.

Provincial (In)efficacy and (Dis)trust

Although it is well established that substantial minorities of Canadians identify with different federal and provincial political parties,[41] relatively little is known about differential feelings of political efficacy and trust at the two levels of government.[42] Is it possible that efficacy and trust are higher for provincial than federal politics, or that regional differences are greater for the former than the latter? If Canadians express greater efficacy and trust about provincial politics, this would accord well with the oft-repeated claims of provincial premiers in federal-provincial disputes that 'their' governments are more responsive to public needs and demands and more trustworthy than is the national government in 'distant' Ottawa. Moreover, large regional variations in these attitudes and beliefs would challenge our thesis that regional differences in efficacy and trust have been overplayed in previous studies of Canadian political culture.

Only the 1983 Political Support and the 1984 CNES surveys asked parallel sets of questions about political efficacy and trust in federal and provincial politics. These data show that levels of efficacy were somewhat higher in provincial politics, with federal-provincial differences being larger in 1983 than in 1984 (Figure 3.7). In both

Table 3.5: Regression Analyses of Political Distrust, Canada and Regions, 1979–1990

Predictor Variables		Canada b	Atlantic b	Quebec b	Ontario b	Prairies b	British Columbia b
Trend		-0.01	-0.00	0.01	-0.01	-0.03d	-0.00
Election Years		-0.15c	-0.01	-0.06	-0.21c	-0.30c	-0.10d
1990 Period Effect		0.60c	0.67c	0.53c	0.65c	0.69c	0.39c
Constant		2.43c	1.95c	1.09	2.76c	4.30c	2.08c
	R² =	.98	.96	.94	.99	.96	.95
	d =	2.63	1.86	2.24	2.71	1.82	1.96

c: p ≤ .05; d: p ≤ .10 (one-tailed test)

years, however, these differences were matters of degree rather than kind since, in almost every case, a majority of respondents failed to report efficacious feelings with respect to either level. Differences in trust were smaller still: the percentages distrusting federal and provincial political authorities varied no more than 10 per cent in either survey, and the average federal-provincial difference was only 4 per cent (Figure 3.8). Similar to their federal counterparts, provincial political efficacy and trust did not vary sharply across regional boundaries or other socio-demographic divisions in the population. Regression analyses of provincial efficacy indices show that Quebeckers and British Columbians exhibited significantly lower external efficacy, whereas non-francophone Quebeckers had lower internal efficacy and Prairie residents had higher internal efficacy. Despite these differences, the predictor variables in the regression analysis collectively explained only 3 per cent of the variance in external inefficacy and 2 per cent in internal inefficacy (data not shown). The comparable 1984 figures were 2 per cent and 1 per cent, respectively. The trust regressions tell a similar story: region accounted for only 3 per cent of the variance in 1983 and 4 per cent in 1984. As for the other socio-demographic variables, well-educated persons and those with higher incomes were more efficacious and trusting, and women were less efficacious and, in 1983, less trusting as well. These relationships are not strong: the several predictors together with region account for 6 to 18 per cent of the variance in external and internal efficacy, and 4 to 6 per cent of that in trust. Overall, then, provincial-level inefficacy and distrust, like their federal counterparts, were commonplace throughout Canadian society in the early 1980s.

Government Performance and Equity/Fairness Evaluations

At least two considerations warrant investigation of people's evaluations of the effectiveness, equity, and fairness of political processes and outcomes. First, and as discussed above, perceptions of the self in the political process have received much scholarly attention in Canada and other countries, although this is only one component of the theoretical framework developed by Almond and Verba. Also important with respect to the viability of the political system are public attitudes about government performance, and the links among such attitudes, perceptions of fairness and justice, trust in government, and sense of citizenship.[43] Second, in Canada, as in other mature democracies, the scope of government activity expanded enormously during the twentieth century, particularly with regard to regulation of the economy and the development of the welfare state. Keynesian demand-management theory stressing the utility of government intervention developed in reaction to the protracted misery of the Great Depression of the 1930s, and it dominated economic thinking until the 1970s. The activist role of the state advocated by Keynesian theory had the widespread support of political élites and ordinary citizens alike. However, in the 1970s and 1980s, the inability of demand-management techniques to alleviate the problems of high rates of both inflation and unemployment coupled with slow or even negative growth eroded élite consensus on, and public confidence in, economic and social policy. Beginning in the late 1970s, neo-conservative politicians who challenged the

Figure 3.7: Inefficacy in Federal and Provincial Politics, 1983, 1984

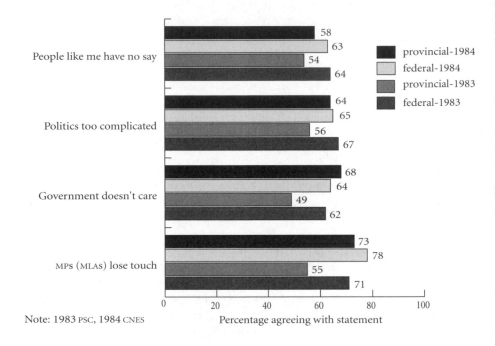

Note: 1983 PSC, 1984 CNES

Percentage agreeing with statement

Figure 3.8: Distrust in Federal and Provincial Political Authorities, 1983, 1984

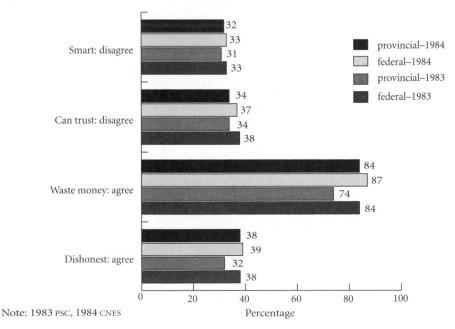

Note: 1983 PSC, 1984 CNES

Percentage

Keynesian orthodoxy and espoused monetarist or neo-classical economic theories led their parties to power in many Western countries. Despite these electoral victories, survey evidence suggests that the resurgence of conservatism as an ideology went largely unheeded by the mass publics of Western democracies.[44] However, the seeming inability of governments to remedy economic and social problems fuelled widespread discontent with politics and politicians.[45]

In Canada, data from the 1983 Political Support in Canada survey shows that many citizens believed that it was important that government be actively involved in economy and society, but they were quite dissatisfied with how government discharged its responsibilities in various policy areas (Figure 3.9). Moreover, public perceptions of the scope, importance, and effectiveness of government activities, as measured on separate 20-point scales,[46] demonstrated little regional variation. A difference of only 1.8 points separated the lowest and the highest mean scores on the scale involving the desired scope of government activity. Regional differences in the perceived importance of governmental involvement also were small, with average scores on a scale measuring the perceived importance of governmental involvement ranging from a low of 12.9 for Prairie residents to 15.2 for non-francophone Quebeckers. Scores on a similar scale capturing satisfaction with the effectiveness of government performance were much lower but, again, regional differences were trivial (ranging from 7.2 in British Columbia to 7.8 in the Atlantic provinces). This pattern of regional similarities in evaluations of government performance was not unique to the 1983 survey;

Figure 3.9: Mean Scope, Importance, and Effectiveness of Government Activities by Region/Ethnicity, 1983

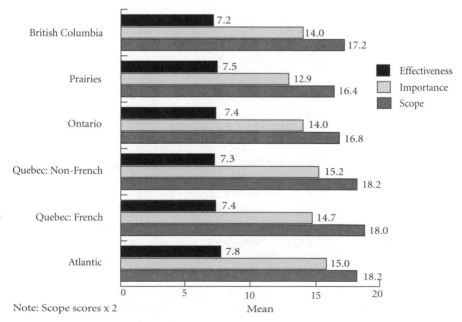

Note: Scope scores x 2

data from the 1988 and 1990 studies (not shown in tabular form) revealed very small regional differences in those years as well.

Table 3.6 reports data from the 1983, 1988, and 1990 PSC surveys on evaluations of government performance in various policy areas. In 1983, the government received, at best, mixed grades, with public satisfaction being highest for health care and education: 32 per cent and 22 per cent, respectively, said that the government performed 'very well' in these areas. The lowest levels of satisfaction were recorded for activities regarding employment opportunities, inflation, and the environment: less than 10 per cent thought that the government was doing 'very well'. Similarly, only 10 per cent to 16 per cent said that it was doing 'very well' in the remaining five policy areas. Substantial dissatisfaction also was evident in 1988, although the 'very satisfied' percentage rose to 25 per cent in the area of welfare services. In 1990, the government's performance elicited the most satisfaction in health care (27 per cent said 'very well'), and the least satisfaction with its handling of the federal deficit (2 per cent), the environment (5 per cent), inflation (6 per cent), and national unity and employment opportunities (both 7 per cent). In all other areas, only 12 to 19 per cent said that the government was doing a good job.

Levels of satisfaction with government performance in the several policy areas varied across regional boundaries, but these differences tended to be quite modest. For example, in 1988 (Table 3.7), the largest percentage of people who judged that the government was doing 'very well' in protecting lives and property (20 per cent), providing employment opportunities (18 per cent), and controlling inflation (13 per cent) resided in Ontario. Ontarians and non-francophone Quebeckers were the most satisfied with welfare services (31 per cent), while Prairie residents most frequently offered positive assessments of the government's protection of rights and liberties (22 per cent). Maritimers offered the most positive evaluations of government performance in areas of the environment (8 per cent), education (29 per cent), and health care (51 per cent). This last percentage is the only instance in which a regional majority gave a high satisfaction rating in any policy area.

The PSC surveys also included questions that invited respondents to comment on the equity and fairness of the Canadian polity and society generally, the operation of the federal government, the civil service, and the courts, and the representation provided by political parties and Parliament.[47] In each study, large numbers of people stated that the processes and outcomes of the political system were neither equitable nor fair (Table 3.8). For at least seven out of nine items in each of the three surveys, majorities (often overwhelming ones) offered negative judgments. In particular, the federal government was criticized for its treatment of various groups: in 1983, 1988, and 1990, 82 per cent, 87 per cent, and 90 per cent, respectively, said that some groups get too much and others get too little, whereas 77 per cent, 82 per cent, and 86 per cent, respectively, thought that the government treats some groups unfairly. The taxation system also was a major source of discontent; in 1990, 92 per cent of Canadians felt that 'some people don't pay enough taxes, whereas others pay too many'. Other criticisms were made about the representation provided by Parliament and political

Table 3.6: Federal Government Performance Evaluations, PSC Surveys 1983–1990

Performance Area	1983			1988			1990		
	very well	fairly well	not very well	very well	fairly well	not very well	very well	fairly well	not very well
Welfare Services	13	58	29	25	56	19	19	57	24
Employment Opportunities	4	36	60	12	52	36	7	39	54
Lives and Property	16	65	19	17	67	16	14	64	23
Rights and Liberties	15	64	21	19	61	20	12	58	30
Inflation	6	52	42	11	60	29	6	31	63
Health Care	32	56	12	37	49	14	27	56	17
Environment	9	55	36	6	32	62	5	40	55
Education	22	58	20	20	54	26	12	53	35
Armed Forces	10	37	53	t	t	t	t	t	t
Culture and Arts	14	67	19	t	t	t	t	t	t
National Unity	t	t	t	t	t	t	7	34	59
Federal Deficit	t	t	t	t	t	t	2	15	84

Note: horizontal percentages by year; t: question not asked

Table 3.7: Federal Government Performance Evaluations by Region/Ethnicity, 1988 PSC Pre-Election Survey

		Percentage Offering 'Very Well' Evaluations				
Performance Area	Atlantic	Quebec: French	Quebec: Non-French	Ontario	Prairies	British Columbia
Welfare Services	30	12	31	31	30	23
Employment Opportunities	12	6	3	18	10	9
Lives and Property	17	13	8	20	19	18
Rights and Liberties	21	14	8	21	22	19
Control Inflation	12	11	5	13	9	10
Health Care	51	20	43	43	41	37
Protect Environment	8	5	5	6	7	5
Education	29	14	23	22	21	16

Note: underscoring indicates largest percentage

Table 3.8: Equity-Fairness Evaluations, PSC Surveys 1983–1990

	1983		1988		1990	
Equity-Fairness Statement	Agree	Disagree	Agree	Disagree	Agree	Disagree
Taxation unfair	80	20	91	9	92	8
Achievement not ascription	56	44	63	37	54	46
Government treats some groups unfairly	77	23	82	18	86	14
Civil service treats everyone equally	28	72	28	72	20	80
Parties look after everyone's interests	48	52	48	52	31	69
Some groups get too much; others too little	82	18	87	13	90	10
Courts act speedily and fairly	52	48	52	48	44	56
Parliament does not represent everyone fairly	65	35	65	35	76	24
Laws apply equally to everyone	49	51	48	52	32	68

Note: horizontal percentages by year; underscored percentages indicate negative evaluations

parties: nearly two-thirds in 1983 and 1988 and three-quarters in 1990 agreed that 'Parliament does not represent everyone fairly', and large numbers also disagreed with the statement that 'parties try to represent the interests of everyone and not merely those who voted for them'. With respect to the judicial system, majorities in each year did not believe that the laws were applied equally and, in 1990, that the courts acted speedily and fairly.

Although judgments concerning the equity and fairness of the political system and society vary across regional boundaries, negative evaluations are commonplace throughout the population (Table 3.9). Non-Francophone Quebeckers were particularly disapproving—they were most likely to agree that: taxation is unfair; some

Table 3.9: Negative Equity-Fairness Evaluations by Region/Ethnicity, 1988 CES Pre-Election Survey

Performance Area	Atlantic	Quebec: French	Quebec: Non-French	Ontario	Prairies	British Columbia
Taxation unfair (A)	92	92	<u>95</u>	90	91	92
Achievement not ascription (D)	43	27	44	36	<u>51</u>	38
Government treats some groups unfairly (A)	83	78	83	82	<u>85</u>	82
Civil service treats everyone equally (D)	61	71	73	72	77	<u>78</u>
Parties look after everyone's interests (D)	49	46	<u>63</u>	50	<u>63</u>	54
Some groups get too much; others too little (A)	89	87	<u>97</u>	85	87	89
Courts act speedily and fairly (D)	47	50	<u>66</u>	49	46	46
Parliament does not represent everyone fairly (A)	53	65	<u>75</u>	62	73	69
Laws apply equally to everyone (D)	54	45	<u>57</u>	53	56	54

A - "agree" is negative response
D - "disagree" is negative response

Note: underscoring highlights largest percentage

groups get too much while others get too little; and Parliament does not represent everyone fairly. They also were most likely to disagree that: political parties look after everyone's interests; the courts act speedily and fairly; and the laws apply equally to everyone. Residents of the Prairie provinces and British Columbia also were somewhat more dissatisfied in several areas. Overall, however, negative judgments were not peculiar to these groups but, rather, were shared by many Canadians in all areas of the country.

As with the political efficacy and trust analyses performed earlier, we assessed the effects of region and other socio-demographic factors on evaluations of government performance and equity-fairness (Table 3.10). Of the several predictors used in these regression analyses, education, gender, income, and two regional variables had the largest significant effects on evaluations of government performance. Canadians with higher incomes reported more positive judgments, whereas those who were less educated, women, francophone Quebeckers, and British Columbians made more negative evaluations than other respondents. Higher-income individuals also expressed more favourable assessments of the equity and fairness of political institutions and processes, while women, non-francophone Quebeckers, and Prairie residents offered more negative evaluations. However, it is important to note that region explained only 2 per cent of the variance in evaluations of government effectiveness. When the impact of region was combined with other predictors, the total variance

Table 3.10: Regression Analyses of Government Performance and Equity-Fairness Evaluation Indices, 1988 CES Pre-Election Survey

Predictor Variables	Government Performance			Equity-Fairness		
	b	B	t	b	B	t
Age	0.00	.00	0.25	−0.00	−.00	−0.22
Education	−0.17	−.07	−2.81b	0.02	.01	0.53
Gender	−0.60	−.11	−4.91a	−0.35	−.09	−4.03a
Income	0.11	.08	3.28a	0.09	.09	3.61a
Regional						
Ethnicity: Atlantic	0.38	.04	1.67	0.17	.02	1.03
Quebec: French	−0.82	−.12	−5.07a	0.20	.04	1.74
Quebec: Non-French	−0.49	−.02	−1.14	−0.73	−.05	−2.38c
Prairies	0.07	.01	0.36	−0.42	−.08	−3.29a
British Columbia	−0.69	−.08	−3.40a	−0.16	−.02	−1.08
Constant	0.41	—	1.14	3.03	—	11.70a
R^2 =		.04			.03	
Region/Ethnicity Only R^2 =		.02			.01	

a: $p < .001$; b: $p < .01$; c: $p < .05$ (two-tailed test)

explained by the regression analysis remained very small, only 4 per cent. Similarly, the several predictor variables had little explanatory power with respect to equity-fairness judgments, with region accounting for 1 per cent the variance explained, and all variables explaining only 3 per cent of the variance. In sum, the prevalence of negative evaluations in all regions and among all socio-demographic groups indicate that public dissatisfaction with the effective and equitable/fair operation of governmental and broader societial institutions and processes was a pervasive component of Canada's political culture.

The 1990s: Plus Ça Change

Our analyses clearly indicate that, in important respects, regional differences in Canadian political culture have been overstated. But, a critic might say, your findings now must be out of date! After all, the 1990s witnessed the demise of the long-lived 'two-party-plus' national party system[48] and its replacement by a new, regionally fragmented one, that 'looks like Canada'. Other significant events have included the failure of the Meech Lake and Charlottetown constitutional accords and the surge in support for sovereignty that very nearly produced a 'oui' majority in the October 1995 Quebec referendum. Collectively, these events constitute compelling evidence of the regional and ethno-linguistic cleavages that threatened to tear the country apart. Although such a critic would be precisely correct in arguing that these events signified that Canada was a polity on the edge of fragmentation in the 1990s, they are not indicators of sea-changes in the patterns of political culture we have described. Indeed, national surveys conducted in 1993, 1995, and 1997 show that many people in all parts of the country continued to be politically inefficacious and distrusting, and government performance and more general equity/fairness evaluations continue to have a pronounced negative tone, and to vary only weakly by region.[49]

Findings from the most recent surveys with comparable data to those for earlier decades illustrate the point. For example, regardless of region, many people participating in the 1997 CNES expressed a lack of both internal and external political efficacy (see Figure 3.10). By itself, region/ethnicity could explain only 3 per cent of the variance in internal efficacy and only 1 per cent of the variance in external efficacy. Adding other socio-demographic variables raised the explanatory power only slightly, to 10 per cent for internal efficacy and to 3 per cent for external efficacy. The 1995 PSC survey tells the same story about political (dis)trust. As in previous decades, overwhelming majorities in every region believed that government officials waste people's tax dollars, and substantial numbers of respondents doubted the honesty and intelligence of bureaucrats and politicians. Region and the other socio-demographics could explain only 6 per cent of the variance in the political distrust index, and region/ethnicity per se could explain only 1 per cent. Exactly the same stories are told for government performance and equity/fairness evaluations in the 1997 PSC survey. For the former, region by itself explains 2 per cent of the variance, for the latter, 0.2 per cent.

Finally, perhaps the most telling data evaluate the performance of political parties. Surely, a critic might exclaim, the new regionally fragmented party system constitutes strong prima facie evidence that people in different regions have strongly differing opinions about political parties. This, in turn, is important evidence of major regional differences in political culture. Although obviously true as a description of regional

Figure 3.10: Political Inefficacy by Region, 1997 CES

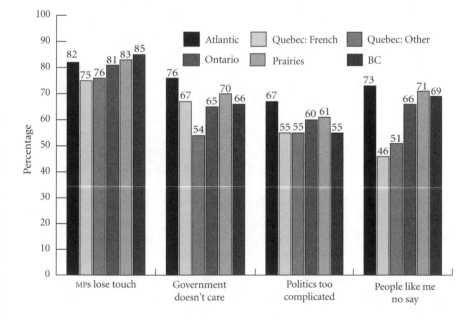

Figure 3.11: Average Number of Negative Party Evaluations by Region, 1993, 1995, 1997 PSC

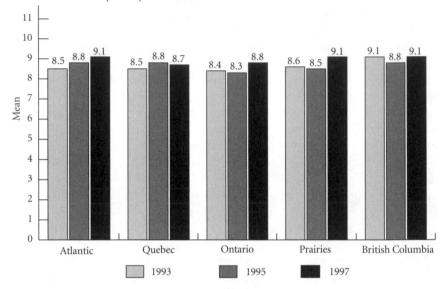

variation in electoral support for *particular* parties, the thesis of strong regional differences in orientations towards parties is false if intended as a characterization of evaluations of the performance of political parties *generally*. In 1993, 1995, and 1997 PSC surveys, respondents were asked if they 'agreed' or 'disagreed' with thirteen statements about Canadian political parties. Respondents were requested to think about parties generally, not about specific parties. Although we will not present the data in detail here,[50] the absence of significant regional differences was truly striking. As Figure 3.11 illustrates, it was not the case that people living in Quebec and the Prairies—the two regions that offered strong support for the new Bloc Québécois and Reform party, respectively—were profoundly negative about parties, while persons living in regions that continued to offer relatively strong support to one or more of the old-line parties were significantly more sanguine. Rather, Canadians in *every* part of the country castigated the parties for a wide variety of misdeeds; in all three surveys positive judgments of party performance were very much the exception, not the rule, in every region. Thus, even with regard to evaluations of party performance, Canadians were much more alike than different. Although comparable data are not available for earlier decades, in the 1990s at least, many residents of every region had tried political parties and found them wanting.

Conclusion: Persistent Political Discontent

The focus of scholarly research on regional variations in Canadian political culture is understandable but problematic. Previous inquiries have used CNES data in an effort to identify provincial and/or regional differences in cultural attitudes that might explain variations in political party support across the regions and, more importantly, problems of national integration that bedevil the polity. However, as we have demonstrated, many Canadians have little regional awareness, and region or province has extremely limited ability to explain a variety of important political attitudes and beliefs. Specifically, similar trends in external and internal political efficacy obtained in several regions, and regional patterns in both attitudes have tended to converge at low levels over time. Political trust also is widespread and manifests only minor regional variations. Canadians' feelings of efficacy and trust, however, do differ between election and non-election years; these attitudes have tended to increase during the former while decreasing in the latter. This latter finding, coupled with the emphasis in democratic theory on the role of elections in mobilizing citizen participation, underscores the need to study public attitudes and beliefs in both election and non-election years. By confining their soundings of these phenomena to the immediate proximity of periodic federal elections, traditional election studies necessarily provide only a limited and misleading portrait of the nature and dynamics of political culture in Canada or elsewhere.

Additionally, our analyses show that beliefs concerning the desirability and significance of government involvement in various policy areas, as well as discontent with government performance and the equity and fairness of political processes and outcomes, are long-standing components of Canada's political culture. Again, widespread negativity is not unique to residents of Quebec and the West, the two regions typically designated as hotbeds of political disaffection. True, many people in these regions are dissatisfied with the operation of political institutions and processes, but so too are their fellow citizens in other parts of the country. The tendency to offer unfavourable judgments is neither a new development nor a transitory reaction to particular policy failures captured in one survey conducted at one point in time. Similarly, the rise of the Bloc Québécois and Reform notwithstanding, Quebeckers and Westerners do not differ significantly when they assess the performance of political parties. Data gathered throughout the 1990s showed that many Canadians in all areas of the country were very dissatisfied with how the parties perform.

In sum, the traditional emphasis on regional variations in Canadian political culture is overstated, and perpetuating the search for regional distinctiveness risks missing the forest for the trees. Future studies need to pay more attention to the low levels of political efficacy and trust and the negative public opinions about political institutions and processes that are hallmarks of Canadian political psychology. The causes of these attitudes and their consequences for the quality of democratic political life in the twenty-first century are important topics for future research. Future studies should also recognize that, despite the paucity of studies that explicitly place Canada in cross-national comparative perspective, widespread public unhappiness with political processes and outcomes is not confined to Canada.[51] The political cultures of other democracies are characterized by dissatisfaction with the performance of government and the activities of bureaucrats and politicians who run them. Comparative investigations likely will reveal patterns of attitudes and beliefs that suggest the existence of a 'political dissatisfaction syndrome', common to many democracies, mature and emerging alike.

We argue that such syndromes are important motors of political change, and a failure to recognize and react to them can have serious, negative, long-term consequences. In Canada, repeated attempts to use processes of élite accommodation and federal-provincial diplomacy to deal with bitter, protracted federal-provincial and inter-provincial conflict and accompanying recurrent threats to national unity have created a set of powerful presuppositions about the nature of desirable and feasible political change. This intellectual legacy has become a central, shared element in élite political culture in Canada, and it poses the danger that the notion of political reform will continue to be conceptualized very narrowly—as tinkering with the constitutional powers and prerogatives of particular provinces or regions. But, to re-emphasize, public discontent with existing political institutions and practices and with the role of the citizen in the political process also is pervasive and profound. Accordingly, constitutional reform as it is typically conceived—as a legalistic log-roll among the federal government and the provinces, involving limited substantive and symbolic concessions to various actors—will do little to dispel Canadians' dissatisfaction with the political system and their place in it. Nor does 'allowing' citizens to react to such deals by voting 'yea or nea' change the situation in any fundamental way. Survey data gathered in the 1990s clearly testified that the referendums on the Charlottetown Constitutional Accord and Quebec sovereignty did nothing to change public opinions on constitutional options,[52] let alone reshape the pan-Canadian political culture of discontent.

Although battles over political reform in Canada typically have been fought over constitutional abstractions that prime ministers, provincial premiers, and bureaucratic mandarins claim will advance or protect regional/provincial and ethno-linguistic interests, it may be conjectured that people are more concerned with improving government performance and responsiveness in areas that directly affect their lives. That they should be so is consistent with the fundamental tenet of democratic theory: the purpose of politics is to satisfy public needs and demands. Expanding the role of citizens and enhancing the responsiveness of governments will constitute major steps toward satisfying the cultural norms that animate a democratic polity. Democratic theorists hypothesize that reducing the 'democratic deficit' will, in turn, do much to alleviate the disaffection that long has characterized Canadian political psychology. Whether their conjecture will receive an empirical test in twenty-first century Canada remains to be seen.

NOTES

1. Gabriel A. Almond and Sidney Verba, *The Civic Culture: Political Attitudes and Democracy in Five Nations* (Princeton: Princeton University Press, 1963).

2. David Bell and Lorne Tepperman, *The Roots of Disunity: A Look at Canadian Political Culture* (Toronto: McClelland & Stewart, 1979); Frederick C. Englemann and Mildred A. Schwartz, *Political Parties and the Canadian Social Structure*, 2nd ed. (Scarborough, Ont.:

Prentice Hall, 1975); Seymour Martin Lipset, *The Continental Divide: The Values and Institutions of the United States and Canada* (New York: Routledge, 1990); Mildred A. Schwartz, *Politics and Territory: The Sociology of Regional Persistence in Canada* (Montreal: McGill-Queen's University Press, 1974); Richard Simeon and David J. Elkins, 'Regional Political Cultures in Canada', *Canadian Journal of Political Science* 7 (1974): 397–437; John Wilson, 'The Canadian Political Cultures: Towards a Redefinition of the Nature of the Canadian Political System', *Canadian Journal of Political Science* 7 (1974): 438–84.

3. Donald E. Blake, *Two Political Worlds: Parties and Voting in British Columbia* (Vancouver: University of British Columbia Press, 1985); David J. Elkins and Richard Simeon, *Small Worlds: Provinces and Parties in Canadian Political Life* (Toronto: Methuen, 1980).

4. See Russell J. Dalton, *Citizen Politics: Public Opinion and Political Parties in Advanced Western Democracies*, 2nd ed. (Chatham, NJ: Chatham House Publishers, 1996), 263–66.

5. Russell W. Neuman, *The Paradox of Mass Politics: Knowledge and Opinion in the American Electorate* (Cambridge, Mass.: Harvard University Press, 1986).

6. Almond and Verba, *Civic Culture*, 480–4.

7. Gabriel A. Almond and Sidney Verba, eds, *The Civic Culture Revisited.* (Boston: Little Brown, 1980); Ronald Inglehart, 'Changing Paradigms in Comparative Political Behavior' in *Political Science: The State of the Discipline*, Ada W. Finifter, ed. (Washington, DC: American Political Science Association, 1983), 433; John R. Gibbins, ed., *Contemporary Political Culture: Politics in a Postmodern Age* (London: Sage Publications, 1989).

8. C.B. Macpherson, *The Life and Times of Liberal Democracy* (Oxford: Oxford University Press, 1977); Carole Pateman, *Participation and Democratic Theory* (Cambridge: Cambridge University Press, 1970); David Held, *Models of Democracy* (Stanford: Stanford University Press, 1987), 254–64.

9. Almond and Verba, *Civic Culture Revisited*, 402.

10. Although subsequent survey-based studies have not overcome the level-of-analysis problem, they have attempted to discern how political efficacy and trust are related to attitudes and behaviours that might affect regime stability. Thus, several studies have measured attitudes toward and involvement in various forms of political participation, ranging from election-related activities to non-violent and violent protests. These investigations also have gauged people's support for regime institutions and willingness to comply with laws and other authoritative edicts of government. See, e.g., Samuel Barnes and Max Kaase et al., *Political Action: Mass Participation in Five Western Democracies* (Beverly Hills, Calif.: Sage Publications, 1979); Allan Kornberg and Harold D. Clarke, *Citizens and Community: Political Support in a Representative Democracy* (Cambridge: Cambridge University Press, 1992); Edward N. Muller, *Aggressive Political Participation* (Princeton: Princeton University Press, 1979).

11. Ronald Rogowski, 'Political Support for Regimes: A Theoretical Inventory and Critique' in *Political Support in Canada: The Crisis Years*, Allan Kornberg and Harold D. Clarke, eds (Durham, NC: Duke University Press, 1983); M. Stephen Weatherford, 'Measuring Political Legitimacy', *American Political Science Review* 26 (1992): 149–68.

12. It also is an important intellectual precursor to contemporary studies of the causes and consequences of social capital, such as Robert Putnam, *Making Democracy Work: Civic Traditions in Modern Italy* (Princeton: Princeton University Press, 1993); Robert W. Jackman and Ross A. Miller, 'Social Capital and Politics' in Nelson W. Polsby, ed., *Annual Review of Political Science* 1 (Palo Alto, Calif.: Annual Reviews, 1998); and John L. Sullivan and J. E. Transue, 'The Psychological Underpinnings of Democracy: A Selective Review of Research on Political Tolerance, Interpersonal Trust, and Social Capital' in J.T. Spense, J.M. Darley, and D.J. Foss, eds, *Annual Review of Psychology* 50 (Palo Alto, Calif.: Annual Reviews, 1999). According to social capital theorists, social interaction generates socio-political trust, which is highly instrumental to civic engagement. This engagement, in turn, fosters compliance with laws, reduces transaction costs, and bolsters economic growth. The stock of social capital is hypothesized to change slowly and, hence, countries that have little social capital also have low probabilities of building effective democratic institutions.

13. Schwartz, *Politics and Territory*; See also Mildred A. Schwartz, *Public Opinion and Canadian Identity* (Berkeley: University of California Press, 1967).

14. See also Simeon and Elkins, 'Regional Political Cultures'; Wilson, 'Canadian Political Cultures'; Bell and Tepperman, *Roots of Disunity*; Elkins and Simeon, *Small Worlds*.

15. Simeon and Elkins, 'Regional Political Cultures', 420–1.

16. Wilson, 'Canadian Political Cultures', 446.

17. Schwartz, *Politics and Territory*, 146–58.

18. For example, Marianne C. Stewart, Allan Kornberg, Harold D. Clarke, and Alan Acock, 'Arenas and Attitudes: A Note on Political Efficacy in a Federal System', *Journal of Politics* 54 (1992): 179–96.

19. Donald V. Smiley, *Canada in Question: Federalism in the Eighties*, 3rd ed. (Toronto: McGraw-Hill Ryerson, 1980); Garth Stevenson, *Unfulfilled Union: Canadian Federalism and National Unity*, 3rd ed. (Toronto: Gage, 1989).

20. Russell J. Dalton, Scott C. Flanagan, and Paul Allen Beck, eds, *Electoral Change in Advanced Industrial Democracies: Realignment or Dealignment?* (Princeton: Princeton University Press, 1984); Russell J. Dalton and Martin P. Wattenberg, 'The Not So Simple Act of Voting' in *Political Science: The State of the Discipline II*. Ada W. Finifter, ed. (Washington, DC: American Political Science Association, 1993).

21. Seymour Martin Lipset and Stein Rokkan, *Party Systems and Voter Alignments* (New York: Free Press, 1967).

22. William Irving and H. Gold, 'Do Frozen Cleavages Ever Go Stale? The Bases of the Canadian and Australian Party Systems', *British Journal of Political Science* 10 (1980): 187–219.

23. See, relatedly, Roger Gibbins, *Prairie Politics and Society: Regionalism in Decline* (Toronto: Butterworths, 1980).

24. See, for example, Harold D. Clarke and Alan C. Acock, 'National Elections and Political Attitudes: The Case of Political Efficacy', *British Journal of Political Science* 19 (1989): 551–61.

25. This is not to say that national elections in Canada or elsewhere adequately perform the several functions ascribed to them by democratic theorists. For critical analyses of elections and their impact on public attitudes, see Benjamin Ginsberg, *The Consequences of Consent: Elections, Citizen Control and Popular Acquiescence* (Reading, Mass.: Addison-Wesley, 1982); Benjamin Ginsberg and Alan Stone, *Do Elections Matter?* (Armonk, NY: M.E. Sharpe, 1986).

26. Harold D. Clarke, Jane Jenson, Lawrence LeDuc, and Jon H. Pammett. *Political Choice in Canada* (Toronto: McGraw-Hill Ryerson, 1979), 49–53.

27. Angus Campbell, Gerald Gurin, and Warren E. Miller, *The Voter Decides* (Evanston, Ill: Row Peterson, 1954), 187.

28. Robert Lane, *Political Life: Why and How People Get Involved in Politics* (New York: The Free Press, 1959).

29. The wording of the efficacy statements has varied slightly over time. A primary difference is that those in the earlier CNES and other surveys do not refer to a specific level of government, whereas the statements in the 1983–90 PSC surveys and the 1984 CNES explicitly mention the federal government. For example, the statements asked in Political Support surveys are: (a) 'Generally those elected to Parliament in Ottawa soon lose touch with the people' (b) 'I don't think that the federal government cares much what people like me think' (c) 'Sometimes, politics and government in Ottawa seem so complicated that a person like me can't really understand what's going on' (d) 'People like me don't have any say about what the federal government does'. Stewart et al. present confirmatory factor analyses validating the use of available measures to distinguish between internal and external political efficacy. Marianne C. Stewart et al., 'Arenas and Attitudes', *Journal of Politics* 54 (1992): 179–96.

30. We employed data from 1965, 1968, 1974, 1979, and 1984 CNES, and other national surveys. The 1980 and 1988 CNES do not contain political efficacy measures. The 1977 and 1981 data were gathered in the 'Quality of Life: Social Change in Canada' study by Tom Atkinson and his associates. The data were gathered in surveys conducted in 1977, 1979, and 1981, and are available from the Institute for Social Research, York University, Toronto, Ontario. The 1983, 1984, 1988 pre-election, 1988 post-election, and 1990 surveys were conducted by Clarke and Kornberg in conjunction with the Political Support in Canada Study. The study was funded by the National Science Foundation (USA), and is described in the Appendix to Kornberg and Clarke, *Citizens and Community*.

31. Schwartz, *Politics and Territory*; Simeon and Elkins, 'Regional Political Cultures'.

32. For example, Pateman, *Participation and Democratic Theory*.

33. Note that the decline in regional differences in responses to the efficacy statements occurred in the mid-1970s—several years before the change in question wording, that is, the explicit reference to the federal government in the 1983 and later surveys.

34. The external political inefficacy index (range 0–2) consists of the number of 'agree' responses to the 'MPs lose touch' and 'government doesn't care' statements. The internal political inefficacy index (range 0–2) is the number of 'agree' responses to the 'politics too complicated' and 'no say' items.

35. The region/ethnicity dummy variables use the conventional 0–1 scoring, with Ontario as the reference category. Age is measured in years; gender is: women = 1, men = 0; level of formal education is: elementary or less = 1, some secondary = 2, completed secondary or technical, community college = 3, some university = 4, completed university (B.A. or B.Sc. or more) = 5; annual family income is a set of categories scored 1 for the lowest, 2 for the second lowest, etc. The number of income categories varies across the surveys.

36. Political methodologists have debated the utility of R^2. Although we recognize the potential for misinterpreting the meaning of the statistic, we agree with Luskin's argument that it is not enough to 'know that the model as a whole explains some non-zero portion of the variance in the dependent variable. We want to know how much the model explains. Other things being equal, a model that explains more smacks less of underspecification. The coefficient of determination [R^2] estimates the proportion of variance explained.' Accordingly, those who argue for the theoretical importance of their preferred explanatory variables (in this case the region/ethnicity dummies) should be able to buttress their arguments with statistics showing that their models fit their data well. R^2 is not the only possible candidate for this task, but it is a useful one. See Robert C. Luskin, 'Abusus Non Tolit Usum: Standardized Coefficients, Correlations and R^2', *American Journal of Political Science* 35 (1991): 1032–46.

37. Post-election surveys are scored 1; non-election year surveys and the 1988 pre-election survey, 0. The 1990 period effect is scored 1 for that year; 0 for other years.

38. The statements in the 1983–90 Political Support surveys are: (a) 'Many people in the federal government are dishonest' (b) 'People in the federal government waste a lot of the money we pay in taxes' (c) 'Most of the time we can trust people in the federal government to do what is right' (d) 'Most of the people running the government in Ottawa are smart people who usually know what they are doing'. The items in the 1979 survey do not mention the federal government but refer only to 'government'.

39. The distrust index is constructed by assigning scores of 1 to 'agree' responses and 0 to 'disagree' responses to items (a) and (b) in note 10 above. For items (c) and (d), 'disagree' responses are scored 1, 'agree' responses are scored 0. The four recoded variables are summed to form the index.

40. The conjecture that, if the 1965–68 question wording had been maintained in subsequent surveys, stronger regional differences in trust would appear, is not supported. Constructing a similar distrust index using the 1965 data shows that, although residents of the Atlantic provinces and Quebec were less trusting than other Canadians, region/ethnicity explained only 1 per cent of the variance. Nor do the other predictors perform especially well. Well-educated and higher income persons were most trusting, and older ones were less trusting but, overall, the several predictors jointly accounted for only 5 per cent of the variance in the trust index. Thus, even more than for political efficacy, levels of political trust do not vary widely across regional or other socio-demographic groups in the Canadian population. This was true circa 1965 when the first national election study was conducted, and it remains so today.

41. Blake, *Two Political Worlds*; Clarke et al., *Political Choice*; Harold D. Clarke, Jane Jenson, Lawrence LeDuc, and Jon H. Pammett, *Absent Mandate: Canadian Electoral Politics in an*

Era of Restructuring, 3rd ed. (Toronto: Gage, 1996); Eric M. Uslaner, 'Splitting Image: Partisan Affiliations in Canada's "Two Political Worlds"', *American Journal of Political Science* 34 (1990): 961–81; Marianne C. Stewart and Harold D. Clarke, 'The Dynamics of Party Identification on Federal Systems: The Canadian Case', *American Journal of Political Science* 42 (1998): 97–116.

42. Ronald D. Lambert, James E. Curtis, Steven D. Brown, and Barry J. Kay, 'Effects of Identification with Governing Parties on Feelings of Political Efficacy and Trust', *Canadian Journal of Political Science* 19 (1986): 705–28; Stewart et al., 'Arenas and Attitudes'.

43. Paul M. Sniderman, 'The New Look in Public Opinion Research' in Ada W. Finifter, ed., *Political Science: The State of the Discipline*.

44. Harold D. Clarke, Marianne C. Stewart, and Gary Zuk, eds, *Economic Decline and Political Change: Canada, Great Britain, the United States* (Pittsburgh: University of Pittsburgh Press, 1989); Ivor Crewe and Donald D. Searing, 'Ideological Change in the British Conservative Party', *American Political Science Review* 82 (1988): 361–84; Barry Cooper, Allan Kornberg, and William Mishler, eds, *The Resurgence of Conservatism in Anglo-American Democracies* (Durham: Duke University Press, 1988).

45. Clarke, Stewart, and Zuk, eds, *Economic Decline*; Harold D. Clarke and Allan Kornberg, 'Evaluations and Evolution: Public Attitudes Toward Canada's Federal Political Parties, 1965–1991', *Canadian Journal of Political Science* 26 (1993): 187–312.

46. The 'scope of government activities' index is created by summing the number of 'should' responses to questions asking respondents if they thought the federal government should or should not be involved in a variety of policy areas. Respondents who believed the government should not be involved in an area are scored 0 for that area. The 'importance of government activities' index is created by assigning scores of +2, +1, and 0 to respondents who thought that the activity in each area was 'very important', 'fairly important', or 'not important', respectively, and then summing the resulting scores. The 'government effectiveness' index is constructed by giving scores of +2, +1, and 0 to respondents who judged that government was doing 'very well', 'fairly well', or 'not very well', respectively, in each area. Persons saying that they 'didn't know' are scored +1 on that activity. The resulting scores are summed to create the index.

47. The government effectiveness index is described in note 14 above. The equity-fairness index is constructed by summing the number of responses ('agree' or 'disagree') indicating that the respondent believed that the political or social systems operate in an equitable and fair fashion.

48. Leon D. Epstein, 'A Comparative Study of Canadian Parties', *American Political Science Review* 58 (1964): 46–60. See also R. Kenneth Carty, ed., *Canadian Political Party Systems: A Reader* (Peterborough, Ont.: Broadview Press, 1992).

49. In addition to the 1997 CNES, we employed data gathered in 1993, 1995, and 1997 as part of the Political Support in Canada project. The latter study is supported by grants from the National Science Foundation (US), and the surveys are described in the appendix to Harold D. Clarke, Allan Kornberg, and Peter Wearing, *A Polity on the Edge: Canada and the Politics of Fragmentation* (Peterborough, Ont.: Broadview Press, 2000).

50. Clarke et al., *Polity on the Edge.* See also Clarke and Kornberg, 'Evaluations and Evolution', 287–312.

51. Neil Nevitte, *The Decline of Deference: Canadian Value Change in Cross-National Perspective* (Peterborough, Ont.: Broadview Press, 1996); Paul M. Sniderman, Joeseph F. Fletcher, Peter H. Russell, and Philip E. Tetlock, *The Clash of Rights: Liberty, Equality, and Legitimacy in Pluralist Democracy* (New Haven: Yale University Press, 1996).

52. Clarke et al., *Polity on the Edge*, chs 4 and 6.

Chapter 4

Revisiting Western Alienation: Towards a Better Understanding of Political Alienation and Political Behaviour in Western Canada[1]

Shawn Henry

Western alienation has been a theme in Canadian politics for a number of years. Although the term itself is relatively recent, the attitudes and emotions behind it can be traced back to the mid-1800s.[2] Today, over 150 years later, Western alienation is as much of a force as ever. For example, in a survey in late 1997, the Environics Research Group found that over 50 per cent of the respondents from the four Western provinces strongly agreed with the statement that 'the West usually gets ignored in national politics because the political parties depend mostly upon the voters in Quebec and Ontario'. Environics has been asking western Canadians this question and others relating to Western alienation since 1979, and at no time during this period has the proportion of western Canadians agreeing (somewhat or strongly) with this statement fallen below 80 per cent.[3]

Many commentators have discussed Western alienation, its perceived roots, and its implications for the Canadian political landscape.[4] However, only a few studies have tried to quantify Western alienation and identify its correlates and driving factors.[5] A further issue is that some of the studies have collected survey data relating to Western alienation in Alberta and then generalized the results to the rest of the Western provinces.[6] To date, there have been no studies which have measured regional alienation attributes outside of the four Western provinces, and only one study has made a conscious effort to compare it to a more general model of political alienation.[7] This chapter extends the scope of analysis beyond the borders of the West to explore the possibility that Western alienation may be better classified as a more generic form of regionally based political alienation found in varying degrees in the peripheral regions of Canada.

The Roots of Western Alienation

On the Prairies . . . an almost conspiratorial view of national politics has existed, one in which political decisions by the national government are unfortunately seen as being all too predictable. In the eyes of the alienated Westerner, systematic and predictable political patterns are clearly discernible; and the West consistently gets shortchanged, exploited, and ripped off.[8]

As Gibbins notes above, western Canadian culture and politics has been pervaded by the feeling that Canadian Federalism promotes a dysfunctional, asymmetrical relationship among the various regions in Canada. In general, there seem to be three pillars supporting Western alienation: economic inequality, political inequality, and regionalism. These pillars are directly related in such a way that as one strengthens or weakens, the others tend to follow suit, and so too does Western alienation.

Economic Inequality

There are five commonly cited economic issues that have created conflict between the Western provinces and the federal government and promoted Western alienation: control of land and natural resources upon entering Confederation, tariff policies, transportation policies, the National Energy Program (NEP), and Federal procurement and spending. Of these five issues, the first three are rooted primarily in a previous era, while the last two are more recent complaints. All five have arguably contributed a great deal to the political culture of western Canada and the general feeling that the West is shortchanged in the zero-sum business of federal economics.[9]

Political Inequality

The structure of the Canadian parliamentary system is the root cause of the political inequality felt by western Canadians. As long as Canada employs a parliamentary system controlled by a House of Commons whose representation is based on population, the West will not have the political weight needed to counterbalance the two populous Central provinces. According to the 1996 census, Ontario comprises 37.3 per cent of Canada's population, while Quebec has 24.8 per cent. By comparison, the four Western provinces together have only 29.6 per cent of Canada's population. An oft-cited example of how the population distribution puts the West at a disadvantage is the 1980 election, in which the Liberal party had already formed the government before even one ballot had been counted west of Ontario. Given that this kind of election outcome is possible, and has happened in recent memory, the results of the Environics studies cited earlier are not surprising.

Regionalism

In terms of the Western alienation literature, regionalism in the West is driven by three primary factors: unique provincial cultures, the practice of province building, and opposition to Quebec's constitutional demands. A number of researchers have noted the impact that immigration patterns have had on the different provincial cultures in the various provinces in Canada.[10] Others point to the influence of key industries on provincial culture.[11] Still others have argued that the unique political culture of each province is in part defined and actively encouraged by provincial governments.[12]

'Province building' is a term that describes a process whereby the provinces have actively sought to make Canada a more decentralized federal state.[13] Cairns describes the situation as follows: 'Federal and provincial governments are not neutral containers or reflecting mirrors, but aggressive actors steadily extending their tentacles of control, regulation, and manipulation into society.'[14] The reason given by provincial governments for increasing their political power is that they wish to make certain their province is not exploited by the federal government. This argument has proven beneficial for many provincial politicians. One study of Alberta politics posits a model of electability for provincial parties based on their ability to juggle a healthy dose of antifederalism and a smattering of conservative economics.[15]

Finally, there is a long history in the West of opposition to special treatment for Quebec and continued demands for more concessions from the rest of Canada. This sentiment has been well documented, and arguments have been made that the antipathy is directed more toward the attention Quebec has received, and the political weight it carries, then toward the Quebec people per se:[16]

> The new fury of the Westerner demonstrates itself when it strikes home that Quebec's six million plus citizens have turned the country on its collective ear and created an enormous attention to their problems . . . while the West's six million plus citizens (still) can't be heard over the rush and scramble to accommodate Quebec. Sometimes the West's frustration and rage is misconstrued as anti-Quebec in nature. It is not. It is, in most cases, envy of Quebec's political prowess combined with fury at the West's own impotence on the national scene.[17]

All of these factors—inequality of federal government economic policy vis-à-vis the provinces, political inequality, and regionalism (particularly opposition to Quebec's constitutional demands and official bilingualism)—fall together into a political amalgam called Western alienation. The predominant view of Western alienation is that it extends beyond political alienation, and is instead a cultural expression of discontent and political protest behaviour. Indeed, Gibbins has gone so far as to define it as

> a political creed of regional discontent. By this we mean that western alienation embodies a socially shared, generated, and transmitted set of interrelated beliefs, a set of beliefs with at least some degree of cultural embodiment and intellectual articulation, with a recognized history and constituency, and with recognized spokesmen and carriers of the creed. In these senses, western alienation is the very antithesis of alienation more generally defined, alienation whose very normlessness connotes the absence of ideological structure.[18]

Is It Really Western? Is It Really Alienation?

From this perspective, Western alienation is both unique to western Canada and a unique form of political alienation. However, since the vast majority of the research on Western alienation has focused exclusively on the West, and for the most part, Alberta, these claims are open to debate. A number of studies have explained how political alienation and political protest emerged in regions that were economically and politically dominated by more populous regions in federal states. For example, studies of the Atlantic provinces reveal similar patterns of colonialism, and economic and political oppression by the Central provinces.[19] A key difference between the Western alienation literature and the research findings for the Atlantic provinces is the existence of a protest tradition in the Western provinces, embodied by the West's generation and support of protest parties. It should be noted, however, that Hiller describes a resurgence in nationalism in Newfoundland based primarily on newly discovered sources of economic wealth.[20] While Newfoundlanders did not parlay this into the development of a new regional protest party or a majority seeking independence, it does demonstrate that the conditions leading to protest in the West can also exist in the East.

Other researchers have taken the theoretical framework generated by work on Western alienation and applied it to Western Australia.[21] These studies uncover similarities between Western Australia and western Canada, including an asymmetrical relationship with the politically and economically dominant regions, a quasi-colonial attitude on the part of the government regarding resources, and a protest tradition. The crux of these findings is that regional political alienation based on a perceived structural flaw in federalism, as well as perceived exploitation by larger, more populous, regions does not appear to be unique to western Canada.

Gibbins cites four reasons why Western alienation should not be considered a more generic type of political alienation.[22] First, he argues that 'while Western Canadians may be alienated from Eastern Canada in general and from the federal government in particular, a similar sense of alienation is not evident in citizen attitudes toward the provincial governments in the West.'[23] Second, Gibbins points out that there is generally no concomitant withdrawal from politics; on the contrary, there is a move to more active participation, to the point of being a driving force behind the creation and support of a number of protest movements and parties, the Reform party being the most recent embodiment of that protest tradition.[24] Third, Gibbins argues that those who suffer the highest levels of Western alienation are not 'the usual clientele of alienation—the dispossessed, the poor, and the economically marginal'.[25] Finally, he asserts that rather than seeing the political system as random and difficult to understand in terms of process, those with high degrees of Western alienation have an 'almost conspiratorial theory of politics, one in which the political decisions, particularly those of the federal government, are unfortunately all too predictable'.[26]

As is the case regarding the assertion that Western alienation is unique to western Canada, the argument that Western alienation is not in fact a more generic form of political alienation must be questioned as well. Specifically, David Schwartz argues that it is possible for individuals, particularly in a federal system, to develop partial political alienation.[27] He stated that this is possible when

> 1) the individual perceives that only some of the political institutions, policies, or processes are incompatible with his basic political values (and hence withdraws identification only from these sub-systems of the polity); or 2) he initially withdraws from the polity as a whole but later is able to cognitively differentiate between

the total polity and some part of the system perceived to require and permit reform.[28]

This definition brings a different perspective to Gibbins's arguments against seeing Western alienation as another form of political alienation. Schwartz also notes that

To a well-socialized citizen who identifies with the polity, who regards the political system as 'good', a conflict between his cherished values and his political system is likely to be a most acute one. If the values are too basic to the self to be relinquished, efforts to reform the system are likely to be made.[29]

In light of the arguments put forth by Schwartz, there is need to revisit the concept of Western alienation to determine whether, in fact, it does not make more sense to see it as a subset of political alienation rather than as a phenomenon distinct from political alienation. The next question then becomes whether or not Western alienation is in fact unique to western Canada. Assuming that it is unique to western Canada, we would expect the attributes describing Western alienation to be consistently expressed by western Canadians while significantly less pronounced among non-Westerners. If this is not the case, Western alienation should instead be viewed as a subset of political alienation that is characteristic of peripheral regions in Canada. A more appropriate term for such a phenomenon would then be *peripheral region alienation*.

Data and Methods

The data used in the following analysis are taken from the 1997 Canadian Election Study. This study comprised three different surveys:[30]

1. The Campaign Period Survey (CPS) conducted over the course of the 1997 Federal Election campaign (27 April to 1 June). The CPS used a rolling sample methodology, interviewing approximately 110 respondents per day for each of the thirty-six days of the campaign, leading to a total sample of 3,949 respondents;
2. The Post Election Survey (PES), which attempted to re-survey the participants of the CPS in the eight weeks following the election. Roughly 80 per cent of the respondents in the CPS study also participated in the PES study, for a total sample of 3,170; and,
3. The Mailback Survey (MBS) of those who completed the PES portion of the study. Fifty-nine per cent also completed the Mailback portion of the study (N=1,857).

Analyses in this chapter employ data collected from all three surveys to derive a composite index measuring peripheral region alienation. When the surveys were conducted, every effort was made to re-interview the same individuals in each wave of the study. Where there were inconsistencies in responses to generic socio-demographic data, the respondent was flagged as a potential 'bad link'.[31] Respondents thus flagged were removed from the sample. Given that part of what defines Western alienation in the literature is opposition to Quebec's constitutional demands, the peripheral region alienation index was calculated only for those respondents living outside of Quebec, leaving a working sample of 1,368.[32]

The Peripheral Region Alienation Index

The Peripheral Region Alienation (PRA) index comprises three themes outlined by the Western alienation literature: political inequality/alienation, economic inequality/ alienation, and antipathy towards Quebec's constitutional demands. For each theme, three questions are used to derive an index (i.e., political inequality/alienation index, economic inequality/alienation index, and an anti-Quebec constitutional demands index), which are then combined to derive an index that measures peripheral region alienation. Directional coding is used to recode the variables included in each index, so that high scores on each index indicates strong opposition to Quebec's constitutional demands, or strong feelings of political inequality or economic inequality.[33] As such, when these indices are added together to form the PRA index, the same relationship holds, where higher values indicate someone who holds views consistent with the Western alienation literature.

In order to derive results comparable to previous analyses, which have focused almost exclusively on data collected from Alberta, the PRA index was developed and tested using only the respondents from Alberta. As part of the development and testing of the indices, each index was subjected to standard tests for reliability and internal consistency.[34]

The three component indices for the PRA index comprise the following attributes:

Political Inequality/Alienation[35]
1. On the whole are you very satisfied, fairly satisfied, not very satisfied, or not at all satisfied with the way democracy works in Canada?
2. Those elected to Parliament soon lose touch with the people. Do you strongly agree, somewhat agree, somewhat disagree, or strongly disagree?
3. In general, does the federal government treat your (province/territory) better, worse, or about the same as the other parts of Canada?

Economic Inequality/Alienation[36]
1. How good a job do you think the Liberal government has done in: a) reducing the deficit; b) creating jobs? Has the Liberal government done a very good job, quite good, not very good, or not a good job at all?
2. Have the policies of the federal government made (province/territory)'s economy better/worse, or haven't they made much difference?

3. Have the policies of the federal government made you better off, worse off, or haven't they made much difference?

Anti-Quebec Constitutional Concessions[37]
1. How much do you think should be done for Quebec: more, less, or about the same as now? Is that a lot more, somewhat more, or a little more? Is that a lot less, somewhat less, or a little less?
2. Should Quebec be recognized as a distinct society? Would you change your mind if this keeps Quebec in Canada?
3. For each statement, please indicate if you strongly agree, agree, disagree, or strongly disagree. We have gone too far in pushing bilingualism in Canada.

The indices range from -6 to +6, and when combined to produce the Peripheral Region Alienation index, result in a theoretical range of -18 (very low PRA) to +18 (very high PRA). In an effort to provide a better frame of reference, the PRA index has been converted into an ordinal variable with five categories: very low PRA, low PRA, average PRA, high PRA, and very high PRA. The 20th, 40th, 60th, and 80th percentiles from the Alberta sample were used to establish the relative cutpoints for this procedure.[38]

Figure 4.1 shows the distribution of the PRA index for the Alberta sample. Figure 4.2 shows the distribution of the PRA index for the total sample (excluding Quebec respondents). Both indices are normally distributed, although the distribution from

Figure 4.1: Peripheral Region Alienation Index, Alberta Sample

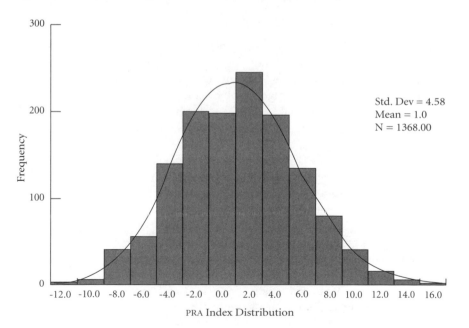

Std. Dev = 4.58
Mean = 1.0
N = 1368.00

PRA Index Distribution

**Figure 4.2: Peripheral Regional Alienation Index,
All Respondents (Excluding Quebec)**

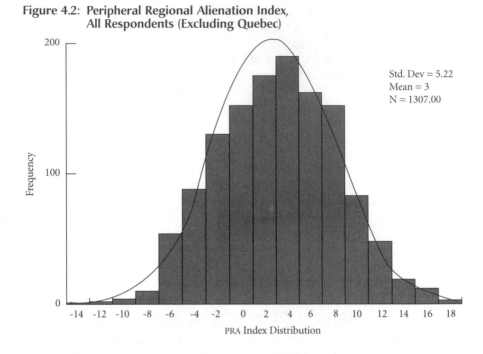

Std. Dev = 5.22
Mean = 3
N = 1307.00

Frequency

PRA Index Distribution

the Alberta sample tends to cluster around higher values than does the total sample (Alberta mean=5.0, Total Sample mean=3.0).

Is It Really Western?

Table 4.1 presents the distribution of PRA index scores across the provinces and territories. The results raise doubts about the degree to which Western alienation or peripheral region alienation can be considered unique to the four Western provinces. Respondents from Alberta had significantly higher scores on the PRA index than respondents from other provinces, with 19.8 per cent of them flagged as having very high levels of PRA (roughly the top quintile of the Alberta sample). British Columbia came in second with 16 per cent of the respondents falling into the very high PRA category, followed closely by Saskatchewan. The proportion of Manitoba respondents showing high levels of PRA was significantly less than the other three Western provinces. In fact, three of the Atlantic provinces and both territories have a higher proportion of respondents falling into the very high category of PRA than does Manitoba.

These results suggest that peripheral region alienation, as measured here, does in fact exist outside of the boundaries of the four Western provinces. In particular, a significant portion of the respondents from Newfoundland and Nova Scotia demonstrated high levels of peripheral region alienation, which in turn provides additional support for those studies finding high levels of regionally based political alienation in

Table 4.1: Peripheral Regional Alienation Index Distributions

Province	Mean	Median	% Very High PRA
Nfld	3.72	3.75	13.04
PEI	1.23	1.00	2.63
NS	3.75	4.00	11.67
NB	2.87	3.25	11.54
Ont.	1.81	2.00	7.21
Man.	2.75	3.00	8.43
Sask	3.97	3.45	11.96
Alberta	4.56	5.00	19.82
BC	3.57	4.00	15.96
Yukon	1.87	1.00	9.76
NWT	2.34	3.00	11.43

the Atlantic provinces.[39] Another issue that these results raise is the uniformity of 'Western' alienation within the four Western provinces. In particular, the results call into question whether Manitoba can be included in the 'Region of the Mind' referred to by Gibbins and Arrison.[40] Finally, the uniquely high levels of PRA found in Alberta raise further questions, since much of the previous research on Western alienation has been based upon Alberta data.[41] In light of these results, the current study does not support the assertion that Western alienation is exclusive to western Canada, nor does it support the idea that it is homogeneous within that region. Rather, the study would suggest that being on the periphery of the Canadian political and economic stage has similar effects both in the West and the East.

Is It Really Alienation?

We now turn our attention to the argument posed by Gibbins that Western alienation is a unique form of political alienation. As shown in Table 4.2, the results seem to support Gibbins's assertion that those with high levels of peripheral region alienation look to their provincial governments as their primary connection to the political system. When asked which level of government does the best job of looking after their interests, three times as many respondents in the very high PRA group chose their provincial government over the federal government.[42] Those respondents on the other end of the peripheral region alienation index were almost evenly divided about which level of government was best suited to looking after their interests. However, it is important to note that over 20 per cent of the respondents in all the categories of the PRA index chose their provincial government over the federal government, which means that the proportion of respondents in the very high category of the PRA index is only 10 per cent higher than the proportion of respondents in the very low category, in terms of saying that they feel closer to their provincial government.

Gibbins's second argument, that those with Western alienation are not withdrawing from politics as would be expected if Western alienation were a more generic form of political alienation, are confirmed by these results. As shown in Table 4.2, a

Table 4.2: Peripheral Regional Alienation Comparisons To Other Key Factors

	Very Low PRA %	Low PRA %	Average PRA %	High PRA %	Very High PRA %
Fed Gov't Better	19.95	16.05	12.50	14.22	8.44
Prov Gov't Better	21.90	24.41	28.88	26.54	31.17
Voting in 97 Fed Election	86.72	81.35	85.81	87.49	90.53
Voting in Last Prov Election	87.10	79.60	81.90	87.20	84.42
Voting Liberal	43.55	26.42	20.26	16.59	6.49
Voting PC	13.38	15.72	13.79	11.37	7.14
Voting NDP	16.30	11.71	14.66	9.00	8.44
Voting Reform	7.79	18.73	32.76	40.28	58.44
Rating Their Interest as 8-10	38.93	33.44	33.19	34.60	42.86
> Than High School Education	62.53	60.20	57.76	50.24	55.19
Laid Off/Unemployed	5.11	2.01	6.03	4.74	7.79
> Than $70k Household Income	28.22	25.08	25.86	27.96	24.68

substantial majority of the respondents in the very high PRA group voted in the most recent federal and provincial elections (91 per cent and 84 per cent, respectively). Further, if part of what defines Western alienation is the urge to protest against the federal government, it is logical to assume that those with very high levels of peripheral region alienation would be more likely to come out and vote against the ruling party. To a large degree, the results reflected this relationship: 91 per cent of the respondents in the very high category of the PRA index voted and only 6.5 per cent of them voted for the Liberals. Over half of those respondents in the very high category of PRA voted for the Reform party in the 1997 federal election.

Finally, the respondents were asked to rate their interest in the 1997 federal election on a scale of 1 to 10, where 10 indicates a very strong interest in the election. Table 4.2 shows the proportion of respondents from each group with a score of 8 or higher on the measure of interest. The results show that the respondents who fell into either the very low or very high categories of the PRA index were the most interested in the election. Almost 43 per cent of those in the very high category gave an 8 or higher out of 10 to express their interest in the election. Thus, Gibbins's assertion that those experiencing Western alienation are not withdrawn from the political components of life is largely substantiated. However, the results do not demonstrate that those with very high levels of peripheral region alienation are substantially more interested or involved in politics than those respondents with very low levels of peripheral region alienation. The results indicate a similar level of participation in the political system (that is, voting) in the two extreme-end groups, as well as similar levels of interest in the political process. In other words, those with high levels of peripheral region alienation do not appear to be unique in terms of political participation or interest in politics.

Concomitant to Gibbins's assertion that those with high levels of Western alien-ation do not drop out of politics is his assertion that these people are also less likely to show other attributes of the socially disenfranchised, such as low income, low levels of education, and being perpetually unemployed. For the most part, these assertions are borne out in our study. Over half of those in the high or very high categories of the PRA index have at least some training after high school. However, the rate of post-secondary education is 10 per cent higher among the respondents in the low and very low categories of the PRA index. Almost a quarter of the respondents in the high/very high PRA groups have a household income of $70,000 or more; however, this is neither higher nor lower than the proportion of the respondents making $70,000 or higher in the low/very low PRA groups. Finally, 7.8 per cent of the respondents in the very high category of the PRA index were unemployed or laid off at the time of the survey. Interestingly, this is the highest unemployment rate of all the PRA groups. Despite these differences, there does not appear to be a strong linear relationship between peripheral region alienation and socio-economic status, thereby supporting Gibbins's assertion that those with Western alienation are not likely to be the socially disen-franchised.

Conclusion

A primary goal of this research was to determine whether Western alienation, as defined in the literature and measured using the 1997 Canadian Election Study, is unique to western Canada and discernible from a more generic form of political alien-ation. The results indicate that 'Western' alienation is not unique to western Canada, and would be better seen as a form of peripheral region political alienation that shows up to varying degrees across Canada. Low levels of peripheral region alienation found in Manitoba combined with the high levels found in Newfoundland and Nova Scotia provide strong evidence that this form of regionally based political alienation is not restricted to western Canada. The fact that Alberta had by far the highest levels of peripheral region alienation raised questions regarding the feasibility of generalizing results of data collected in Alberta to the other three Western provinces, as has been done in some of the previous research on Western alienation.

The current analyses also find that those respondents with high levels of peripheral region alienation are not more socially disenfranchised, nor have they withdrawn from the political system. Of the respondents in the very low category of the PRA index, slightly more show higher levels of income and education, but the relationship between peripheral region alienation and these factors is not entirely linear. In terms of political interest and involvement, only federal party preference stands out as a clear delineator between groups.

The results indicate that peripheral region alienation does exist outside of the confines of the four Western provinces. In light of this, the assertion that Western alienation should not be considered in the same light as a more generic form of polit-ical alienation is weakened. The relationship between peripheral region alienation and the feeling the provincial government does a better job of looking after the interests of the respondents was consistent with Schwartz's definition of partial political alienation. Further, the results indicating that those with high levels of peripheral region alienation are not part of the socially disenfranchised is also consistent with Schwartz's argument that the 'well socialized' citizen is more likely to be proactive in his or her opposition to systemic bias in the political system.

By moving to a definition that focuses on partial political alienation, with a peripheral region focus, Western alienation studies would be able to compare the sociopolitical structure in western Canada that leads to this alienation with examples of alienation and corresponding structural variables existing elsewhere. The benefit of looking to other examples of peripheral region alienation outside of Canada is that new perspectives and possible solutions for old problems could be brought to light. For example, as shown in studies of Western Australia, the existence of an elected Senate has done very little to ameliorate feelings of peripheral region alienation.[43] With this knowledge and further study, insight may be gained as to what specific types of structural changes are necessary to reduce peripheral region alienation in Canada. Large groups of Canadians still feel alienated from the federal government and the two most populous provinces. Retooling Western alienation into a regionally based form of peripheral region alienation may revitalize attempts to understand and address this long-term problem in Canadian federalism.

NOTES

1. Data from the 1997 Canadian Election Survey were provided by the Institute for Social Research, York University. The survey was funded by the Social Sciences and Humanities Research Council of Canada (SSHRC), grant number 412–96–0007 and was completed for the 1997 Canadian Election Team of André Blais (Université de Montréal), Elisabeth Gidengil (McGill University), Richard Nadeau (Université de Montréal), and Neil Nevitte (University of Toronto). However, the Institute for Social Research, the SSHRC, and the Canadian Election Survey Team are not responsible for the analyses and interpretations presented here. The author would like to thank Tom Langford, Richard Wanner, and the editors and three anonymous reviewers of this volume for their helpful comments.

2. J.F. Conway, *The West: The History of a Region in Confederation* (Toronto: James Lorimer, 1983); David Elton, 'Western Grievances—A Long History' in *Politics: Canada*, 7th ed. Paul Fox and Graham White, eds (Toronto: McGraw-Hill Ryerson, 1991).

3. Environics Research Group Ltd. Focus Canada 1997.

4. See Don Braid and Sydney Sharpe, *Breakup: Why the West Feels Left Out of Canada* (Toronto: Key Porter, 1990); Conway, *The West*; Elton, 'Western Grievances'; David Elton and Roger Gibbins, 'Western Alienation and Political Culture' in *The Canadian Political Process*, 3rd ed. Richard Schultz, Orest M. Kruhlak, and John Terry, eds (Toronto: Holt, Rinehart and Winston, 1979); David Elton and Peter McCormick, *The Western Economy and Canadian Unity* (Calgary: Canada West, 1987); Roger Gibbins, 'Western Alienation and the Alberta Political Culture' in *Society and Politics in Alberta*, Carlo Caldarola, ed. (Toronto: Methuen, 1979); Roger Gibbins, *Prairie Politics and Society: Regionalism in*

Decline (Toronto: Butterworths, 1980); Roger Gibbins, *Regionalism: Territorial Politics in Canada and the United States* (Toronto: Butterworths, 1982); Roger Gibbins and Sonia Arrison, *Western Visions: Perspectives on the West in Canada* (Peterborough, Ont.: Broadview Press, 1995); David Kilgour, *Uneasy Patriots: Western Canadians in Confederation* (Edmonton: Lone Pine Publishing, 1988); George Melnyk, 'Region and Reaction: The Western Right' in *Riel to Reform: A History of Protest in Western Canada*, George Melnyk, ed. (Saskatoon: Fifth House, 1992); George Melnyk, *Beyond Alienation* (Calgary: Detselig Enterprises, 1993).

5. Elton and McCormick, *Western Economy*; Gibbins, *Prairie Politics*; Gibbins and Arrison, *Western Visions*.

6. See, for example, Elton and Gibbins, 'Western Alienation'. See also Gibbins, *Prairie Politics*.

7. Robert Gilsdorf, 'Western Alienation, Political Alienation and the Federal System' in *Society and Politics in Alberta: Research Papers*, Carl Caldarola, ed. (Toronto: Methuen, 1979).

8. Gibbins, *Prairie Politics*, 168.

9. For a more detailed discussion of the economic foundations of Western alienation, see Elton, 'Western Grievances'.

10. David J. Elkins, 'The Horizontal Mosaic: Immigrants and Migrants in the Provincial Political Cultures' in *Small Worlds: Provinces in Canadian Political Life*, David J. Elkins and Richard Simeon, eds (Toronto: Methuen, 1980); Nelson Wiseman, 'The West as Political Region' in *From Riel to Reform*; Peter McCormick, 'Regionalism in Canada: Disentangling the Threads', *Journal of Canadian Studies* 24, 2: 5–21.

11. Robert Brym, 'Regional Social Structure and Agrarian Radicalism in Canada: Alberta, Saskatchewan and New Brunswick', *Canadian Review of Anthropology and Sociology* 15, 3: 339–50.

12. Elton and McCormack, *Western Economy*.

13. Edwin R. Black and Alan C. Cairns, 'A Different Perspective on Canadian Federalism', *Canadian Public Administration* 9, 1 (March 1966): 35. The theory behind 'province building' has been refuted by R.A. Young, Philippe Faucher, and André Blais, 'The Concept of Province Building: a Critique' in R.D. Olling and M.W. Westmacott, eds. *Perspectives in Canadian Federalism* (Scarborough, Ont.: Prentice Hall, 1988). They argue (p. 137) that Black and Cairns's theory is too broad and that almost any move on the part of the provincial government can be construed as an act of 'province building'.

14. Alan Cairns, 'The Governments and Societies of Canadian Federalism' in *Perspectives on Canadian Federalism*.

15. Terrence Levesque and Kenneth Norrie, 'Overwhelming Majorities in the Legislature of Alberta', *Canadian Journal of Political Science* (1979): 466.

16. Elton and Gibbins, 'Western Alienation', 90.

17. Stanley C. Roberts, President of the Canada West Foundation in 1979. Cited in Gibbins, *Prairie Politics*, 178.

18. Gibbins, 'Western Alienation', 145.

19. Harry H. Hiller, 'Dependence and Independence: Emergent Nationalism in Newfoundland', *Ethnic and Racial Studies* 10, 3 (1987): 257–74; Robert Brym and R. Sacouman, eds, *Underdevelopment and Social Movements in Atlantic Canada* (Toronto: New Hogtown Press, 1979); R. Matthews, *The Creation of Regional Dependency* (Toronto: University of Toronto Press, 1983).

20. Hiller, 'Dependence and Independence'.

21. Hiller, 'Dependence and Independence'; Harry Hiller, 'Resources and Rebellion: Western Australia and Western Canada', in Bruce Hodgins, John J. Eddy, Shelagh D. Grant, and James Struthers, eds, *Federalism in Canada and Australia: Historical Perspectives, 1920–1988* (Peterborough, Ont.: Broadview Press, 1989); Garth Stevenson, 'Western Alienation in Australia and Canada' in *Western Separatism: The Myths, Realities and Dangers*, Larry Pratt and Garth Stevenson, eds (Edmonton: Hurtig Publishers, 1981).

22. Gibbins, 'Western Alienation'.

23. Ibid., 144.

24. Ibid.

25. Ibid.

26. Ibid.

27. David Schwartz, *Political Alienation and Political Behaviour* (Chicago: Aldine Publishing Company, 1973), 15.

28. Ibid., 15.

29. Ibid.

30. More detail regarding the methodologies employed in the 1997 Canadian Election Study can be found in the Technical Documentation available from the Institute for Social Research.

31. Alan Northup, *The 1997 Canadian Election Survey: Technical Documentation* (Toronto: Institute for Social Research, 1998), 36.

32. The distribution of respondents from each of the provinces/territories is as follows: Newfoundland–47, Prince Edward Island–42, Nova Scotia–64, New Brunswick–55, Ontario–447, Manitoba–89, Saskatchewan–94, Alberta–228, British Columbia–222, Yukon–42, North West Territories–38.

33. For those questions with 5-category ordinal response sets, the values were recoded so that the extreme ends of the scale were equal to 2 (i.e., +/- 2), the moderate values were recoded to 1 (+/-1), and don't knows, refused, middle of the scale responses were recoded to 0. For the 3-category ordinal response sets, the middle of the scale responses and the don't know, refused responses were again recoded to 0, with the other two response sets being recoded to 2 (+/-2).

34. For each index, a factor analysis was undertaken and for all four indices (political inequality/ alienation, economic inequality/alienation, anti-Quebec constitution changes, and peripheral region alienation) the factor analysis yielded only one factor. Reliability analyses were also undertaken, focusing primarily on Chronbach's Alpha. With 3 components, we would

be looking for an Alpha of .40 or higher to be achieving an average inter-item correlation of 0.25 or higher. See Richard A. Zellers and Edward G. Carmines, *Measurement In The Social Sciences* (London: Cambridge University Press, 1980), 56–60.

35. Chronbach's Alpha = 0.41.

36. Chronbach's Alpha = 0.51.

37. Chronbach's Alpha = 0.65.

38. The percentile cut points are: 20th percentile = 0.00; 40th percentile = 3.50, 60th percentile = 6.0; 80th percentile = 9.2.

39. Hiller, 'Dependence and Independence'; Brym and Sacouman, *Underdevelopment*; Matthews, *Regional Dependency*.

40. Gibbins and Arrison, *Western Visions*, 1.

41. For example, Elton and Gibbins, 'Western Alienation'; Gibbins, *Prairie Politics*.

42. Two questions were asked (rotated randomly): In general, which government best looks after the interests of people like you: the federal government or the provincial/territorial government? and In general, which government best looks after the interests of people like you: the federal government, the provincial government, or is there not much difference?

43. John Uhr, 'The Canadian and Australian Senates: Comparing Federal Political Institutions' in *Federalism in Canada and Australia: Historical Perspectives, 1920–1988*, Bruce Hodgins, John J. Eddy, Shelagh D. Grant, and James Struthers eds, 130–46.

Chapter 5

Regionalism, Political Culture, and Canadian Political Myths

BARRY COOPER

Nations do not make myths. Myths make nations.
F.W.J. Schelling, *Philosophie der Offenbarung,* 1856

Both the formal institutions of government in Canada and the somewhat less formal means by which governments make decisions have come under considerable stress in recent years.[1] By formal institutions, I have in mind the Parliament of Canada, the constitutional division of powers or federalism, and what has come to be known as the citizens' constitution, expressed chiefly in the Canadian Charter of Rights and Freedoms. Among the less formal institutions may be included the political parties and other means of citizen participation in politics, as well as what Canadians usually call regionalism, regional identity, or regional political consciousness, which political scientists often analyze in terms of political culture. I will try to sort out these terms below.

The 1993 national elections brought into focus, for the first time since the 1920s, the connection between regional identity and the representativeness of the party system.[2] The connection was confirmed in 1997, and the travails of the Reform party in search of a United Alternative added further evidence. Consider the long-term historical perspective as well: during the 1920s, the combination of the farmers' parties, the Progressives, and the Maritime Rights movement put considerable strain on the customary 'brokerage' role of political parties in Canada. Instead of trading off regional and other interests within the government, these interests, fortified by ideological visions, clashed openly across the floor in the House of Commons. Notwithstanding this challenge to traditional party government, the Liberal party of Canada under Prime Minister William Lyon Mackenzie King was able to swallow and digest regionalism, and much else besides.[3] Partly as a consequence of this adroitness, King was able to transform the Liberal party into the Government party. The 1993 eclipse of the Conservatives, and the replacement of the two constituent elements of that party by the Western-based Reform party of Canada and the nationalist Bloc Québécois, provided Prime Minister Jean Chrétien with a problem and an opportunity not dissimilar to that faced by King during the 1920s and 1930s. Changes in the political economy of the West and in the structure of federalism over the past two generations have made Chrétien's task in some respects easier, but in others much harder.

Dissatisfaction with the style of Prime Minister Brian Mulroney and with some of the policies of his government, as well as mistakes made during the campaign, can account for the defections of many voters who had previously supported the Conservatives. However, it was not preordained that the beneficiaries would chiefly be the regional parties. In this context the Liberals, too, must be considered a regional party, their region being Ontario. We will see, however, that the 'regionalism' of Ontario is peculiar insofar as it expresses itself as a (pseudo) pan-Canadian myth. A further nuance to the elections of the 1990s was the demise of the New Democratic Party, particularly the defection of so many 'left-wing' NDP supporters to the 'right-wing' Reform party. These defections appear less paradoxical if the regional bases of support of the NDP are kept in mind and its ideological position on a left-right spectrum is somewhat devalued.

As a first approximation I will endeavour to describe the 'limited identities' that were expressed at least in part through the party system in the 1993 election and confirmed in 1997.[4] For purposes of this chapter, we may as well regard 1997 as the late show to 1993. More specifically, I will begin by distinguishing regional identity and political unity and then consider the contrasting, and often conflicting, regional myths that express those limited identities. The stability of these myths, in contrast to the well-known and oft-deplored electoral volatility of Canadians, is what allows them to be described as political institutions. The regional political cultures—and I will concentrate chiefly on the West in this connection—reinforce as well as express the several political myths.

Having on other occasions argued for the legitimacy of considering political myths, I will take it as given that regionalism or regional identity in Canada is both a symbol that expresses an important element of political reality and a term that can be critically clarified to the point that it can bear a limited theoretical meaning within the cognitive discourse of political science.[5] Political culture, to adopt a conventional understanding, refers to a more or less taken-for-granted framework or context for action. As David Elkins put it, 'political cultures differ, among other ways, in the range of actions deemed appropriate, possible, plausible, or decent'.[6] To simplify somewhat, it seems to me that the distinctive attribute of western Canadian political culture, which is reinforced by political myth, is populism. Populism, I will argue, has important implications for the formalities of government.

Let us begin, however, with political myth, which should be distinguished from political history. As Northrop Frye once said, history aims at telling what happened, whereas myth aims at telling what happens all the time. The privileged discursive vehicle for recounting political myths is imaginative literature. In Canada, it is fair to say, there is no writer (and no literature) of whom one can say he or she belongs among the classics. This is not, however, to be deplored, at least not by political science. Canadian literature records what the Canadian imagination has experienced as meaningful, and it tells readers about those meanings in a way that nothing else could do. Chief among the questions literature answers is, as Frye also remarked, 'where is here?' The 'answer' is found not in an awareness of a factual array or the conceptual grasp of a deployment of data, but in an imaginative and participatory knowledge, a knowledge of reminiscence and reflection, not of reductive transformation and scientific restatement.

To put this point abruptly: when someone says, 'I am a Westerner', he or she means *something*. Specifically, the person is making an imaginative or metaphorical identification of place and meaning, and answering the question: 'where is my here?' To understand Canadian regionalism properly, one must take into account not only voting data and economic interests but also texts and speeches that express regional imaginative consciousness. Only in such places can one find questions of meaning presented, often indirectly.

For many years, a book by an American man of letters, Edmund Wilson, was the most important critical work on Canadian literature. This is what the author said: 'In my youth, of the early nineteen-hundreds, we tended to imagine Canada as a kind of vast hunting preserve convenient to the United States.'[7] Summer visitors to fishing lodges in the Northwest Territories or to the goose pits around Rose Valley, Saskatchewan, will recognize the element of truth in that image.

In addition, however, there are the interpretations of Canadian critics, of whom Frye is the most eminent. For him, literature expressed a sense of identity. 'Identity is local and regional, rooted in the imagination and in works of culture; unity is national in reference, international in perspective, and rooted in a political feeling.'[8] The distinction between regional identity and national unity is, in my opinion, of considerable importance and theoretical significance. According to Frye, 'the essential element in the national sense of unity is the east-west feeling . . . expressed in the national motto, *a mari usque ad mare*'. Suitably qualified, Frye's observation undoubtedly applies to Western regionalism, political culture, and myth.

The devil is in the qualifications. First, it should be emphasized that the tension between cultural identity and national unity is not just unresolved for the time being, but is incapable of resolution. Second, the 'east-west feeling' is not simply or necessarily a positive one. Third, unity is not only distinct from uniformity but is opposed to it. Political unity rejoices in dissent and in variety of outlook, tradition, and myth. In part, this understanding of Canadian unity is expressed in the celebration of linguistic duality, and clearly the symbolism can include Westerners who are overwhelmingly English speaking. At the same time, however, the symbol of bilingualism expresses most perfectly an important aspect only of the old colony of Canada, Upper and Lower Canada, Canada East and Canada West, the Canada of the St Lawrence valley, not the entire country. To distinguish the identity of Canadians living in what was the old colony of Canada from the identities of other Canadians, I would like to employ the venerable term 'Laurentian'. As I shall indicate below, it refers not just to the Innis-Creighton-Lower approach to Canadian history, but to an important regional myth.

Frye emphasized clearly the distinction to be drawn between unity and uniformity; for Westerners the connection between national unity and decentralization is self-evident. Consider this charming political anecdote.[9] On 25 March 1983, Joe Clark of High River, Alberta, described William Davis of Brampton, Ontario, as a regional candidate for the leadership of the Progressive Conservative party, which leadership Clark eventually won. On 7 June, four days before the convention voted to select a new leader, Premier Davis hosted a dinner at another Toronto club, the Albany, for 150 people who had helped in his bid for the leadership. In his remarks to his supporters that night he commented on Clark's statement, which had been made some ten weeks earlier. 'I am not a regional candidate,' he said. 'I believe in Canada, not a community of communities.' The latter was a term that Clark had borrowed from Frye and had used to describe his understanding of Canadians' limited identities. As one observer noted, 'Davis's eyes filled with tears as he spoke of his commitment and his audience was visibly moved.' The image of a weeping Ontario premier, and of the hearts of his otherwise hard-nosed political supporters at the Albany Club swelling with patriotic pride is an index of the power that comes from the identification of a genuine but limited 'Canadian' identity with the non-existent but evocative pan-Canadian alias. A Westerner would be puzzled by all the emotion or just write it off as Toronto-centric arrogance unable to confront a genuine challenge to its own self-understanding and self-satisfaction. No Westerner, not even the accommodating Mr Clark, would have taken Premier Davis's words at face value.

The difference between Davis's Laurentian and Clark's Western image of Canada can be brought out theoretically by considering the limited applicability of what Frye considered the 'essential element' of unity, the 'east-west feeling'. In *Divisions on a Ground*, a later collection of his writings on culture, Frye wrote:

> In Canada there is a single gigantic east-west thrust down the St Lawrence, up the Great Lakes, and across the prairies, then through whatever holes a surveyor could find in the Rockies to the west coast. . . . One enters Canada through the Strait of Belle Isle into the Gulf of St Lawrence, where five Canadian provinces surround us, with enormous islands and glimpses of a mysterious mainland in the distance, but in the foreground only sea and sky. Then we go down the waterway of the St Lawrence, which in itself is only the end of a chain of rivers and lakes that starts in the Rockies. The United States confronts the European visitor: Canada surrounds and engulfs him, or did until the coming of the airplane.[10]

Notice, however, a number of things that go to the heart of the Laurentian perspective. First, the Maritimes—and especially Halifax and its history—stretching south to the Caribbean and east to Europe are eclipsed. Second, the history of the West prior to the history of Canada's interest in the West is symbolically non-existent; after all, the Hudson's Bay Company was named after something, and it was not the St Lawrence River. Third, the desire of Westerners in the twentieth century, before the Free Trade Agreement, for a north-south connection as well as an east-west one is ignored, as is the mere fact of how many flights have been made across the Pacific in more recent years.

In an essay that originally appeared as the Conclusion to the first edition of the *Literary History of Canada*, Frye summarized his impression of how what he now called the *Canadian* imagination has developed. The Canadian imagination, he said, is characterized by 'what we may provisionally call a garrison mentality'. The earliest maps of the country showed only forts. Simcoe had read his Tacitus and established outposts along the Niagara frontier to keep the Aboriginal and the American *feri* at bay until they swore allegiance and became *socii*. The cultural maps of a later time also showed only forts, according to Frye. Now, a garrison is a closely knit—because beleaguered—society, held intact by unquestionable morals and authority. Motives count for nothing. One is either a fighter or a deserter. As Margaret Atwood, one of Frye's most gifted pupils, put it: 'The central symbol for Canada—and this is based on numerous instances of its occurrence in both English and French Canadian literature—is undoubtedly Survival, *la Survivance*.'[11] The point of garrison life, evidently, is to survive. Garrisons are also sites of military and administrative rule.

The limited applicability of Frye's position can be emphasized with the observation that Frye maintained *both* that identity is regional, local, and imaginative, *and* that there is a Canadian mentality expressed imaginatively in a Canadian literature. If one holds to the first insight, the survival of the Laurentian imaginative garrison, which is by all arguments the symbolization of an identity of some kind, has become an expression of a national identity. In the quotation given above, the 'country' is identified with the abstract political unit and not with the concrete and etymological sense of land lying opposite an observer, which is to say, a local meaning. The point I wish to make is not what lawyers would call a quibble; it concerns conceptual clarity.

Consider first the Maritimes. As one student of Maritime self-understanding observed, 'Frye's Laurentian paradigm of Canada can, in fact, be seen as an incidental demolition of the Maritimes and that region's vision of the reality it constitutes.'[12] Margaret Atwood was also in error: 'Maritime fiction possesses almost no trace of what Margaret Atwood has pronounced as typically Canadian—the sense of forever being "immigrants to the place, even if we were born here"—and little trace of any beleaguered garrison mentality.'[13] Instead of imagery depicting savagery, emptiness, and cold, the neo-classical 'book of nature' features prominently in Maritime symbolism, along with invincible backwoodsmen capable of reading it.

Recall Frye's imagery: Canada has no Atlantic seaboard; arrival in Laurentian Canada is a recapitulation of the story of Jonah being swallowed by the whale. For the people who actually inhabit the area, such images simply do not express the reality of Maritime experience. Not only does the country have an Atlantic seaboard, but the experiences native to it constitute the 'headwaters of Canadian literature'.[14] Furthermore, Frye's Laurentian imagery implied that, because a search for imaginative Canada could never start with the Maritimes, what one found there (if anything) was unlikely to be 'Canadian', in the Laurentian mythic sense. If the Maritimes were, in one way or another, to be swallowed by the Laurentian/Canadian whale, that happy event would signal that the region had at long last become imaginatively 'Canadian'. Maritimers, however, see things rather differently. Their parochialism is a defence against imaginative 'Canada', to say nothing of the West.

If, Janice Kulyk Keefer wrote, 'there were a historical type native to the Maritimes, surely it would be that of the pawn or born loser'.[15] The historical evidence is clear enough: the exiling of the Acadians, the reception of exiles from the Thirteen Colonies and the Scottish Highlands. Even if one traces the social patterns of twentieth-century Maritime experience to an otherwise admirable eighteenth-century conservatism,[16] the fact remains that stagnation and decadence remain the most prominent features of pre-modern communal life to have survived into the present.[17]

The political consequences of this heritage for contemporary Canada usually appear in a context of controversy and polemic in which statistics on income or unemployment feature prominently. In making sense of these indicators, a somewhat more profound conflict of interpretation comes to light. On the one hand, Maritimers have long maintained second thoughts about Confederation; on the other, outsiders have long been puzzled by the economic ineptitude and inertia of the region. To give an example from the 1990s, an MP from British Columbia wondered whether federal policies that redistribute wealth from productive individuals and regions to the Maritimes had not turned them into dependent 'charity cases'. He was roundly criticized for his insensitivity and within a week had issued an apology.[18] Only recently have Maritimers begun to question the desirability of federal transfer payments to the region,[19] though their fellow citizens in other parts of the country have long held serious reservations about the deliberate creation of economic dependency by the federal government.

Even this brief excursus into the symbolism and identity of the Maritimes supports the interpretation that Frye misused his own distinction between unity and identity. A plausible account of why this occurred is contained in the discourse of another literary critic, Dennis Duffy. In the concluding remarks to his fine study of Upper Canadian/Ontario literature,[20] he said that the evidence he had just reviewed made imaginatively articulate not Canada and not even the contemporary political unit of Ontario but, more narrowly still, the heartland of Upper Canadian Loyalism, the wedge of land between the Ottawa River and Lake Huron. In that place, the myth of exile (from the American colonies), covenant (loyalty to the Crown), and return to a garden (the transformed wilderness) fully expressed the regional identity of an imaginative 'Canada'. To be more precise: 'Canada', understood as a symbol of identity and not as a political body, is centred in the Loyalist heartland, is full of garrisons concerned about survival, and is indeed moved by feelings of a meaningful east-west axis. This 'Canada', which is imaginatively real, is, however, imaginatively unconnected with even the Loyalist Maritimes, and is connected still less with the West. Duffy sensed this, though his account of those differences remained regrettably undeveloped. To put the matter bluntly: Canada, the imaginative reality centred in the Loyalist heartland, became Canada, the political reality. By so doing, imaginative 'Canada' betrayed its own regional identity and was rewarded, as it were, with control of the political unit.

Making Duffy's hints explicit reveals, in a larger context, how unoriginal they are. This is not a criticism, because in that unoriginality is found a great insight. The expansion of political and economic power from the St Lawrence valley, and especially from the Loyalist heartland, carried with it the attempt to replace the local sense of identity of the inhabitants of the proto-West with that of the newcomers, the imaginative 'Canadians'. It is not to be wondered at, therefore, that the Métis, and the other inhabitants of the Red River Settlement as well, did not greet the representatives of Canadian administrative rule as the bringers of light, culture, and civilization, which was how the newcomers understood themselves. The story of this cultural conflict, which is the foundation myth of the West, has been played out time and again. Differences in culture and in identity, as I mentioned above, are just what are expressed in myth. And myths are not lies: they are stories that express and give shape to the meaning of individual and of collective lives.

Employing Frye's terminology consistently leads to the conclusion that there is indeed a 'Canadian identity', and that it is located geographically in the Loyalist heartland of Ontario. The political unit, Canada, of course embraces the Loyalist heartland but much else besides. Our present concern, however, is with regionalism, political culture, and myth. From what has been learned from Frye, it is clear that just as there is no pan-Canadian identity, neither is there a pan-Canadian culture. This is not to say that 'Canadian identity' and 'Canadian culture', in the precise (and restricted) sense of the identity and culture of the Loyalist heartland does not mistake itself for a pan-Canadian, sea-to-sea equivalent. It does—all the time. Moreover, within the highly compatible Laurentian myth that gives form and meaning to the old colony of Canada, the identification of national identity with the foundation of a federal, bilingual Dominion is easy enough to make. The myth of a Loyalist garrison can easily be accommodated to the image of a French linguistic, cultural, ethnic, historical, or religious garrison as the foundation myth of nationalist Quebec.[21]

The nationalist myth of Quebec took on recognizable form in the wake of Lord Durham's famous *Report on the Affairs of British North America* (1839). Durham shocked a generation of French Canadian political and intellectual leaders by pointing out the inherent bad faith of being themselves urban and educated liberals but liberals who appealed to the non-liberal sentiments and emotions of their rural and ignorant supporters; as well, Durham pointed to the obvious solution to this ongoing political problem, namely greater liberalization.[22] In 1840, François-Xavier Garneau published *Louise: Une légende canadienne* and five years later his *Histoire du Canada*. The *Histoire*, in particular, set the pattern for nearly all subsequent French Canadian historiography, inspiring a school of patriotic poetry and the plot lines of innumerable historical novels: the English desire to suppress the French was the desire of evil to destroy goodness—and yet goodness survived and endured, and one day would triumph. The key to survival was to cling to tradition, to change nothing, and to resist the temptation of 'English' liberalism. Liberalism was a temptation because it promised prosperity, just as Durham had said.

The formular French Canadian novels of the mid-nineteenth century offered a variation on the following story: a young man abandons the farm, lured by an urban *anglaise* temptress. In the city he is degraded: he learns to swear, drink, smoke, and brawl but is saved by a virtuous French Canadian girl who brings him back to the rural paradise, saves his soul, and ensures continued survival. The plot was a central theme as late as Abbé Groulx's *L'Appel de la race* (1922), and Groulx is often identified as the patron of contemporary Quebec nationalism.

A generation later, the contrast between the corrupt but rich urban English and the virtuous but poor rural French had turned into the contrast between rich corruption and poor virtuousness *within* the city. If it were not God's will that only the rural poor would be virtuous, then another explanation had to be sought. Sociologically inclined historians, heirs to the novelist-priests, supplied one. Michel Brunet, for example, explained the relative poverty of French Canadians in 1950 by way of the conquest of New France nearly 200 years earlier. The logic of Brunet's position was simple: the English are a majority and majorities rule in their own interest, which means suppressing the French. No need to examine evidence contrary to the thesis ever arose; indeed, historical facts, if chosen with sufficient care, could easily confirm it. The single cause of French poverty—the English—was balanced by a single solution for French poverty—independence, or failing that, as much political jurisdiction as possible. Castigating *les Anglais* has always been, and remains, preferable to proclaiming the need to reform Quebec's own 'distinct' political practices.

In the generation after Brunet the same story was told—or rather, the same myth was retold. For example, there is Charles Taylor's curious (and in my opinion, spurious) distinction between 'first-level diversity' and 'deep diversity'.[23] Taylor is a federalist, and his views are prudently qualified. This is much less true with an avowed sovereignist such as the late Fernand Dumont, whose most influential work, *Genèse de la société québécoise* has influenced a host of Quebec commissions and a generation of intellectuals and politicians.[24] His language, no less than his doctrine, was heavily influenced by Hegel.[25] In the autobiographical preface, which he called his 'mise en scène', Dumont adopted a voice of great confidence. What he had to say is unambiguous, not to say self-evident.

It is obvious (*c'est entendu*) that the present state of a society, he said, can be understood only by again raising (*remonter*) the question of its past, which meant both returning to the historical and elevating it to the dignity of a true story. History, he said, is not a chain of events, punctuated by a few dramatic episodes, that somehow ends up in the present, but the story of a decisive 'turning' (*un tournant*)[26] from an unfocused collectivity to a society, even a 'distinct society', but then from society to a state, which was for Dumont the last historical hurdle to be overcome, to be achieved through a re-examination of the genesis of the collective identity as set out in *Genèse de la société québécoise.*

And yet (to repeat), this final overcoming has not taken place. Dumont was able to evoke a goal or a purpose, which he called a 'utopia', but he could only predict its achievement. That is why his book is called The Genesis of Quebec Society, not The Genesis of the State of Quebec. The history of Quebec, therefore, is the story *not* of the birth of a state but of the genesis of a society awaiting transfiguration into a state.

But this 'idealist' or purposive element in Dumont's argument also means that his is not a *serious* Hegelianism,[27] and the results, therefore, remain incomplete. To retain the metaphor of birth, Quebec history is a series of abortions, beginning with the failure of New France to convert the Indians.[28] Of course, Dumont argued, Quebec survived, but the catalyst for its survival was the otherness of the 'English', and survival preserved the old problems without abolishing them. There was no *Aufhebung*. The nineteenth-century opportunity, which *was* attended by the violence of 1837, seemed, according to Dumont, lost forever; the late-twentieth-century alternative, a utopian ethnic enclave dedicated to survival, could never move beyond a purely 'defensive strategy'.

Dumont simply dressed up the traditional Garneau-Groulx-Brunet myth in the brighter colours of Hegelian philosophy of history. The new look has had great appeal to the secular intellectuals of contemporary Quebec. Indeed, the political religion of Quebec's sovereignists looks like nothing so much as chirping within Hegel's *geistige Tierreich*, the spiritual bestiary, a discourse forever poised on the brink of an apocalypse. This consciousness, which is expressed in a subdued and scholarly way in Dumont, is given more enthusiastic expression in popular tracts: 1988, *Le Prochain Rendez-vous: essai sur l'avenir du Québec* (Louis O'Neill); 1990, *Maintenant ou jamais!* (Pierre Bourgeault); 1990, *Ma terre, Québec: essai sur le Québec en marche* (Jean-Charles Claveau); 1992, *Demain, la république: le projet du Québec Profond* (Jean-Louis Bourque); 1993, *Gouverner ou disparaître* (Pierre Vadeboncoeur). The titles are meant both to present the apocalypse in thought and to evoke the apocalypse in deed. The strong words—and Vadeboncoeur goes so far as to speak of genocide, a *génocide en douce*—do not, however, refer to the reality of strong deeds. Instead, these writers express the longing of the spiritual bestiary evoking the 'naturalness' of the evolution of Quebec towards an independent state.

On the other side, the federalist nationalists among Quebec intellectuals, with the possible exception of Stéphane Dion, have grown quiet. Meech Lake and Charlottetown did a great deal to undermine the credibility of the myth of two founding peoples. At the same time, those defeats enhanced the appeal of the 'Dumont paradigm', as Nemni called it. Because *les Anglais* had thwarted the aspirations of Quebec society once again, the only alternative must be pursued. In 1999, in his speech opening a session of the Quebec legislature, Premier Bouchard provided his own version of this double-sided dialectic of self and other:

> So, let's be clear. A few years ago, English Canada kept asking: 'What does Quebec want?' Now their message is: 'Who cares what Quebec wants?' This is a message Quebeckers must ponder. . . . English Canadians have decided they want to be governed as a single, unified nation. Good for them. We in Quebec have no quarrel with that new resolve . . . as long as we are not bullied into following someone else's vision.[29]

Bouchard's evocation of Quebec alone against 'English Canada', no less than the Anglophobic symbols, *Québécois pure laine* or *de la vielle souche*, was at least as divisive as the evocations of 'Laurentian nationalism', especially economic nationalism, with their pseudo-Loyalist, anti-American sentiments.

Turning now to the West, one finds actual rather than imaginative forts, but very little trace of the garrison mentality. Critics who have analyzed the literary texts of western Canada have nearly all emphasized the importance of the landscape. 'All discussion of the literature produced in the Canadian West', Henry Kreisel announced, 'must of necessity begin with the impact of the landscape upon the mind.'[30] Donald Stephens made a more explicit contrast: 'The "garrison mentality" so obvious in the writing of Eastern Canada (in the Maritimes, Quebec, and Ontario) is not prominent in that of Western Canada (the Prairies and British Columbia).' The reason, he said, is that 'the prairie is a landscape that makes them [the inhabitants] greater than [garrison] life; it is an environment that brings out the best, and the worst, in man.'[31] Finally, the land is not, as it is in the imaginative Canada described by Frye and Atwood, chiefly a threat. 'Prairie man', wrote Ricou, 'may feel insignificant or immensely self-confident; he may feel free or inescapably trapped; he may be deeply religious or a rebel against all authority; his imagination may be stifled or stimulated. In each case, however, his nature or outlook will be linked to his curiously abrupt position in a vast and uninterrupted landscape.'[32] Plenty of additional critical and imaginative evidence could be cited. The point, however, is plain: the West is not a transplanted imaginative Ontario garrison.[33]

The imaginative prairie landscape has both a spatial and a temporal dimension. Spatially it extends, as David Carpenter said, 'from the dryland to the Promised Land', that is, from Manitoba and Saskatchewan to Alberta.[34] Imaginatively, Alberta is the quintessential West, *le far-west*, as they say in French cinematographic circles. And British Columbia, as Edward McCourt called it in his classic study, is the near east.[35] However that may be, changes over time are more important for our purposes than changes over space.

The historical theme of Western identity consists in variations in the response of European groups and individuals to a non-European landscape. The new land did not have an impact on an empty head but on a conscious one filled with the old culture. Right from the beginning, British words such as *meadow, red deer,* and *snow* proved inadequate to the reality experienced. Only recently have cultural geographers and historians devoted much attention to the problem of how the Western landscape was articulated by the pre-settlement explorers.[36] After the early explorers, who were more interested in markets than landscape anyhow, descriptions turned technical or fictional; from about the mid-nineteenth century, economics and calculative reason parted company with imagination and emotion. Explorers were supplanted by expeditions, and hastily scribbled journals gave way to official reports, to scientific accounts and scientific speculations about rainfall, flora, and isotherms. Maps were drawn on grids. From the start, then, the West has felt the impact of the most advanced contemporary technologies. Moreover, unlike the great technologies of central Canada, Western ones were concerned directly with resource extraction, not industrial manufacturing. At the same time, however, they were subordinated to central Canadian technologies. Consider, for example, the prairie town. Wallace Stegner's 'hugeness of simple forms' congealed, in towns, into the mass production of identical elevators, banks, and railway stations, a main street called Main Street, and a dirt road beside the tracks called Railway Avenue. It was as if the CPR had one blueprint and people had to fit it.

The early settlers, chiefly from Britain and Ontario, and the earliest writers clung to the cultural forms they left behind. Consequently they often made 'inappropriate' responses to the new environment. The settlement experience was in many respects a frontier experience, though it was not seen that way by the literary imagination. On the contrary, the West was part of an imperial civilization whose most idyllic fictional characters, the policeman, the preacher, and the teacher, were its agents. When, during the 1920s, the 'realistic' novels of F.P. Grove or Sinclair Ross began to displace the romantic and pastoral adventures of an earlier day, a new awareness of Western experience had achieved articulate form. The chaste, sunlit, and superficial garden myth was rejected, along with the spirit of empire. Constriction and isolation, the dark effects of conquering rather than cultivating the land, became major themes of western literature. The closest the West ever came to creating a garrison mentality was probably in a Depression-era novel such as Ross's *As For Me and My House*.[37]

Contemporary Western literature—the comedy of W.O. Mitchell, Robert Kroetsch, W.P. Kinsella, Jack Hodgins, Aritha van Herk, or Guy Vanderhaeghe, for example—offers less a rejection of sentimental romance, as did Ross and Grove, than a self-conscious new beginning. 'The habit of beginnings, of starting again', wrote Dick Harrison, 'is deeply ingrained in the Western consciousness, and comedy is its necessary expression.'[38] The same can be said even of Margaret Laurence, whose great novels are almost never considered to be Western, and the rich array of BC writers who are hardly known beyond the provincial borders.

The conclusions to be drawn from this brief consideration of Western self-understanding may be summarized as follows: first, the West has not been part of imaginative 'Canada'; second, there is scant evidence of a garrison mentality; third, survival is not the dominant theme, save under extreme and adverse conditions; and fourth, it soon enough gives way to the spirit of new beginnings.

This account of the tensions among the several regional myths or regionally based images and understandings of the shape of the Canadian body politic is far from complete. We have said little of the distinctiveness of British Columbia and Newfoundland, and even less of the North and the pre-political as well as pre-modern self-understandings of the many Aboriginal communities in the country. For those who seek them, there are a large number of what Jeffrey Simpson called 'faultlines' from which to choose.[39] I would like to conclude by indicating the connection between the Western sense of identity and the formal and constitutional implications of it as they resonate with the political culture usually identified as populism.

A few years ago, Saskatchewan Premier Allan Blakeney told a surprised audience at the Canadian Club in Toronto that the only natural resources extensively regulated by the federal government were those that were Western staples: oil, gas, uranium, and wheat:

> We in the West find it passing strange that the national interest emerges only when we are talking about Western *resources* or Eastern *benefits*. If oil, why not iron ore and steel products? If natural gas, why not copper? If uranium—and we in Saskatchewan may well be Canada's biggest uranium producer in a few years—if uranium, why not nickel?

Premier Blakeney was clearly rejecting the myth of the nation derived from the experiences of the Loyalist heartland, a myth that somehow always manages to justify the interests of the inhabitants of southern Ontario who do not, after all, constitute the whole of the Canadian body politic. One could adduce a similar stance from the speeches of Premier Peter Lougheed of Alberta, particularly during the period of the National Energy Program. On occasion, rejection of the garrison myth, particularly when heavily freighted with conflicting regional interests, has led to a rejection of the forms of parliamentary government.

The conventional understanding of Western politics is based on the obvious: the usual alternation of Liberal and Conservative governments, which is almost the rule elsewhere in the country, has been modified beyond recognition west of the Ontario frontier. There are Liberal and Conservative governments, of course, but there have also been the United Farmers of Manitoba, the Co-operative Commonwealth Federation, the United Farmers of Alberta, Social Credit, and several coalition governments as well as New Democratic Party governments, the NDP being the nominal successor to the CCF. On the federal scene, many MPs from the West have been identified with parties other than Liberal and Conservative—notably the Progressive party, Social Credit, the CCF and the NDP, and more recently, the Reform party/Canadian Alliance.

Many commentators have taken note of this peculiarity of Western political life and, having called these parties 'third parties', rendered an obvious political judgment: third parties are 'protest parties'. Notice, however, that these 'third parties' can become the major parties in a two-party system. In British Columbia, for example, Social Credit and the CCF/NDP for over a generation constituted the Government and Opposition. In other words, the Western parties that are neither Liberal nor Conservative are 'third' only in the context of the Parliament of Canada—and even there the Canadian Alliance, having become official opposition, must provide a modest and perhaps temporary challenge to the term.

It is no doubt accurate enough to call the Western parties 'protest parties'. Most people find the identification obvious and self-evident, and see no need to ask the next question: against what are these parties protesting? And why have the Liberals or the Conservatives been unable to capture that protest and turn it into support for their own party? Or, if they do capture the 'protest party', as the Conservatives conceivably may have done under Brian Mulroney or the Liberals may have done with the Progressives during the 1920s, why don't the voters remain loyal, once they have been captured? Why did the Progressive voter switch to the CCF or Social Credit? Why did the Western Conservatives desert to Reform and the Canadian Alliance?

Two related and general answers have been proposed to these questions. One concerns the limited ability of 'national' brokerage politics to represent regional interests, particularly when Western interests conflict with those of Laurentian Canada. The NEP and gun registration are recent examples. Such legislative initiatives are claimed by the governments that enacted them to be splendid instances of laws designed to effect the common good, and, indeed, may appear that way to some sections of the country. The mere fact that these policies have been opposed by Westerners exposes the fraudulence of the claim and the deceptiveness of appearances. To Westerners such policies look like sectionally-based exercises of regional administrative control by Laurentian Canada.

The logic of Westerners' response to the Liberal and Conservative parties in Ottawa may therefore be summarized as follows: first, Westerners have rejected the Laurentian myth that Canada is a garrison; second, supposedly 'national' public policies have often simply given legislative expression to the Laurentian myth; third, the 'national' policies have been imposed on the West by parties temporarily or semi-permanently under the sway of the Laurentian myth; fourth, those policies have harmed Western interests and have insulted Western pride—pride in being Canadians, their own kind of non-garrison Canadians, among other things. Thus, fifth, Westerners have pursued a multi-pronged strategy, both inside and outside the Liberal and Conservative parties, to find a political vehicle that represents their interests and their vision in the national government. This logic is a skeletal expression of politics in a complex, politically articulate society with diverging as well as converging interests. In this respect, Westerners may be compared to Quebeckers, who have followed a similar strategy (but with greater success) and have seen their share of non-Liberal and non-Conservative MPs and provincial governments.

This account, or one very much like it, of the specific flavour of Western politics has often been repeated. There is another reason, which has seldom been made explicit, that Westerners have undertaken the political responses they value. It concerns the heart of Canadian political institutions—or rather, it shows how easily those institutions can be, and have been, subverted to serve the sectional interests just indicated. Most Canadians know that Canada is not a republic and that Parliament and the provincial Legislative Assemblies are not congresses. Beyond that, things get a bit hazy, and Canadians are likely to speak about their country as a liberal democracy or a constitutional democracy. This is undoubtedly correct: Canada is a constitutional (or a liberal) democracy, but so too is the United States, and it has a Congress, not a Parliament. The distinction between the two kinds of government, congressional and parliamentary, is formal. The central formality, so far as Western political life is concerned, is the crown as the locus of sovereignty.

A second institutional observation concerns one of the main conventions of parliamentary government, the ability of the legislature to control the executive by granting or withholding supply. This ability depends on the prior ability of the legislature to raise funds. Historically, the chief source of funds for the provinces, namely the benefits to be derived from natural resources, either through their sale or through the collection of on-going royalties, were withheld from the North-Western Territorial government and from the successor prairie provincial governments. As early as 1884, Frederick Haultain, the territorial permier, made the point that, as soon as responsible government came to the North-West, the administration of public lands should be assumed by the government, whether territorial or provincial, whether one big province or several. The story has been told in great detail by Lewis H. Thomas in his book, *The Struggle for Responsible Government in the North-West Territories: 1870–97*. The word *struggle* in the title was well chosen, and it did not end in 1897, with the North-West Territories Act.

Peter Lougheed once observed that 1930—the date of the passage of the Natural Resources Transfer Acts—not 1905, marked the creation of the Prairie provinces as members of Confederation. The timing, however, could not have been worse, inasmuch as the entire country was about to endure a decade of severe deflation. The Prairie provinces were the hardest hit part of Canada so that, even if the provinces did control their resources, there was little revenue to be earned from them. The conclusion to be drawn from the absence of responsible government from the Prairie provinces for the sixty years prior to 1930 is that political leaders were deprived of the education in parliamentary government that their colleagues in the East had experienced for at least a generation before 1870. In addition to being neophytes in the arts of parliamentary democracy, Prairie politicians, for two additional generations, were effectively stunted by the federal government. In response they sought alternative forms of self-government.

Ottawa's refusal to grant responsible government to the Prairie provinces was matched by the experience of many Western MPs and premiers of the malignant consequences of party government. In terms of constitutional forms, political parties are simply a means of expediting the conduct of government in much the same way that elections are simply a means of securing representatives in an assembly. It bears repeating that, historically, parliamentary government has been two-party government, a Government-and-Opposition arrangement. The grave defect of a two-party system, as successive political movements, from the Progressives through Social Credit and the CCF to Reform and the Canadian Alliance, is that they seldom serve the interests of articulate and regionally concentrated minorities.

This aspect of Western political experience was most clearly demonstrated by the operation of political parties in the House of Commons. One of the paradoxes of parliamentary government is that, although a member is elected as a representative of the entire body politic and is thus theoretically free to exercise his or her independent judgment, that freedom is compatible with cabinet government only so long as the majority of members identify the common good or the national interest with the good of their party. As Norman Ward once observed, MPs 'must use their freedom to subjugate themselves'. The operation of party discipline, in turn, is understood by the leaders of the large parties that expect to form the Government or the Opposition to be entirely in keeping with the common good. After all, they are trying to win the next election by pleasing the electorate and accept as unproblematic that what pleases the electorate is by definition in the national interest and constitutes the common good.

The great problem for Western MPs, however, was that, for 'national' political parties—historically, for the Liberal and the Conservative parties—the electorate was disproportionately concentrated in the St Lawrence valley. In caucus, therefore, even the most loyal MP would, when regional issues divided the party, invariably be out-voted and would then have an awkward task ahead: to explain to the individuals that elected him or her why a particular policy was in the common interest when, for example, it didn't look like it was in the interest of the people who voted for the member. What in caucus looks like majority rule back on the farm looks like a member Ottawashed.

Because they have been denied the experience of responsible government in the provinces and, coupled with that, have experienced a certain disenchantment with the actual operation of responsible government in and by Ottawa, a significant number of Westerners have questioned the usefulness and, indeed, the legitimacy of parliamentary government. This has led them to advocate changes to the electoral system, and to support non-partisanship and regional parties, of course, but also to favour direct democracy and 'populism'. However, these demands to change, to reform, or even to destroy parliamentary government have never been wholeheartedly supported across the West. It should be borne in mind, for example, that even during the miserable seven lean years of the great depression, when the CCF and Social Credit were on an upward curve, the two old parties still attracted the support of over half of the electorate.

Even so, the logic of Western support for populism is obvious. Having been excluded from the political education that accompanies the operation of responsible government, and having been persistently out-voted and out-muscled by the operations of the party system and the first-past-the-post electoral system, a significant number of Westerners found in populism a coherent explanation for their condition. In one way or another, populism identifies public virtue with the will of the people, and the people are one. From this assumption, which to a populist is a self-evident verity, the conclusion can be drawn that divisions are not the reflection of genuine diversity of interest or of different visions and experiences of political reality. On the contrary, to a committed populist, divisions and conflicts are, in principle, artificial and manufactured by self-interested and mischievous outsiders. From the Progressives during the 1920s to the supporters of Reform/Canadian Alliance of today, 'the common sense of the common people' (to use the formula that opens the

Reform Party's 1993 *Blue Book*) has been strongly contrasted with the manipulative and Machiavellian activities of 'élites', mostly Eastern élites. Reform proposed to put its populism into practice by advocating direct democracy through the great trinity of initiative, referendum, and recall. But direct democracy and the legal and constitutional changes required to enact populist measures are wholly incompatible with the operations of parliamentary government. Most Reformers either ignored this awkward problem or didn't know it was there.

The fact is, popular sovereignty has no place in a parliamentary regime. When populist measures have nevertheless been passed, it comes as no surprise that they have not withstood the scrutiny of the courts. The most notorious example was the Manitoba Initiative and Referendum Act of 1916, which was appealed all the way to the Judicial Committee of the Privy Council. At each step in the appeal process, the incompatibility of direct and parliamentary democracy was pointed out. To serious populists, this result only confirmed their opinion that parliament would have to be changed along with 'partyism'. After the futility of the comparatively modest constitutional changes proposed by the Meech Lake and Charlottetown accords, however, the prospect of a major constitutional change that would transfer sovereignty to 'the people' and replace Parliament with a congressional system is remote in the extreme. Perhaps more to the point, there is no guarantee that, in a populist regime, the interests of the West would be any better protected than they are at present, nor that the Western understanding of Canadian federalism would prove persuasive to Easterners.

Recently even Reformers and Alliance party members have had to rethink the long-term effectiveness of populism as a strategy. Early in 1999, Ian McClelland, a Reform MP for Edmonton Southwest, questioned the coherence and the desirability of maintaining even a nodding allegiance to populism. 'The logical outcome of "pure" populism', he wrote, 'is a party with no political principles at all. . . . Populism does not allow for principled decision-making, as leadership defers to majority public opinion in all major (and also, theoretically, minor) respects.' The answer, Mr McClelland argued, to a parliament populated by five regionally based parties, is a recovery of responsible government. As a first, but major, step in that direction he proposed a 'less government' party as the seed around which opposition to the 'more government' Liberal party could crystallize. Mr McClelland, who learned of the virtues of parliamentary government after becoming an assistant deputy speaker, was predictably denounced by hard-core populists in the Reform party as an 'élitist'.

The significance of the realization by a sitting Member of the difficulties of squaring the populist appeal of the Reform/Alliance party with the responsibilities of representation is a portent more than an achievement. Populists in office are compelled by the demands of responsible government to conform to constitutional conventions and practices that contradict their fond belief in the sovereignty of the people. In the absence of radical constitutional change, Mr McClelland's change of heart would eventually happen to the party as a whole, should the Canadian Alliance or any other populist party ever become a parliamentary majority. Mr McClelland's anticipation of the difficulties is a portent because it may presage an end to the historical pattern of Western protestation and the start of a politics of Western leadership. That, too, expresses the emphasis on open horizons and endless possibility that is such an important element in Western regional identity.

NOTES

1. In *Derailed: The Betrayal of the National Dream* (Toronto: Key Porter, 1994), David Bercuson and I discussed at some length the context for the present analysis.

2. Previously the topic had been examined indirectly, by means of an analysis of the Canadian electoral system that combined single-member constituencies, a plurality needed to elect, and disciplined parliamentary parties. See Alan C. Cairns, 'The Electoral System and the Party System in Canada, 1921–1965' reprinted in Douglas E. Williams, ed., *Constitution, Government and Society in Canada: Selected Essays by Alan C. Cairns* (Toronto: McClelland & Stewart, 1988), 111–38.

3. His actions are described clearly in the standard histories of the various regional protests. See, for instance, Ernest R. Forbes, *Maritime Rights: The Maritime Rights Movement, 1919–1927, A Study in Canadian Regionalism* (Montreal: McGill-Queen's University Press, 1979), ch. 8; W.L. Morton, *The Progressive Party in Canada* (Toronto: University of Toronto Press, 1950), ch. 6.

4. The term 'limited identities' is taken from J.M.S. Careless, 'Limited Identities in Canada', *Canadian Historical Review* 50 (1969): 1–10.

5. Particularly useful in this respect are the remarks of Rudolf Heberle, 'Regionalism: Some Critical Observations', *Social Forces* 21 (1943): 280–6.

6. David Elkins, 'British Columbia as a State of Mind' in Donald E. Blake, ed., *Two Political Worlds: Parties and Voting in British Columbia* (Vancouver, University of British Columbia Press, 1985), 53.

7. Edmund Wilson, *O Canada: An American's Notes on Canadian Culture* (New York: Farrar, Straus and Giroux, 1965), 11.

8. Northrop Frye, *The Bush Garden: Essays on the Canadian Imagination* (Toronto, Anansi, 1971), ii.

9. P. Martin, A. Gregg, and G. Perlin, *Contenders: The Tory Quest for Power* (Toronto, Prentice Hall, 1983), 53.

10. James Polk, ed., *Divisions on a Ground: Essays on Canadian Culture* (Toronto: Anansi, 1982) 58.

11. Frye, *The Bush Garden*, 225–6; Margaret Atwood, *Survival: A Thematic Guide to Canadian Literature* (Toronto: Anansi, 1972), 32. In 1976, Frye wrote 'National Consciousness in Canadian Culture'. Here the identification of imaginative, that is, regionalized, Canada, and the political unit is even more pronounced. The essay is reprinted in *Divisions on a Ground*, 41–56.

12. Janice Kulyk Keefer, *Under Eastern Eyes: A Critical Reading of Maritime Fiction* (Toronto: University of Toronto Press, 1987), 27.

13. Keefer, *Under Eastern Eyes*, 36.

14. See Arthur MacMechan, *Headwaters of Canadian Literature* (Toronto: McClelland & Stewart, [1924] 1974).

15. Keefer, *Under Eastern Eyes,* 16, 94.

16. D.C. Harvey, 'The Heritage of the Maritimes', *Dalhousie Review* 14 (1934): 28–32.

17. See William S. MacNutt, *The Atlantic Provinces: The Emergence of Colonial Society, 1712–1857* (Toronto: McClelland & Stewart, 1965), 267–8; Silver Donald Cameron, *The Education of Everett Richardson: The Nova Scotia Fisherman's Strike, 1970–71* (Toronto: McClelland & Stewart, 1977), 30.

18. See *Alberta Report,* 4 July 1994, 6–7.

19. See Fred McMahon, *Looking the Gift Horse in the Mouth: The Impact of Federal Transfers on Atlantic Canada* (Halifax: AIMS, 1996).

20. Dennis Duffy, *Gardens, Covenants, Exiles: Loyalism in the Literature of Upper Canada/Ontario* (Toronto: University of Toronto Press, 1982).

21. William Johnson has provided the most thorough, and controversial, discussion of the French ethnic garrison in two books, the first written in French; *Anglophobie, Made in Quebec* (Montreal: Stanké, 1991), and the second written in English: *A Canadian Myth: Quebec, Between Canada and the Illusion of Utopia* (Montreal: Davies, 1994). Neither has received much attention from Quebec or Canadian intellectuals or scholars.

22. This interpretation of the *Report* was recently restored to public visibility by Janet Ajzenstat in her splendid study, *The Political Thought of Lord Durham* (Montreal: McGill-Queen's University Press, 1988).

23. Charles Taylor, *Reconciling the Solitudes: Essays on Canadian Federalism and Nationalism,* ed. Guy Laforest (Montreal: McGill-Queen's University Press, 1992), 183.

24. Fernard Dumont, *Genèse de la société québécoise* (Montreal: Boréal, 1993). A very helpful discussion of Dumont's work is Max Nemni, 'Post-Ethnic Nationalism in Quebec: A Promise of History?' presented at the sixty-sixth meeting of the CPSA, Calgary, June 1994. Dumont is an important intellectual force in Quebec and is well known in the French-speaking world of scholarship. In addition to major sociological and cultural studies, he has written on Christian theology as an *homme de foi,* and is a published poet.

25. Taylor, as well, is known internationally for his interpretation of Hegel. Indeed, an account of the importance of Hegel in Canadian intellectual life, which is more sensed than understood, has yet to be written. See, however, David MacGregor, 'Canada's Hegel', *The Literary Review of Canada* (February 1994); or Peter C. Emberley, *Values, Education, and Technology: The Ideology of Dispossession* (Toronto, University of Toronto Press, 1995), ch. 4.

26. The 'turning' is the Heideggerian *Kehre* writ large.

27. According to Hegel, the social elements awaiting transfiguration will remain external to one another so long as the society in question is shielded from the experience of violence. Dumont does not discuss this *zauberisch* aspect of Hegelian political science, which, because it would lead back to the arguments of Pierre Vallières and the violence of the FLQ, may be just as well.

28. Dumont, *Genèse*, 55.

29. Lucien Bouchard, as reported in *The Globe and Mail* 4 March 1999, A4.

30. Henry Kreisel, 'The Prairie: A State of Mind', *Transactions of the Royal Society of Canada* Series IV, 6 1968, 1973. Consider the opening sentence of one of the most famous western Canadian novels, W.O. Mitchell's *Who Has Seen the Wind*: 'Here was the least common denominator of nature, the skeleton requirements simply, of land and sky—Saskatchewan prairie'.

31. Donald G. Stephens, 'Introduction' to Donald G. Stephens, ed., *Writers of the Prairies* (Vancouver: University of British Columbia Press, 1973), 2.

32. Laurence Ricou, *Vertical Man/Horizontal World: Man and Landscape in Canadian Prairie Fiction* (Vancouver: University of British Columbia Press, 1973), 173.

33. Greg Thomas and Ian Clarke, 'The Garrison Mentality in the Canadian West', *Prairie Forum* 4, 1 (1979): 83–104, discussed the Hudson's Bay Company forts and the tree-planting palisades of prairie homesteads. They said nothing, however, of the 'many tender ties' that joined the men of the HBC and the women of the country; palisade trees, which also acted as windbreaks, were in any case characteristic only of Ontario settlers' homesteads. See also Sylvia Van Kirk, *Many Tender Ties: Women in Fur-Trade Society in Western Canada, 1670–1870* (Winnipeg: Watson & Dwyer, 1980); Barry Cooper, *Alexander Kennedy Isbister: A Respectable Critic of the Honourable Company* (Ottawa: Carleton University Press, 1988) for further discussion of Western self-understanding before the arrival of Canadians.

34. David C. Carpenter, 'Alberta in Fiction: The Emergence of a Provincial Consciousness', *Journal of Canadian Studies* 10, 4 (1974): 17.

35. Edward A. McCourt, *The Canadian West in Fiction* (Toronto: Ryerson, 1949), vi. We will not consider British Columbian regionalism here. Elkins's essay is a useful starting point.

36. A selection of these early writings is in John Warkentin, ed. *The Western Interior of Canada: A Record of Geographical Discovery, 1612–1917* (Toronto: McClelland & Stewart, 1964). Discussion of the writers excerpted by Warkentin may be found in: D.W. Moodie, 'Early Images of Rupert's Land' in Richard Allen, ed., *Man and Nature on the Prairies*, Canadian Plains Studies 6 (Regina: Canadian Plains Research Center, 1976), 1–20; B. Kaye and D.W. Moodie, 'Geographic Perspectives on the Canadian Plains' in Richard Allen, ed., *A Region of the Mind: Interpreting the Western Canadian Plains*, Canadian Plains Studies 1 (Regina: Canadian Plains Research Center, 1973), 17–46; G.S. Dunbar, 'Isotherms and Politics: Perception of the Northwest in the 1850s' in A.W. Rasporich and H.C. Classen, eds, *Prairie Perspectives* 2 (Toronto: Holt, Rinehart and Winston, 1973), 80–101; R. Douglas Francis, 'Changing Images of the West', *Journal of Canadian Studies* 17, 3 (1982): 5–17. See also Doug Owram, *Promise of Eden: The Canadian Expansionist Movement and the Idea of the West, 1856–1900* (Toronto: University of Toronto Press, 1980) and Doug Francis, *Images of the West: Responses to the Canadian Prairies* (Saskatoon: Western Producer Prairie Books, 1989).

37. At the same time, two things ought to be borne in mind. In 1941, when Ross's book was published, it sold only a few hundred copies. And second, those who have certified Ross's

novel as a 'prairie classic' were critics for whom garrison literature was most familiar, that is, Easterners. Certification was as much a political as an artistic judgment.

38. Dick Harrison, *Untamed Country: The Struggle for a Canadian Prairie Fiction* (Edmonton: University of Alberta Press, 1977), 179. See also Laurence Ricou, 'Field Notes and Notes in a Field: Forms of the West in Robert Kroetsch and Tom Robbins', *Journal of Canadian Studies* 17, 3 (1982): 117–23; and Robert Lecher, 'Bordering On: Robert Kroetsch's Aesthetic', ibid., 124–33.

39. Jeffrey Simpson, *Faultlines: Struggling for a Canadian Vision* (Toronto: Harper Collins 1993).

Part 3

Regionalism and the Contemporary Canadian Party System

Introduction

The four chapters in this section try to come to terms with the apparent regionalization of the Canadian party system since the federal election of 1993. Taken as a group, these chapters illustrate the elusive character of Canadian regionalism. On the one hand, they demonstrate that political competition in Canada has become regionalized to a remarkable degree, with campaigns that are segmented into distinct regional battles and parties that have come to rely on regionally based patterns of support. On the other hand, in their studies of the Reform party, the Liberal party, and the New Democratic Party, respectively, David Laycock, Joseph Wearing, and David Stewart argue that these political parties are not regional parties, in the sense of parties acting primarily as agents for or representatives of a particular region. Rather, the logic of political competition and the electoral system have forced parties to develop regional strongholds in their pursuit of electoral success.

In Chapter 6, William Cross sets the stage by examining patterns of regionalization in the election campaigns of 1993 and 1997. Following the work of R.K Carty, Cross argues that election campaigns during the third-party system years—from 1957 to 1988—were characterized by national campaigns that were aided by the rise of a national medium of communication: television. In 1993 and 1997, however, this pan-Canadian approach to campaigning was shattered by the rise of the Bloc Québécois and Reform. As a result, the federal election campaigns in both years were 'a collection of largely discrete regional contests'. Even the Liberal party, which was the only party to run credible campaigns in every region of the country, approached the 1997 election prepared to highlight different issues in each region and to defend itself from different directions, depending on the Liberals' main competitor in that region.

It might appear to follow from Cross's analysis that the Reform party, which was one of the catalysts for change in the party system in 1993, could be characterized as a predominantly regional party. According to David Laycock, however, this characterization would be inaccurate. Laycock examines the party's policy stances, its conduct in Ottawa, and its effort to reformulate itself, and concludes that the party has allowed its right-of-centre ideological bearings to override its fealty to Western themes and concerns. Laycock's account of the Reform party leadership's effort to expand the party's bases of support by emphasizing ideological rather than regional issues illustrates Mildred Schwartz's observation in *Politics and Territory* that large parties wishing 'to maximize their electoral appeal are constrained from making excessively particularistic approaches to voters, since what attracts one group may actively antagonize another. In this way, a party's desire to govern may propel it to discover larger, nationally appealing issues and thereby push it away from narrow concerns with regionalism.'[1]

Laycock concludes that Reform's efforts to transcend its regional origins are doomed to fail. Even though the party's leadership is acting on precisely the impulse that Schwartz identified, a substantial segment of its followers are unwilling to sacrifice regional concerns on the altar of national success. Moreover, there is little evidence to suggest that voters outside western Canada are willing to see Reform and its successor, the Canadian Alliance, as a genuinely national party distinct from its Western roots. Although Laycock's chapter was written before the 2000 election campaign, his predictions regarding the party's inability to expand beyond its regional base were certainly borne out by the election's outcome.

Despite the Liberal party's increasing reliance on Ontario, Joe Wearing argues in Chapter 8 that the one-party predominance in Ontario is an illusion. The outcome of the elections of 1993 and 1997, he argues, do not reflect Liberal strength in Ontario as much as they demonstrate the weakness of the other parties. Ontario voters were punishing Conservative candidates for the sins of the Mulroney government and New Democrat candidates on electoral outcomes for their party's term in office provincially. Wearing also notes the distorting effect on electoral outcomes of the single member plurality electoral system employed in Canada. The Liberals were able to win 98 per cent of Ontario seats with only 49 per cent of the popular vote because of this institutional arrangement. With Reform and the Conservatives splitting the vote on the right, the Liberals were able to dominate the province with a slim majority in the popular vote.

In his account of the NDP's rise to prominence in Atlantic Canada, David Stewart joins Wearing in rejecting the argument that a profound realignment in regional support has taken place among the Canadian electorate. According to Stewart, the Atlantic region has been distinctive in its unwavering rejection of parties other than the Liberals and Conservatives. This distinctiveness is rooted in precisely the social and economic differences that Schwartz casts as preconditions to differences in the party system: Maritimers, writes Stewart, are more likely to be churchgoers, Protestant, poor, of British descent, and living in non-farming rural communities. In both 1993 and 1997, however, voters in Atlantic Canada departed from old patterns, and support for the NDP rose. Stewart attributes this change to the confluence of a number of short-term factors, including the NDP's popular leader from Atlantic Canada, widespread perceptions that the federal government's program cuts were unfair, and competition between the Conservatives and Reform on the right of the spectrum. The results of the 2000 election supported Stewart's contention. The Liberal party, having reviewed its reforms to Employment Insurance, regained support in the region. NDP support in Atlantic Canada dropped, reducing the party from eight seats to four.

NOTE

1. Mildred A. Schwartz, *Politics and Territory: The Sociology of Regional Persistence in Canada*, 136.

Chapter 6

The Increasing Importance of Region to Canadian Election Campaigns

WILLIAM CROSS

Much about competition among political parties in Canada has changed in the past 10 years. Today there are five official parties in the House of Commons, up from three a decade ago. For all five of these parties, these have been eventful years, with none of them now occupying a position similar to that held at the start of the 1990s. The rise of Reform/Canadian Alliance and the Bloc Québécois and the sharply diminished positions of two of the three traditional parties have resulted in a dramatic increase in the importance of region to Canadian party competition. The combination of these changes to the party system and the parties' mastery of new communication techniques has facilitated a highly regionalized approach to campaigning. This chapter explores how these developments have increased the importance of region and how the parties have adapted their campaign strategies to this changing electoral playing field.

The Changing Political Landscape

As the 1980s drew to a close, the Progressive Conservatives were enjoying their second consecutive majority mandate; by 2000, they were the fifth-place party in the House of Commons and had both a 10 million dollar debt and a leader recycled from the 1970s. The Liberals, meanwhile, had rebounded from their electoral drubbings of 1984 and 1988 to win three successive majority governments, leading all other parties by at least a two-to-one margin in all three elections. However, as the new century begins, the Liberals increasingly look like a party of Ontario—the province was represented by two-thirds of their parliamentary caucus after the 1997 federal election, and 100 of the party's 172 MPs after the 2000 election. The New Democrats entered the 1990s on a high, having won a record number of seats in the 1988 election, electing their first ever member from Quebec in a 1990 by-election, and leading the other parties in some national public opinion polls. Today the New Democrats continue their rebuilding efforts from a disastrous 1993 election in which the party won the votes of only slightly more than one-in-twenty Canadians and lost official party status in the House of Commons.

The two parties that have shared the Official Opposition role in the past three parliaments were virtually non-existent at the beginning of the 1990s. After failing to elect any candidates in its maiden campaign in 1988, the Reform party emerged as the party of choice in western Canada, winning 52 seats in 1993, 60 in 1997, and 66 in 2000; all but three of these were from west of the Ontario–Manitoba border. At the same time, nationalist Quebeckers turned their allegiance away from the Conservatives to the upstart Bloc Québécois. The Bloc won a majority of Quebec seats in its maiden campaign in 1993 and again in 1997 and 2000 while not contesting any ridings outside the province.

The Rise of Regionalism in the Party System

While Reform/Canadian Alliance and the Bloc agree on little ideologically, both find their roots in the articulation of regional interests. The Bloc has no federal aspirations beyond being the party of francophone Quebeckers and accordingly has no willingness to accommodate other interests within the party. Reform began as a party of western Canada. This is exemplified by their first election slogan: 'the West wants in'. While the party has since expressed a desire to move beyond the West, it has failed completely in this regard.[1] Both Reform/Canadian Alliance and the Bloc feed off strong regional tensions and have often exacerbated these divisions in their self-interest.

The rise of Reform and the Bloc as regional parties marks a significant change from the style of party politics dominant in Canada since at least the 1960s. The Liberals and Progressive Conservatives (and to a lesser degree the New Democrats) practised an ideological flexibility driven by a desire to stitch together broad, national electoral coalitions that transcended the country's regional and linguistic cleavages. The Conservative government from 1984 to 1993 was perhaps the ultimate example of a brokerage party seeking to accommodate divergent regional interests under one tent. Brian Mulroney courted both strong Quebec nationalists and champions of Western regionalism. Both groups had been particularly disaffected from the previous Liberal government and questioned the value of Canadian federalism.[2]

Ironically, while the Mulroney government can be held up as a classic example of brokerage politics, it was also fertile ground for the formation of two regionally based parties that were philosophically opposed to the accommodative approach. It was the implosion of the Mulroney coalition, substantially pitting Western regionalists against Quebec nationalists, that provided much of the initial spark for the birth of both of these regional parties.[3] The result was not only the existence of two regionally based parties, but also a new emphasis on region by the three traditionally national parties, forced to respond to strong electoral challenges from the Bloc and Reform/Canadian Alliance.

In many ways, this emphasis on region is reminiscent of electoral campaigns from the first half of the twentieth century.[4] Until the late 1950s, Canadian election campaigns were rarely driven by national debates; instead, most were a collection of local contests. For the first fifty years after Confederation, political communication was characterized by the lack of a national media, without which the parties and their leaders were dependent upon local media and personal contact to convey their messages to voters. Michael Nolan has observed that during this period, 'platform speeches were probably the most important means of direct communication for politicians at election time'.[5]

While whistle-stop train tours allowed the leaders to travel to many parts of the country and to attract local media attention, they had no opportunity to deliver a simultaneous message to voters nation-wide. Rather, the parties often developed local pitches that were made by the leader during his visit and by the local candidates. The parliamentary parties were loose collections of local notables who were dependent on their ability to dispense local patronage and not on national campaign strategies devised by communication experts.[6]

In the 1930s, the introduction of radio made it possible for parties to communicate simultaneously with large numbers of voters from different areas. Given the strong attention to region in the Liberal governments of King and St Laurent that dominated this period, it is not surprising that radio was used primarily to deliver regional messages. The focus of political communication shifted from the local community as radio allowed voters from different parts of a region, and sometimes even different provinces, to listen to a single speech at the same time. The governments of the day used radio as a campaign tool to support their approach to governing, which centred on strong regional representation in the Cabinet.[7]

With the advent of television as a national medium and the rise of a pan-Canadian approach to governing, the style of national election campaigns changed dramatically in the late 1950s. As television coverage of campaigns reached Canadians from coast to coast, it encouraged 'the trend begun by radio to regard elections as more than a local event, with the country seen as a single electoral district'.[8] Just as the advent of radio had facilitated a shift from constituency-based campaigns to a regional focus, television encouraged the parties to shift 'the focus of their attention from region to nation'.[9] David Smith refers to this method of campaigning and governing as 'pan-Canadianism'. Smith identifies television as playing an important role in this development as it provided the method by which parties could communicate concurrently with all Canadians. Television had a nationalising effect on political communication, 'with a consequent sacrifice of regional perspective'.[10]

The national parties were able, for the first time, to set a national agenda for campaigns and to present a common front to all voters. This was accomplished through television commercials broadcast on the national networks, national leaders' tours with reporters following along to capture common footage for broadcast on both local newscasts and the national networks, and events such as leaders' debates broadcast across the country. All Canadians, regardless of their location or the activities of their local party associations, were provided with a base of common political information. The influence of this pan-Canadian approach is evident in the public policy issues with an inherently national scope that dominated political discourse during this era: issues such as bilingualism and biculturalism, constitutional reform, and social policy expansion.

After more than three decades of pan-Canadianism, leaders of the traditional parties were surprised to watch the 1993 federal election develop into a series of unique, regional contests. While the old-line parties had often stressed different issues in different regions, there had never before been an election quite like 1993, in which the parties that won the second and third largest numbers of parliamentary seats effectively ignored as much or more of the country than that in which they aggressively competed.[11] In this regard, the 1997 election reaffirmed the 1993 result. Instead of one national election with similar party competition across the country, the campaign was a collection of largely discrete regional contests.

The change in this regard is evident in an examination of federal party competition by province in 1988 and 1997, which illustrates significantly increased fragmentation in the later election. In 1988, the Liberals and Conservatives were competitive across the country, with the New Democrats significant players from Ontario westward. There appear to be two or three models of party competition operative in 1988: two-party Conservative-Liberal competition in Quebec and Atlantic Canada; and three-party competition with the New Democrats joining the fray in Ontario and western Canada. (A third model might be competition between the Conservatives and New Democrats on the prairies.)

As illustrated in Table 6.1, the story was very different in 1997. Atlantic Canada appeared to be a three-party contest among the traditional parties; Quebec was dominated by the Bloc and the Liberals, with the Conservatives holding on to a small foothold; Ontario was dominated by the Liberals; Manitoba was the only province with four-party competition; Saskatchewan had three-way competition among the Reformers, New Democrats, and Liberals; Alberta was dominated by Reform; and British Columbia was contested between Reform and the Liberals. There were, in fact, seven different models of party competition evident in the 1997 election, with every province outside Atlantic Canada having a different constellation of competitive parties.

Parties' Campaign Objectives

In 1997, the strategic imperatives of each party dictated that they target their campaign efforts to certain parts of the country, while virtually ignoring others, and prepare different strategies for each targeted region. As Table 6.1 illustrates, the Liberals were the only party to compete effectively across the country. Liberal campaign strategists anticipated that the party would face different opposition in each region and would accordingly have to be prepared to talk about different issues and defend itself from different directions in each region.[12] For example, in the 1997 campaign, the Liberals were attacked from the right by the Conservatives and Reform on economic issues in Ontario, while both the New Democrats and Conservatives were fighting them from the left on health care and social policy in Atlantic Canada; meanwhile the Liberals were fighting off Reform from the right and the New Democrats from the left in western Canada. Given this electoral context, it quickly

Table 6.1: Comparison of Election Results, 1988 and 1997

1988 Federal Election

Province	Party Winning Most Votes	Parties Winning at Least Half as Many Votes
Newfoundland	Liberal	Conservative
Prince Edward Island	Liberal	Conservative
Nova Scotia	Liberal	Conservative
New Brunswick	Liberal	Conservative
Quebec	Conservative	Liberal
Ontario	Liberal	Conservative, New Democratic
Manitoba	Conservative	Liberal, New Democratic
Saskatchewan	New Democratic	Conservative
Alberta	Conservative	
British Columbia	New Democratic	Conservative, Liberal

1997 Federal Election

Province	Party Winning Most Votes	Parties Winning at Least Half as Many Votes
Newfoundland	Liberal	Conservative, New Democratic
Prince Edward Island	Liberal	Conservative
Nova Scotia	Conservative	New Democratic, Liberal
New Brunswick	Conservative	Liberal, New Democratic
Quebec	Bloc Québécois	Liberal, Conservative
Ontario	Liberal	
Manitoba	Liberal	Reform, New Democratic, Conservative
Saskatchewan	Reform	New Democratic, Liberal
Alberta	Reform	
British Columbia	Reform	Liberal

became apparent to the campaign's leadership that one standard campaign plan would not suffice. National Liberal Campaign Chair Gordon Ashworth reported that it was the first time in his long experience with the Liberal party that the campaign was perceived in regional terms.[13] All of the other parties quickly came to the same conclusion and what was billed as a national election campaign became, instead, seven different regional contests.

While the Liberals prepared regional strategies primarily out of an expectation that they would have different competitors in each province who represented different positions on the political spectrum, the other parties had additional strategic imperatives pushing them towards regionally targeted strategies. One common characteristic shared by the other four parties was that none of them was seeking to form a government. The working of Canada's electoral system encourages parties (especially those with modest electoral objectives) to focus their efforts on those regions where they have the greatest concentration of support and to ignore those where their support is insufficient to win a plurality of the vote in individual ridings.[14] Each of these parties found its support concentrated in discrete regions and faced large areas of the country where it had little voter support.

The Reform party entered the 1997 campaign with the objectives of expanding on its Western base, gaining some ground in Ontario, and finishing second overall.[15] With more limited campaign funds than its principal opponents, Reform needed to stretch its resources and accordingly decided that a regionally focused campaign would provide more potential 'bang for the buck'.[16] Money spent on delivering a national message, it was reasoned, would be largely wasted because the party had no realistic hope of winning seats in Quebec or Atlantic Canada. The party also realized that the messages it used to attract voters in western Canada might not be appealing to voters in Ontario. Thus the party decided to prepare different messages for its targeted voters in different regions.[17]

As for the Bloc Québécois, it was once again only contesting Quebec's 75 seats and had little interest in the results elsewhere in the country. The party restricted its campaigning and advertising to the province of Quebec.

The principal objective for the New Democrats in the 1997 election was to regain official party status in the House of Commons. The party saw its traditional share of the popular vote reduced by two-thirds in the 1993 election and its parliamentary complement cut from 44 to 9. Parliamentary rules require that a party have at least 12 seats in order to qualify as an official party and be entitled to increased parliamentary funding and routine speaking rights in the House. Accordingly, party strategists decided early on to focus their resources on the three to four dozen ridings where its candidates were competitive.[18] The party's support was concentrated in Nova Scotia, New Brunswick, Manitoba, Saskatchewan, and small pockets of urban Ontario and British Columbia. The New Democrats were not competitive in Quebec, Alberta, Prince Edward Island or much of Ontario or British Columbia. Spending large sums of money on national advertising was perceived by party strategists as a waste of scarce campaign resources.[19]

The Progressive Conservatives also had regaining official party status as their first objective. Since the Reform party had captured the vast majority of their former supporters in the West, the party focused its energies on Ontario, Quebec, and Atlantic Canada: three regions where it had a chance to win individual ridings. The Conservatives also made a deliberate decision to focus on different issues in each of these three regions.[20] In effect, the party prepared and executed three different campaign plans, while virtually ignoring the three western-most provinces that had provided its electoral base in recent decades.

It is possible, then, to conclude that the parties' decisions to approach the 1997 campaign with regional strategies resulted both from the complexion of contemporary Canadian party competition and from the increasingly fractured views of Canadian voters (at least as expressed in their choice of a preferred federal party). It is also true, however, that several advances in communication practices were converging with this changing political climate to facilitate the adoption of these campaign strategies.

Pollsters and Campaign Strategies

The parties, faced with the challenge of developing and implementing appropriate campaign strategies focusing on each of the targeted regions, have increasingly come to rely on pollsters and television advertising experts. The increased importance of regionalism in party competition has made political polling more essential to the parties' electoral strategies than ever before. Because the parties are now tailoring specific messages to narrow, targeted groups, the pollster must identify the key groups and the message most likely to attract their support. The contemporary party pollsters' task is largely threefold:

1. Identify regions of the country where the party has a sufficient concentration of potential supporters to offer the likelihood of winning a plurality of the vote in individual ridings.
2. Identify the regional and socio-economic status of those voters who, though undecided or leaning toward another party, may be persuaded to vote for their party (swing voters).
3. Determine which issue the party should emphasize in its conversations with each target group and what the best positioning of the party's policy is on that issue.

The parties have limited resources and are competing in a fragmented market in which a vote share of 38 per cent for the Liberals in 1997 resulted in a majority government. No campaign team was concerned with winning the support of a majority of Canadians heading into the 1997 election; instead, each was preoccupied with identifying and communicating with those swing voters in key ridings who might be persuaded to support their candidates.

The parties rely on the results of large, baseline polls conducted in the months before an election campaign to determine which regions of the country they should target and which they should ignore. Parties normally will conduct two or three baseline polls in the run-up to an election, using large sample sizes so that regional sub-samples are still large enough to produce meaningful data: that is, results with small margins of error to increase confidence in the result. All of the parties in the 1997 campaign decided, on the basis of their pre-election polling, to substantially ignore large parts of the country where they did not believe they could win a plurality of votes in individual ridings. Even the Liberals, the only party to run something approaching a national campaign in 1997, effectively wrote off most of British Columbia outside Vancouver and Victoria, and all of Alberta outside Edmonton. The party strategists knew from polling results that it was highly unlikely they would be able to win in these areas of solid Reform support.

Once the party pollster has identified those regions of the country where the party is competitive, attention is turned to the question of which market groups to target within these regions. The pollster develops composites of groups that are over-represented in the swing voter category and the result is the identification of several different groups of voters with whom the parties want to communicate. The pollster will identify the characteristics of voters who have not yet committed to voting for the party but likewise have not ruled it out. Party leaders and strategists do not want to spend resources talking to those who are ardent supporters of other parties or with those who are already committed to supporting them (though some effort will be made with these voters to ensure they actually vote).

The parties do not enter the campaign prepared to engage in a general dialogue with all Canadians. Instead, they wish to pursue a focused dialogue with selected voters in selected ridings. For example, in the 1997 campaign, the Reform party targeted young male voters living in Ontario's 905 area code (the suburban belt surrounding Toronto). Other Ontario voters, including young males living a few miles away in downtown Toronto, were of lesser interest to the party's campaign efforts.

Once the pollster identifies the party's targeted voters, attention is then turned to ascertaining which campaign themes would be most effective in pushing each specific group of targeted voters into the category of committed supporters of the party. The themes will differ by region and by targeted group within the region. For example, in 1997, Reform decided that the following issues would be effective for the groups they had targeted in their key regions: in British Columbia and Alberta, national unity and political accountability; in Saskatchewan, tax relief, national unity, and political accountability; and in Ontario, establishing Reform as a national party and national unity.[21] Similarly, the Conservatives concentrated on different messages in their targeted regions: in Ontario, tax relief and health care; in Quebec, national unity and leadership; and in Atlantic Canada, health care and social policy.[22]

The parties rely not only on their baseline polls, but also on tracking polls. Tracking polls are polls conducted on a daily basis during the course of a campaign. Because they are conducted daily, they allow the pollster to measure shifts in public opinion and to estimate the effects of various campaign stimuli—such as television advertisements—on voter opinion. Indicative of the importance of regional data to the 1997 campaign was the fact that the Liberal party increased the size of its daily tracking sample from a few hundred to 1,500 in order to have significant results by region. Because the party was essentially fighting a series of regional campaigns, national polling numbers were of little use in 1997. Liberal pollster Michael Marzolini reports that the regional tracking poll was the most effective tool available to the party during the 1997 campaign.[23]

After determining the issues on which to concentrate in each targeted region, the research turns to discovering the best positioning of the party's policy on these issues. The parties use focus groups to provide them with this information. A focus group is a gathering of about a dozen voters from a party's target group. The group is usually led by a professional moderator in a discussion of the campaign issues in an attempt to determine what these voters think about the various positions being staked out by the parties. Parties will often screen their planned television advertisements during focus group sessions in order to gauge the reaction of targeted voters before airing their ads publicly. Focus groups enable the campaign strategists 'to put flesh and emotion on the stark numbers of the polls'.[24] The sessions allow strategists to hear what voters are thinking in far more detail than a poll allows. While the information received is not necessarily representative of public opinion at large, if the same pattern recurs at several of these sessions the strategists have greater confidence they are discovering something that may be generalizable.

Besides helping to determine the best positioning of a party's policies, focus groups can assist a party in identifying its most effective spokespersons on various issues. For example, in 1997 the Liberals learned that Paul Martin had great credibility with voters and would be effective in delivering their economic message. As a result, Martin was used as a public spokesperson on this issue. Party members are often found to have varying degrees of credibility in different parts of the country: an effective spokesperson for the Liberal party in Alberta may not be effective in Quebec. The focus groups help the parties determine which of their parliamentary leaders to spotlight in each region.

Campaign Communications

The primary use of the polling and focus group data is to inform the parties' communication strategies. Television remains the dominant method of campaign communication between parties and voters. More voters will see a party-sponsored television advertisement or watch an excerpt from a leader's speech on the evening news than will meet a candidate, attend a political rally, or read a party mailing. Four factors converged in the 1990s to produce a significant change in the way parties are using television to communicate with voters. These factors are:

1. the increasing regionalisation of party competition;
2. use of more sophisticated polling techniques, providing the parties with detailed information on regional and socio-demographic blocks of voters;
3. the changing nature of Canadian television, offering viewers 50-plus cable and specialty channels from which to choose;
4. the parties' increasingly sophisticated use of television, as evidenced by their greater reliance on time-buyers to reach particular audience segments.

Parties no longer use television simply to send a single message to all voters, but rather use it as a primary tool in their efforts to send targeted messages to particular voting groups. Contemporary party strategists put together a television marketing plan for each campaign, including both paid and free advertising, the leader's tour, and participation in leaders' debates and town hall forums, all aimed at communicating specific messages to their targeted voters.

The media advisers, like the pollsters, talk about the 1997 campaign in regional terms. The parties created regionally targeted advertisements that responded to the issues of interest to their swing voters in each region and the nature of party competition within the region. The campaign of 1997 was the first in which the Liberal party made use of regionally targeted television advertising instead of relying exclusively on national television advertisements.[25] In 1997, all of the parties spent a much smaller percentage of their advertising budget on national television buys than had been the norm in earlier elections. Most of the budget was spent on local and regional broadcasts.[26] The result of this was, for example, that television viewers in Atlantic Canada and Ontario received very different messages from the Conservative party during the 1997 campaign. The Conservatives emphasized tax relief and health care in television advertisements aired in Ontario, and social policy in Atlantic Canada.[27] More than any other party, the Conservatives came the closest to offering different electorates contradictory messages. After the campaign, the Liberals' Gordon Ashworth was highly critical of the national media for paying little attention to the messages broadcast by the Conservatives outside of central Canada, and for failing to criticize the apparent contradiction in a Conservative campaign that called for tax relief in Ontario and increased spending in Atlantic Canada.

Advertisements are targeted not only by region but also by socio-demographic group. For this purpose, the parties use time buyers who employ computer programs to track the demographics of each television show's audience and then match up a campaign's target audience with a television show's viewership. This process has become more sophisticated and effective as more speciality channels have been made available to Canadians. Even if the technology had been available and the electoral context had called for this type of targeted campaigning, it would not have been particularly effective in Canada a decade ago. Before the spread of cable television, most Canadians chose their television viewing from among the three national networks. Today, the offerings include all-sports networks, nature channels, cooking channels, country and western music channels, religious networks, and scores of local stations. The audience for the World Wrestling Federation on TSN is certainly different from that for Martha Stewart Living on the Life Network. The time buyers know the demographics of each show's audience and purchase party advertising time accordingly. New cable networks such as CTV Sportsnet now offer different programming—and thus discrete advertising opportunities—in the country's different regions.

The parties' use of free media is also part of their master communications strategy. For example, leaders' tours are structured to complement and reinforce parties' paid advertising. Polling data influences decisions concerning which ridings the leaders visit, the theme of the visit, and the content of the leaders' speeches.[28] For example, while the party leaders normally visit each province at least once to provide the appearance of a national campaign, they spend most of their time in targeted ridings where the party is concentrating its advertising efforts. The events in which the leaders participate are often chosen to correspond thematically with local advertising. For example, if a party is running commercials in British Columbia about the quality of health care, its leader may well visit a health-care facility during his or her visit to the province. Thus, the leaders' tours are orchestrated so that free media coverage will appear to reinforce the party's message to its targeted voters.

Conclusion

A seamless relationship binds the work of the party pollster, the advertising consultant, the time buyer, and the tour director. The campaign relies on the polling and focus group data to identify its target audience; the advertisers then develop an advertisement aimed at the targeted audience; the advertisement is tested before focus groups; time buyers purchase advertising time for that particular spot on a television program with a large viewership among their targeted audience; and the tour director structures the leader's activity to reinforce the local advertising message. The result is that the parties no longer engage in national communications efforts but rather in a series of dialogues with selected groups of voters on issues of particular concern to them. Even in nationally televised events such as leaders' debates, the participants are coached by their advisers on the issues to stress and the phrases to use in order to appeal to their targeted voters. Thus, while television initially had a nationalizing effect on campaign communication, in that it encouraged and facilitated the simultaneous delivery of the same partisan message to Canadians from coast to coast, in its current manifestations it is being used to deliver substantively different targeted messages to particular sub-groups of voters.

This enhanced focus on targeted communication parallels a substantial increase in regionalization of the party system. In this regard, the 2000 campaign was similar to those of 1993 and 1997: the national election was really a patchwork of distinct regional contests. The supposedly national clash over 'values' between the Liberals and Alliance may have occurred in Ontario, but the campaign was waged by different parties, and over different issues, in other regions. Atlantic Canadians again chose chiefly from among the Liberals, Conservatives and New Democrats in a campaign centred on the question of whether it is better to be represented in government or to continue to protest from the opposition benches. For the third consecutive election, the campaign in Quebec was a contest between the Bloc and the Liberals focused on the federal question. In much of western Canada, the campaign was dominated by the Alliance, with modest opposition from the Liberals and New Democrats. While the national media tried hard in 2000 to create a national campaign dynamic between the Alliance and the Liberals, the contest did not look this way to voters east of the Ottawa River, nor likely to many west of the Ontario/Manitoba border.

NOTES

1. In the wake of the 1997 federal election, Reform's leadership appeared to recognize that the party could not be electorally successful outside the West in its present form. Accordingly, Reform party leader Preston Manning championed the United Alternative movement. The culmination of this was a March 2000 vote by party members to wind down the Reform

party and create a new party—the Canadian Conservative Reform Alliance. This change was driven by a belief that many central and eastern Canadians continue to view Reform as a party of western Canada, and that this could only be corrected through the creation of a new party. The new party, with its new leader Stockwell Day, proved unable to make a breakthrough into Ontario in the 2000 election, winning only two seats in the province.

2. In the lead-up to the 1984 election, Mulroney actively recruited supporters (including candidates) from among the Quebec nationalist community. Many of these recruits were outraged by the Liberal government's 1982 patriation of the Constitution without the support of the Quebec government, and were successfully brought into a coalition with the Conservatives' more traditional support base in western Canada. Conservative voters in the West were particularly disenchanted with the federal government in the wake of the Liberals' National Energy Program and perceived general disregard for Western interests.

3. For a full discussion of the roots of the Reform party and the Bloc Québécois, see R. Kenneth Carty, William Cross, and Lisa Young, *Rebuilding Canadian Party Politics* (Vancouver: University of British Columbia Press, 2000).

4. For a good discussion of the early evolution of campaign communication in Canada, see Michael Nolan, 'Political Communication Methods in Canadian Federal Election Campaigns 1867–1925', *Canadian Journal of Communication* 7 (1981) 28–46.

5. Ibid., 31.

6. See R.K. Carty, 'Three Canadian Party Systems' in R.K. Carty, ed., *Canadian Political Party Systems* (Peterborough, Ont.: Broadview, 1992) 563–86.

7. For a discussion of the importance of strong regional representation in Cabinet during this period, see David E. Smith, 'Party Government in Canada' in Carty, *Canadian Political Party Systems*, 531–62.

8. David R. Spencer and Catherine M. Bolan, 'Election Broadcasting in Canada: A Brief History' in Frederick J. Fletcher, ed., *Election Broadcasting in Canada*, (Toronto: Dundurn Press, 1991), 28.

9. R. Kenneth Carty, 'Three Canadian Party Systems: An Interpretation of the Development of National Politics' in Hugh G. Thorburn, ed., *Party Politics in Canada*, 6th ed. (Scarborough, Ont.: Prentice Hall, 1991), 125–43.

10. David E. Smith, 'Party Government in Canada', 552.

11. These assertions, elaborated on below, are based on post-1997 election interviews with senior campaign officials of the Liberal, New Democratic, Progressive Conservative, and Reform parties.

12. Interviews with Michael Marzolini (Liberal party pollster), Gordon Ashworth (Liberal National Campaign co-chair) and Terry Mercer (Liberal party executive director).

13. The party has, however, always treated francophone Quebec as a different region from English Canada for campaign purposes.

14. For a complete discussion of the implications of the Canadian electoral system, see Alan C. Cairns, 'The Electoral System and the Party System in Canada, 1921–1965', *Canadian Journal of Political Science* 1, 1 (1968): 55–80.

15. See Faron Ellis and Keith Archer, 'Reform at the Crossroads' in Alan Frizzell and Jon H. Pammett, eds, *The Canadian General Election of 1997* (Toronto: Dundurn, 1998), 111–33.

16. Interview with Bryan Thomas (Reform party advertising director).

17. Ibid.

18. See Alan Whitehorn, 'Alexa McDonough and Atlantic Breakthrough for the New Democratic Party' in Frizzell and Pammett, *The Canadian General Election of 1997*, 91–109.

19. Interview with Jim Matsui (NDP pollster).

20. Interview with Perry Miele (Progressive Conservative party advertising director).

21. Interview with André Turcotte (Reform pollster).

22. Interview with Perry Miele.

23. Interview with Michael Marzolini.

24. John Laschinger and Geoffrey Stevens, *Leaders and Lesser Mortals: Backroom Politics in Canada* (Toronto: Key Porter Books, 1992), 92.

25. Interview with Gordon Ashworth. Note that the Liberal party has long run separate advertising campaigns in French and English Canada.

26. For example, Reform's advertising director, Bryan Thomas, estimates that 75 per cent of his party's advertising budget was spent on local and regional buys.

27. Interview with Perry Miele.

28. Interview with David Miller (Liberal tour director).

Chapter 7

Making Sense of Reform as a Western Party[1]

David Laycock

In *Politics and Territory*, Mildred Schwartz demonstrates the importance of distinguishing between regionalism as a variable with direct impacts on the party system, and regionalism as a distracting disguise for other factors shaping the behaviour of parties and voters.[2] With this distinction in mind, in this chapter I explore the sense in which Reform was a 'Western party' through two basic questions. First, what did the Reform party's experience tell us about the essentially Western, and contingently Western, dimensions of Reform's agenda? Second, what does the manner of Reform's transformation into the Canadian Alliance suggest about the importance of 'Westernness' to Reform? 'Is Reform a Western party?' has seemed to many commentators to invite an obvious answer.

My argument is that we should press beyond the simple answer in search of useful insights into the Reform party, and into the ironies and complexities of the interplay between regionalism and party politics in Canada. The picture that then emerges shows a party that typically allowed its ideological bearings to override its fealty to Western themes and concerns, and whose leadership attempted to institutionalize such an override with a move to national party status.

Was Reform a Party of the West?

Did Reform's Electoral Support Come From the West?

Yes, Reform's electoral support came primarily from the West. Despite Reform's second-place showing in many Ontario ridings in 1993 and 1997, it failed to attract more than 20 per cent of the Ontario vote and lost its lone 1993 seat in the 1997 election. By stark contrast, in 1997 over 50 per cent of the Alberta vote garnered Reform 24 of 26 seats; over 40 per cent of the British Columbia vote produced 25 of 34 seats; over 30 per cent of the Saskatchewan vote yielded 8 of 14 seats, and just over 23 per cent of the Manitoba vote netted 3 of 14 seats.

It is commonly suggested that the Reform party effectively undermined the ability of both the New Democratic and the Progressive Conservative parties to claim a representational mandate from the West. NDP and Tory party performances in the 1997 election suggest that this claim about Reform's success in the Western regional party system is true, regardless of whether Western NDP voters switched primarily to Liberal candidates rather than Reform[3] or whether Reform actually placed regional issues ahead of its ideological preferences. The Canadian Alliance would have to stumble badly, choose an Ontario Tory as leader, or suffer a major internal rift for either the NDP or the Tories to regain any semblance of their previous Western strength and legitimacy. So, from the perspective of Reform's relative strength in the national party system, its electoral support in 1993 and 1997 translated into a dominant position within the Western component of that system. This allowed Reform to set the agenda for policy debate in the West regarding national issues, thereby reinforcing the marginal status of the Tories and New Democrats.

Did Reform's Organization, Activists, and Leadership Come From the West?
Reform remained a party of the West until its supersession by the Canadian Alliance, despite its major push since 1991 to 'go national' with recruitment and election campaign efforts. Preston Manning's confidants and key advisers were Westerners; in fact, they were mostly Albertans. The notable exception was Rick Anderson, an Ottawa consultant and one-time Liberal organizer. Manning's concentration of power in the leader's office stunted the development of a leadership core,[4] which helps to explain why none of the major candidates for the leadership of the Canadian Alliance came from within the Reform party caucus or organization.

Preston Manning tried to make location of the party's physical and psychological home outside of big-city Ontario seem appealing to voters east as well as west of Manitoba. This strategy met with moderate success in the West, but little success in the East. Locating and retaining party headquarters in Calgary had important symbolic and practical effects on the party's activities. Reform activists at conventions were disproportionately from British Columbia and Alberta, the party's electoral motherlodes.[5]

Despite the recruitment drives of Tom Long and Stockwell Day in Ontario and Quebec during the Canadian Alliance leadership race of 2000, the vast majority of committed activists were western Canadians in the direct leadership vote among Alliance members. This was true even after the party claimed to have boosted its membership from 75,000 to 202,000 between March and 17 June 2000, with many new members coming from Ontario and Quebec. Tom Long's poor showing in the first round of the leadership vote indicates that many of the recently recruited members in Ontario and Quebec felt insufficiently committed to the party or the candidates whose organizations recruited them to bother voting, especially when this had to be done by 'tele-vote'. Western members made up a clear majority of conventional voters in this round. So even after the reinvention of Reform through the Canadian Alliance, the party remained primarily Western in terms of its support base.

Did Reform Articulate Key Elements of Western Political Culture?
Reform always articulated important Western themes. Standing out among these was antipathy towards, or at least depleted patience with, Quebec's demands for 'special

treatment', and the related view that Western interests have been systematically ignored by successive Liberal and Conservative governments.[6] But this argument for Reform as the expression of Western political culture has to be made carefully. For example, the idea that social and moral conservatism are much stronger elements of Western than other regional political cultures in Canada, widely believed within the Reform party, has shakier foundations than the media generally suppose.[7]

One issue on which this image may reflect the reality is tolerance for gays, and willingness to protect gays through provincial human rights legislation. A 1999 study conducted by Joseph Fletcher found that while 65.9 per cent of Prairie respondents supported such legislation, this was a full 10 per cent below the level of support in British Columbia and Ontario, and 12 per cent below the national average. And willingness to allow gays to teach in public schools was also lowest in the Prairies, at 68.3 per cent, compared to 77.7 per cent in British Columbia, 72.6 per cent in Ontario, and 76.1 per cent overall.[8] Willingness to let gays teach jumped 16 per cent between 1987 and 1999 in the Prairies, and by 25 per cent nationally. Given the clear pattern for younger respondents to be far more tolerant of gay teachers than older ones,[9] one can safely predict that, in another decade, the intolerance championed by Day and his supporters in the Alliance rank and file will be very unpopular, even in Alberta. Joe Clark's victory in Calgary Centre in the 2001 federal election may be a harbinger of this trend.

Socially and morally conservative currents certainly found a more effective partisan vehicle in the West with Reform—and in Alberta with Ralph Klein's Conservative party—than in other regions. But this had more to do with the representational distortions of the single-member plurality electoral system, both federally and in Alberta, than with the distinctively and broadly conservative cast of Western political culture.

In Alberta, rural over-representation gives Ralph Klein's government a huge incentive to appeal to electorally powerful rural moral traditionalists. For example, they publicly considered use of the notwithstanding clause to override a Supreme Court of Canada decision, in the Vriend case, to protect gays from discrimination through changes to Alberta's human rights code. Not all of the Alberta Cabinet were willing to pursue the matter so zealously, and Premier Klein eventually decided not to deploy the notwithstanding clause to overturn the Court decision. But by strenuously advocating this course of action, Stockwell Day satisfied rural social conservatives in Alberta, and propelled himself to national prominence, well before he appealed to urban fiscal conservatives with his introduction of a 'flat' provincial income tax.

Just as this kind of provincial policy position misrepresents Alberta to urban Albertans, and Alberta generally to the rest of Canada, Reform's representational dominance in Parliament misrepresents Western political culture inside and outside western Canada. As Roger Gibbins and Sonja Arrison have shown in the book *Western Visions,* and as a review of daily newspapers in western Canada confirms, such misrepresentation has significant effects on the social and political self-perceptions of

Westerners, and their sense of the practical political horizons available to them and the national polity.

Did Reform's Core Policies Make It a Party of the West?

Did the core policy concerns and underlying ideological orientations of the Reform party express an 'essential Western-ness', or something else of greater import to the party?[10]

Two of Reform's key commitments were the Triple-E Senate and constitutional equality of the provinces. The Triple-E Senate was intended to counteract the majoritarian basis of central Canadian advantage in interregional policy conflicts and related battles in Parliament. The commitment to constitutional equality was designed to serve the same objective, with special emotional significance attached to ending Quebec's blackmail of the federal polity and the rest of Canada.

Historically, both are almost exclusively and hence almost essentially Western concerns. They have been aimed at disaffected Westerners who understand that the majoritarian tilt of Canadian parliamentary institutions guarantees that central Canadian voter firepower will always win when regionally defined interests are in a shootout. Westerners' sense of the futility of zero-sum regional confrontations in the federal system has been expressed in many ways over the past century, including third-party formation and support for direct democracy. In recent years, this has found expression in widespread Western support for contra-majoritarian instruments in the heart of the federal parliament.

The Reform party also frequently called for an end to poor treatment of the West by the federal government. This is obviously an exclusively Western concern. But as we will see below, it is more an article of faith than a consistent guide to Reform policy, because when push came to shove, it did not typically trump ideological concerns more generally associated with the post-1970s 'New Right' in Western democracies. Reform also demanded substantial decentralization of power from the federal to provincial governments, in most major policy areas.

Western support for decentralization has substantial yet often exaggerated historical roots. The exaggeration can be illustrated with an analogy by considering how incorrect it would be to read Social Credit's attack on the federal power, with its origins in a desire to implement financial reform over Ottawa's head, into all of post-World War I populism. Social Credit founder and Alberta Premier William Aberhart was a financial reform enthusiast first, with few thoughts about federalism or any centralized power, save that of the financial 'octopus'. His frustrations with the exercise of political power in a federal polity[11] that allocated responsibility for financial regulations to Ottawa were responsible for his eventual view that Ottawa should exercise power only with interprovincial consensus and permission.[12]

Similarly, it would be misleading to disconnect Reform's advocacy of decentralization from its leader's and core activists' strong preference for market over state determinations of economic activity. After all, Tom Long's strenuous case for decentralization of power in the federal system during his run for the Canadian Alliance leadership had nothing to do with an antipathy to Ontario's power in the federal system. Rather, it had everything to do with his desire to produce a leaner and meaner, more business-friendly government at the federal level, to complement the policy agenda of the Harris Tories. Were it the case that contemporary provincial rather than federal governments regularly indulged in egregious 'interference' in the market and with private property, we probably would have seen Reform advocating selective centralization of state power to enhance human freedom. Of course, given this federal scenario in Canada, we would likely not have a Reform party at all.

Centralized state power was problematic for Reform primarily because it constrained a New Right ideological variant of economic freedom, not because it was centralized. Why would Reform conventions continually call for constitutional entrenchment of private property rights—which would, in practice, give tremendous power to the same courts the Canadian Alliance now follows Reform in wishing to 'curb'—if their concern for decentralization were on a par with their classical liberal conception of marketplace freedom?

The long history of anti-federal antagonism in western Canada does not reduce to this conception of freedom. Indeed, much of the populist antagonism to the federal government until the 1960s stemmed from Westerners' view that their freedom was diminished because old-line party governments in Ottawa did too little to constrain powerful market forces. A good deal of this antagonism still exists, but gets little attention from the major media.

But while Westerners' greater current support for decentralization did not make this core article of Reform faith essentially Western, it was an important part of Reform's appeal in West. This is clearly revealed in the two major behavioural studies done of Reform activists and supporters.[13] Especially after the 'old-line parties' joined in an unholy alliance to support the Charlottetown Accord, Reform supporters were certain that the Liberals, the New Democrats, and the Mulroney Conservatives lacked credibility as Western-sensitive parties. The Mulroney government's program downloading and transfer payment reductions had major decentralizing effects. However, the Meech Lake and Charlottetown Accords were seen by both the Reform and many post-1993 Reform voters in the West as insufficiently decentralist, and too determined to constitutionalize the whip hand of central Canadian political forces—Ontario and Quebec—in the federal polity.

Reform had a strong policy commitment to fiscal conservatism. This involved a preference for radical reductions in the level of state intervention in the market, tax cuts combined with severe cuts to social programs, a major assault on the deficit and debt to restore order to Canada's 'fiscal house', and opposition to non-market political determinations of social resource allocation.

Outside of the daily press, fiscal conservatism began its ascent to broader interregional public support in the West.[14] It was championed first by the early Reform party, then in Ralph Klein's popular efforts to eliminate the deficit without raising taxes. But the enthusiasm with which parties of the right pursue—and parties of the centre emulate—this agenda, tells us that there is nothing essentially Western about this package of fiscal conservatism.

Another way of reaching this conclusion is to note a key part of the pitch by United Alternative organizers and enthusiasts in the two years prior to the Reform party's metamorphosis. They repeatedly argued that the supra-Western appeal of this brand of fiscal conservatism had been demonstrated in Mike Harris's election and continuing popularity, which then proved that Reform could evolve into a party with substantial non-Western support. When the Reform party became the Canadian Alliance, tax cuts jumped to the top of the platform and media campaign. This will likely remain an important part of the Canadian Alliance's appeal in the West, but there is nothing essentially Western about this priority. During the Alliance leadership race, the three major candidates gave tax cuts priority over all other issues, including 'democratic populism'. This sounds much more like the 'Common Sense Revolution' agenda of the Ontario Tories and American Republicans than it does of Reform party conventions during the 1990s.

Reform has a strong policy commitment to social or moral conservatism, advocating recriminalization of abortion, restoration of capital punishment, a return to traditional family structure and values, and an arrest of the slide into secular value pluralism and 'multiculturalism'. Some of this is clearly portrayed in the party's Blue Sheet, and some of it, like the strong party sentiment against secularism and multiculturalism, was expressed by prominent Reform activists inside and outside party meetings, without forming explicit party policy. As portrayed both in the Toronto-based 'national' media and in *Alberta Report*, social conservatism often appears to be disproportionately important to the western Canadian political agenda, relative to other regions. But beyond misinformed media spin, this appearance has largely been an artifact of the prominence given to social and moral conservative positions by the Reform party.

Reform benefited disproportionately from the single member plurality electoral system, both in terms of parliamentary representation, and its ability to set a tone in the Western political culture. While not all Reform activists were social conservatives, the party had a substantially higher percentage than other parties.[15] These activists were more conservative than the average Reform voter,[16] and considerably more so than the average western Canadian.[17] As citizens who felt threatened by an urban, secular, and ethnically diverse culture, these Reformers were also, unsurprisingly, more vocal than western Canadians for whom this dynamic culture is less problematic.[18]

As Roger Gibbins has argued for twenty years, western Canadian society is no longer dramatically more rural, less culturally modern, or inclined to support a return to traditional values than central Canadian regional societies.[19] Although it seems counter-intuitive to many inside and outside the West, the success of a party with a high-profile regionalist message is consistent with his thesis of 'regionalism in decline'. Encountering regionalism in decline at a time of regional party success leads us to recall Mildred Schwartz's guidance on unpacking the meaning and significance of regionalism. There are many politically and sociologically relevant meanings for 'regionalism', so we must be careful to avoid generalizing in a way that masks and mixes complex phenomena.[20] With this in mind, it becomes easier to appreciate why the social conservatism of Reform was not primarily an expression of its Westernness, but rather of the prominence of social conservatism within the party itself.

Support for direct democracy figured prominently in Reform party policy, and was overwhelmingly endorsed by its 'anti-party' members.[21] Reform promoted national citizen's initiatives, and recall campaigns against MPs as accountability-enforcing endruns around an unresponsive party system and related political, bureaucratic, and judicial élites. This promotion had and has stronger Western than non-Western roots, and more contemporary appeal in the Western provinces than elsewhere in Canada. This is to be expected in a party system with a long history of federal élites who have been perceived as acting contrary to Western interests.

But direct democracy's Western roots must be qualified in several important ways, as must Reform's promotion of direct democracy. These roots are primarily in pre-1920 grain grower and labour politics, before the rise of viable third parties in the West. Direct democracy had ceased to be significant in Western politics well before William Aberhart's chastening experience with recall's deployment by his own constituents in 1937.[22] In 1991, a desperate Social Credit government inserted ballots on citizens' initiatives and recall into the 1991 British Columbia election.[23] The victorious New Democrats were saddled with a large majority vote supporting such mechanisms, and introduced a restrictive Initiatives and Recall Act in 1994.

The result has been a delight for enemies of the NDP, despite the failure of the first three recall campaigns in 1998, and a failed attempt to mount a 'total recall' campaign, targeting all NDP MLAs, in the spring of 1999. In Alberta, Premier Ralph Klein has refused to support such regime-tweaking headaches. Enthusiasts of his vague promotion of federal-level direct democracy in his keynote address to the February 1999 United Alternative convention should be chastened by his provincial record. Since becoming premier, Klein has rejected three private members' bills supporting legislative foundations for citizens' initiatives, even refusing to be in the legislature for the votes.[24] Neither Saskatchewan nor Manitoba has legislatively enabled recall or citizens' initiatives.[25]

Alienation from political élites and party politics per se[26] is not dramatically greater in western Canada than elsewhere in the country.[27] Consequently, we must dispense with the argument that direct democracy will be promoted primarily in response to unusually high levels of citizen alienation from political life. The greater contemporary appeal of direct democracy in the West stems from several sources. The historical resonance of pre-1930 campaigns for direct democracy is undeniable. Effective promotion of direct democracy by Reform since 1987 has been important. Underlying the success of this promotion is Westerners' broad acceptance of the view that, so long as federal governments are formed without having to rely on Western support and can marginalize Western concerns when push comes to shove, some institutional threats should be available to force Ottawa to address such concerns.

Referendums, recall, and the Triple-E Senate are prima facie instruments of such threats.

There has been a Western experience with and enthusiasm for direct democracy on both sides of the forty-ninth parallel. But Reform's approach to direct democracy is not central to western Canadian experience. In Canada and most western American states, promotion of direct democracy before the late 1970s was part of an overall package of popular democracy. This package included various forms of delegate democracy, exercises in what we might call the 'democratic corporatization' of the policy process, and/or other forms of extra-parliamentary popular power. The package also typically extended into the economic realm through agricultural co-operatives, proposals for workplace democracy, and other challenges to the market's role in social resource allocation.[28]

Even in early Social Credit practice, advocacy of direct democracy was not detached from what were presented as popularly controlled challenges to the distribution of power in the prevailing political economy. From this perspective, if we look both at and beyond Reform's experiments with 'electronic town halls' and pay-per-call, party-sponsored local referendums,[29] the Reform party detached its advocacy of direct democracy from a broader agenda of democratic reform comparable to those of earlier Western populisms.

Perhaps by focusing on the substantive footsteps and understandings of earlier prairie populists we are looking in the wrong place. Another picture emerges if we recall the long-standing Reform party promotion of constitutionally entrenched private property rights. This demand rounds out 'Resolution #2', concerning economic and fiscal themes, in the statement of basic principles for the February 1999 United Alternative convention.[30] It became clause #21 in the 'Canadian Alliance Declaration of Policy', adopted in January 2000.[31]

If we attach the right amount of symbolic importance to this demand, and link it to the major outlines of the party's post-1987 economic and fiscal agenda, Reform's advocacy of direct democracy can be seen as organically linked to its campaign to transform the prevailing political economy. This time around, the prevailing political economy is seen as a predacious welfare state, not a national economy dominated by central Canadian railways, financial interests, grain companies, and tariff-sheltered manufacturers.

Reform's reasons for supporting direct democracy[32] becomes clearer if we consider the parallels Reform advocates regularly drew between consumer and citizen sovereignty.[33] Reform spokespeople typically made the case for direct democracy with reference to the venality and unaccountability of 'old-line party' politicians. For these charges to be made with such conviction, a key assumption must have been necessary: that elected officials are thwarting the people's will, a will consistent with Reform policy as outlined in its *Blue Sheet*, especially as this policy presented a direct challenge to the political economy and normative legitimation of the modern welfare state.

From a certain angle, then, Reform's advocacy of direct democracy appears to sit squarely in the tradition of western Canadian populism and political culture. This perspective on Reform's continuity with earlier Prairie populism turns the earlier populists' antagonism to the capitalist political economy/party system nexus on its head. In the new perspective, we identify the 'rational kernel' of direct democracy as opposition to the prevailing political economy, regardless of the latter's historically idiosyncratic content.

Such historical revisionism concerning the central traditions of western Canadian populism offers the additional benefit of adding fuel to the fire under which Canadian parties, politicians, and indeed much of public life are currently being roasted. The ease with which direct democracy has been presented in North America, as the best mechanism for holding governments accountable, to citizens encouraged to understand themselves primarily as besieged taxpayers, suggests that this roast is far from over.

The majoritarian logic of referendums could easily backfire for the Canadian Alliance. Of the two 'issues of personal conscience' that Reform's *Blue Sheet* suggested were appropriate for national referendums, the party was in sync with public opinion on capital punishment, but well out of sync on abortion. The ease with which the Liberals used Alliance support for a referendum on abortion as an effective 'wedge issue' in the 2000 federal election is ample proof of this matter.[34] National votes on social issues 'which change Canada's basic social fabric', such as immigration and language policy, could go either way, depending on the wording of the questions.[35]

On economic issues identified with regions, even a strong majority in the West could not best central Canada in direct popular votes. Imagine, for example, if there had been a referendum in 1980 on the federal Liberals' National Energy Policy, a classic zero-sum pitting of region against region according to Reform's account of the reasons for a Triple-E Senate.[36] One has only to pose this example to see the problem with referendums as a tool of hinterland economic defence.

In Reform's *Blue Sheet* and the Canadian Alliance *Statement of Principles*, successful national referendums have been identified as necessary conditions of either federal budget deficits or tax increases. Despite current public opinion in this regard, such votes will not be foregone conclusions. They would, however, place real political constraints on the state's ability to sustain existing social programs and business regulations or introduce new ones. My sense is that the attractiveness of such constraints is the main reason that the party is posing such referendum requirements, not the attractiveness of citizen sovereignty per se.

Was Reform a Party of the West in Its Choice of Issues?

Reform party policy and the issues it highlighted in Parliament were by no means identical. In the House of Commons, Reform focused considerable attention on regional grievance issues, including the treatment of the oil industry, the distribution of federal contracts and largesse, and the central Canadian focus of CBC programming. Reform MPs spoke frequently about their regional constituents' virtues and challenges. Coverage of what Reform MPs chose to focus on in the House thus generated a picture of regionalist politics, and to the media, of essential regionalism.

But the picture was actually more nuanced than this. Consider Reform's substantial attention, in February 1999, to the tax penalties 'traditional families' carry in comparison to dual-income families with mothers working outside the home. Was this position taken because the proportion of 'traditional families' who live in western Canada is substantially higher than the proportion of 'traditional families' living in the rest of Canada? No. Was Western public opinion regarding this tax treatment markedly different? It seems unlikely. Reform MPs were not acting as their Western constituents' delegates on this issue; they were acting, as Edmund Burke would have it, as their trustees.

Nor is there anything particularly Western about the early Reform case against social insurance programs and Medicare, or the continuing Reform campaign against high taxes and federal government profligacy with tax revenues. Reform criticism of the (un)employment insurance program may have been regionally motivated in part, since Quebec and Atlantic Canada appeared to benefit disproportionately from this program. But the main thrust of the Reform critique was to deplore government intervention in the market, labour or otherwise. This critique portrayed employment insurance premiums as a means of denying the benefits of market discipline to many Canadians, including those who would have to relocate if the program were slashed. Reform party attacks on federal immigration policy, and the party's abiding desire to roll back affirmative action programs by eliminating section 15.2 in the Charter of Rights and Freedoms,[37] seem also to elude classification as essentially Western.

Consider now a potentially revealing counterfactual—the Reform party's consistent orientation to, and 'non-selection' of, agricultural policy issues. *Blue Sheet* policy always pronounced in favour of vaguely qualified 'free market' orientations on agricultural policy. Quite uncharacteristically for a Western party, it was strikingly silent over the past decade as prairie farmers' transportation and other subsidies or farmer-friendly programs were dismantled. Recently, prairie farmers have faced low commodity prices and high foreign state subsidies to their international competitors. As this crisis deepened in western Canada's agricultural community over the past several years, Reform focused on their free-market and family values agendas—calling for tax cuts, more social program cuts, and changes to the tax treatment of families with stay-at-home mothers.

I am not taking issue here with the substance of Reform policy. Their position on free-market agricultural policy may have been the logical extension of free trade. It may not be socially just to distribute federal monies to farmers instead of, say, single-parent mothers. What seems obvious, however, is that Reform's agricultural policy was dramatically out of step with historic prairie farmer organizations' demands, and with the expressed current desires of a majority of prairie farmers.

In what sense, then, was Reform representing Western farm families? The answer may be that Reform believed it knew what was best for them in the long run and was thus representing their long-term interests. This response presents an interesting substantive matter for debate. But it does not yield a positive answer to the question, did Reform party agricultural policy express something essentially Western about the party? It does suggest that elements central to Reform's ideological core trumped both its purported populism (assuming broad regional support for prairie farmers in crisis), and its western Canadian regional advocacy, when either of the two came into conflict with the ideological core. When this happened, Reform MPs became trustees, and populist representational orientations became residual, contrary to their party doctrine on representational practices.[38] Following a federal election in which the Alliance party suffered embarrassment over its ambiguous commitments to direct democracy, and in which its leader made up policy on the fly rather than stick to delegate-sanctioned party policy, we have been given no good reasons to believe that the same will not be true of Canadian Alliance MPs.

This diversion into agricultural policy leads to the rhetorical question posed in the next section of this chapter.

Was Reform More a Right-Populist Party than a Party of the West?

Did Reform's social and economic policy objectives not share considerably more with the right wing of the US Republican party than with any prior western Canadian populisms, including early Social Credit? Tom Flanagan's excellent analysis of Reform party strategy in *Waiting for the Wave*[39] claimed that the Reform party engineered its 'invasion from the right' with both an impeccable sense of timing (taking advantage of the post-Meech Lake unravelling of Brian Mulroney's unstable coalition between Québécois nationalists and conservative Westerners) and a conscious decision to aid and profit from this unravelling by presenting Reform as 'the party of the West'. Yet, while Flanagan spoke of Reform's successful 'invasion from the right' in the 1993 election, he denied that Preston Manning is ideologically committed to the right.[40] Rather, Flanagan argued that Manning was clearly more ideologically flexible than many of the party's activists, and that his rhetorical commitment to populism placed constraints on how rapidly a program of the right would be implemented, were Reform to gain power.

Evidence that Manning is prone to thinking about politics in terms of conflict resolution and the neutralization of significant differences emerged at the end of his speech to the 1999 United Alternative convention. 'I have a dream,' he told delegates, 'that some day—just once—perhaps to begin the new millennium—this country can have one big family meeting—a meeting like we've never had before . . . at which every region and every principled interest truly committed to redefining our politics and our federal union is truly represented.'[41]

This is not, however, an instance of non-ideological speech. It exemplifies what Manning had been doing very well since 1988. He defined Reform's position as expressing either 'truly principled interests' (the views of 'one big family') or 'the common sense of the common people'. Audiences were meant to understand that those who do not accept the Reform position are not truly principled interests but 'special interests'. They cannot, by definition, be part of 'the people', and were opposed to the interests of the 'one big family' that the people (a.k.a. Reform supporters) were advocating with things like the five resolutions that launched the United Alternative.[42]

This rhetorical tactic is of course classically populist, but it is also, like all populism, not realistically seen as ideologically neutral once put into its proper political context. The policy agenda Manning promoted was not ideologically indeterminate. One cannot have read the *Blue Sheet*, attended policy debates at Reform Assemblies, listened to the vast majority of Reform MPs, or pursued the 'links' to other conservative parties and right-wing think tanks offered on Reform's Web page, without thinking that the party Preston Manning dominated so effectively for more than a decade must have been closely related to the Newt Gingrich-led New Right Replublicans to the south.[43]

If the Reform party had such clear right-wing ideological bearings, why would a leader who dominated it not be best understood as right-wing in some important sense? Compared to the right wing of the Republican party, or for that matter to either Tom Long or Stockwell Day, Manning may appear a moderate. But our relevant context is the Canadian political competition. In this competition, Reform appealed to voters that were consistently grouped on the far right of the electorate.[44] The Reform party's major achievement is arguably to have pulled political discourse and policy debate substantially to the right over the past decade.[45] It is not plausible to argue that Preston Manning, who exercised such strenuous and effective control over the party, was not supportive of this re-orientation.

Clarity about Reform's ideological bearings also requires us to question Manning's 1999 claim that the politics of left-right identification are largely irrelevant to contemporary partisan choices. He argued that such considerations would not hamper the United Alternative's move beyond Reform's support base. The United Alternative could move beyond left-right politics, he suggested, by uniting the right and all those 'committed to reforming the federation on the basis of equality and individual autonomy, as well as through a rebalancing of powers and bottom-up grassroots democracy'.[46]

This argument suggests that when push comes to shove, conservative ideological approaches to policies will co-exist with regionalist or majoritarian-populist approaches to policies, in some kind of higher synthesis. My reading of Reform policy choice and issue emphasis since 1987, however, points to a different conclusion: when a choice had to be made, New Right ideology trumped regionalist or decentralist or populist concerns. That this is widely understood outside of Reform circles may explain why the February 1999 United Alternative meeting drew so few from the non-right, despite organizers' efforts to portray it as an ideologically diverse meeting of opponents to one-party dominance at the national level.

Realizing that for Reform, New Right ideology normally prevailed also helps to explain Stockwell Day's massive upset on the first round of Canadian Alliance's leadership vote. He won not just by recruiting ex-Conservatives in Ontario, but also by appealing to an impressively organized range of those on the party membership's socially and economically conservative right wing, especially those from Alberta.

For most Canadians who have not already voted for Reform, the Canadian Alliance would be widely seen as a Trojan horse for the non-moderate political right.[47] To some

Ontario backers of the Harris 'Common Sense Revolution' whose new memberships before the Alliance leadership race were not exclusively contingent on a Tom Long victory, this is a good thing. What remains to be considered is whether the Canadian Alliance party can shed the Western regional image that secured Reform's invasion from the right.

Will the Alliance Retain Its Western Support?

Is there any prospect of the Canadian Alliance party becoming other than a Western regional party? Or has Reform been seen so much as a party of the West that the Alliance would face a huge challenge in becoming anything else? If we recall the earlier discussion regarding the primary concerns of Reform, we can think briefly about the consequences of giving certain among them less prominence.

The 2000 Canadian Alliance election campaign, and current parliamentary priorities, soft-pedalled traditional Reform positions on the Triple-E Senate and the poor treatment of the West by the federal government. Many long-time Reform supporters and activists could feel somewhat abandoned by these changes. Granted, concern with moral principles in government and concern with the deficit and economic problems were important reasons for members to join Reform. However, many Reform members left the Conservative ranks because the Tories appeared willing to put Quebec and Ontario concerns before those of the West.[48] How will these activists and voters respond, as alienated Westerners, to a party seeming to back away from regional concerns? Some may well decide to vote for splinter parties, such as Christian Heritage, and some may vote for a Reform 'rump' party, if one arises in reaction to a 'de-Westernized' Alliance party. The odds on this latter development occurring before the next federal election seem much higher following the disappointing 2000 federal election performance of Stockwell Day and his Ontario candidates than they did before that election.

The old Reform party core membership made a strong association between a right-populist agenda with opposition to a strong/centralized state, and/or 'special rights' for Quebec.[49] If the twin themes of equality among provinces and ending Quebec's blackmail of federal polity is detached from the anti-central Canadian themes and watered down to broaden the Alliance's appeal, there could be some losses owing to non-voting in western Canada. But unless a rump Reform party is assembled before the next federal election, these voters may still feel more at home in the Canadian Alliance party than any other party.

We may also see some decline in Alliance party activism in the West in the next federal election campaign. Almost 40 per cent of Reform party members voted 'No' in the first February 1999 party referendum on the United Alternative, and half didn't bother to vote at all. With Stockwell Day as Alliance leader, activists in organizations of the religious right were instrumental in pushing him above Preston Manning on the first leadership ballot.[50] They might take up the activist slack created by soft-pedalling old Western alienation themes. This could, of course, alienate more voters than it attracts. Reform was already overwhelmingly the vote choice of Christian fundamentalists and social conservatives in English Canada west of Quebec, so it seems unlikely that there are many new votes to harvest in this constituency.

Shortly after the United Alternative resolution passed at the 1999 UA convention, GUARD (Grassroots United Against Reform's Demise) was formed by several high-profile Reform party activists, and was initially endorsed by more than one dozen of its Western MPs. Through the summer of 1999, the party was wracked by Manning's expulsion of Manitoba MP Jake Hoeppner from Reform's federal caucus, and by considerable opposition to this move within the caucus. Hoeppner refused to stop criticizing party advisor Rick Anderson for his pro-United Alternative work, especially after he discovered Anderson's attempt to get Hoeppner's local party association to expel him. He continued for over a year to denounce the United Alternative plan as a disaster for Reform's Western identity and populism.[51]

Eventually, Preston Manning scored a major victory for Reform dissolution and broadening out, when 92 per cent of party members voted in favour of accepting his preferred option in a March 2000 internal party referendum. At that time, the only person thought likely to challenge Manning for the new party's leadership was Stockwell Day, the telegenic and well-known finance minister in the Alberta Conservative government. How this vote would have turned out if party members in the Western provinces had thought that Tom Long would enter the leadership race as a Bay Street-financed opponent to Manning is anyone's guess.

The Progressive Conservative party under Joe Clark has distinguished itself from the Alliance party partly with reference to its asymmetrical and Quebec-accommodating view of Canadian federalism. This could help the Alliance to retain its Western regionalist support, even if 'Western rights' is a love that dare not speak its name in the Alliance party.

Can the Alliance Appeal to Other Regions?

Can the Alliance's anti-politician, anti-statist populism appeal broadly outside the West? Continued support for Mike Harris outside of Toronto seems to ride as much on anti-politician populism as on tax cuts, fiscal austerity, and the backlash against 'special interests' and the welfare state.[52] But even though the Alliance obtained more votes in Quebec than the Progressive Conservatives in 2000 (6.2 per cent to 5.8 per cent), Quebec support for the Alliance is very weak. It was, arguably, made weaker by the membership-buying scandal in the Gaspé that did so much to handicap Tom Long's leadership bid in the last week of the campaign. Alliance support in the Maritimes in 2000 rose slightly, but will be stalled unless it moves much closer to the centre on social programs and regional equalization issues.[53] This seems unlikely. Of votes cast in the first round of the Alliance leadership race, Maritime votes accounted for only 1.47 per cent of the national total.[54]

Can Ontario Voters Be Wooed?

Several scenarios can be sketched here.

Was Manning's Departure Enough?

As we now know, replacing Preston Manning with Stockwell Day did not lead to significant electoral gains in Ontario, even after an all-out and hugely expensive Alliance campaign in Ontario throughout the 2000 campaign. In the eyes of the Ontario business establishment, Preston Manning symbolized not just Reform's Western-ness, but also the party's knee-jerk opposition to Ontario interests whenever they appear to conflict with Western interests. The presence of long-term Conservatives on corporate boards was also clearly a barrier to their embrace of Manning. As founding party leader, Manning came to symbolize the party's refusal to budge on 'the Quebec question'. Ontario business élites have seen this as pandering to Western prejudice, not as a promising strategy for dealing with a problem that reduces domestic and international confidence in the Canadian economy.

Finally, it is worth noting that among Ontario Alliance voters, Preston Manning finished a relatively weak third in the first round of the Alliance leadership race. Manning picked up 25 per cent of non-tele-vote ballots, compared to Stockwell Day's 39 per cent and Tom Long's 35 per cent.[55]

Although Reform's fundraising failure among central Canadian business was often portrayed in positive terms to its Western right-populist supporters, this appeal cannot work for the Alliance, which seeks and needs support from the Ontario business community. In a 19 June 2000 breakfast meeting at the Toronto Stock Exchange, Stockwell Day advertised himself as the 'candidate who could unite both Bay Street and Main Street'. As he put it, 'Clearly Wall Street likes what I did in Alberta, and I know that Bay Street feels the same way.'[56]

Tom Long's campaign was lavishly financed by Bay Street and policy-tilted in its direction. While unwilling to identify any of his backers, he presented the Bay Street support as an indication that he could 'win Ontario' for the Alliance, and thus dump the Chrétien Liberals. However, it is now apparent that, even when combined with the legendary organizing skills of the Mike Harris strategic brain trust in which Long was so pivotal, Bay Street money was not enough to secure an Ontario leader for the Common Sense Revolution outside of Ontario.

As Stephen Harper and Tom Flanagan note, 'If Reform knew how to break into Ontario, it would have done so by now.'[57] They say that it is Reform's 'populism' that is alien to Ontario political culture and explains Ontario voters' reluctance to embrace Reform and the Alliance to date. But was it Reform's populism that Ontario voters have trouble with? Or was it Reform's other stances: anti-federal government and anti-Quebec feelings, as well as visceral anti-statism and prominent elements of anti-secular social conservatism? Anti-federal government feeling, social conservatism, and anti-statism are contingent elements of Reform's populist package that have been wholeheartedly adopted by the Alliance under Stockwell Day's leadership. The results of the 2000 election—that is, that these views are not accepted beyond the core Reform vote in Ontario—were in a sense foreshadowed by Rick Anderson and André Turcotte, respectively Reform's chief strategist and pollster. Both men were Manning loyalists during the leadership race, and both made a point between the two leadership ballots of warning that a Day victory would eventually shrink rather than expand the Alliance vote relative to Reform's 1997 vote. In light of Stockwell Day's remarkable incompetence and bad judgment as party leader during and after the 2000 election, it now appears that these claims were not merely strategic.

The other contingent element of Reform's populism, antagonism towards Quebec, has little support in Ontario. Under Day's leadership, the Alliance tried to shed some of Reform's anti-Quebec reputation. But so far Day has not been able to convince either Québécois or Ontarians that their interests are promoted in a radically decentralized federalism of the type Day endorses.

In sum, more than a leadership change is necessary for an Alliance breakthrough in Ontario.[58]

How Can an Alliance Leader Have Broader Appeal?

If Preston Manning had been replaced by Tom Long, this would not have played well among Western voters, who would have felt uneasy about an Alliance party led by an Ontarian seeking broader support in Ontario. If this meant de-emphasizing traditional Western concerns, many committed Western regionalists who moved from Reform to the Alliance would have believed that their party had been hijacked. As many Reformers said about the Conservative party after 1982, 'We didn't leave the party—it left us.'

It is worth remembering that only 55 per cent of the 1999 United Alternative convention delegates voted to create a new party. This leaves many—a majority of Western Reformers in particular—having to accept Ontario members' swing votes as first step in a process that by mid-2000 would replace the Western delegates' party. Concerns about this replacement began to emerge when stories about the Long campaign's purchased and often bogus memberships gained national prominence one week before the first leadership ballot. As more than one prominent Western Reformer remarked, 'We don't do things this way in the West.' Long's membership recruitment tactics deeply offended many old Reform members, who had joined and sustained the party at least partly because they believed that Reform was above the corrupt party practices they associated with 'old-line parties'.

Did Stockwell Day manage to remove the stain of 'Western-ness' from the Alliance party's new clothing in the eyes of potential Ontario supporters? It appears that some Ontario voters hoping for a fresh start beyond regionalism may see him as less problematically Western than they see Preston Manning. The Alliance party surpassed Reform's 1997 popular vote by 4.5 per cent in 2000 (19.1 per cent for Reform to 23.6 per cent for the Alliance). Manning's role as Reform party founder, combined with his evident domination of its Western parliamentary caucus, guaranteed that this image problem attached itself to Manning almost as much as to the party over the past decade.

It is highly unlikely that any new Alliance leader, even one from the West, will continue to emphasize Reform's traditional regional concerns. In his July 2000 leadership victory speech,[59] Stockwell Day did not allude even indirectly to Reform's Western roots or to the regional grievances that were so central to Reform's birth and life. Day had very good reasons to avoid emphasizing Reform's traditional regional concerns prior to the 2000 federal vote and during the fall election campaign. He and his handlers clearly felt that such behaviour would seriously cut into whatever potential room for voter growth the Alliance had in Ontario by demonstrating its inability to transcend its regional roots. The Alliance would be viewed, legitimately, as little more than a new name for the Reform party,[60] and a failure at its primary objective— creating an interregional party of the right. Despite these efforts to transcend its regional roots, the Alliance did in fact fail to achieve this objective, with only 2 of its 66 seats coming from Ontario.

When the new party option prevailed among Reform party members,[61] Preston Manning felt constrained to drop Reform's explicitly regionalist agenda. This had already begun by the February 1999 United Alternative convention, with the quiet replacement of a call for a Triple-E Senate for a merely 'elected' Senate in the resolution on 'democratic and governance themes'.[62] One can also see it in Manning's United Alternative convention speech, which pressed none of the symbolic or explicitly pro-Western buttons that had previously offered comfort and an esprit de corps to activist Reformers. Manning referred to Western grievances only in passing, suggesting that 'because the West wasn't present or represented at the founding of Confederation, it has not always felt the same sense of ownership for the federal system that the founding fathers and provinces have felt.'[63]

Reducing profound regional alienation to a matter of pop-psychological 'ownership' offered thin gruel to Reform activists for whom 'Ottawa' is a dirty word, and in whose moral geography central Canadian élites of all kinds are inherently suspect. One can assume that many members who voted 'No' in the first party referendum on the creation of a new party fall into this category.

A leader who moves much beyond symbolic olive branches to central Canada must do so seriously for the party re-creation gamble to be have been worth the effort. He or she then risks being seen as a turncoat by many core Reform voters in the West, especially if he or she gives in to Ontario Alliance operatives' and financial supporters' pressure to drop the moral conservative and direct democracy enthusiasms that sustain many Western Alliance activists, but have no potential for expanded electoral appeal in Ontario. The premise of the Alliance gamble was that whatever sacrifices needed to be made to mount a national appeal would be more than offset by major Alliance gains, and debilitating body blows to the federal Conservative party, in Ontario. How plausible is this scenario?

Only one scenario would lead to a rapid folding of tents in the national Conservative party, and to a steady growth of a 'non-regional' Alliance party: a new Alliance leader who would drop the regional agenda, pick up substantial support in Ontario, look like a viable alternative to the Liberals nationally, and keep enough core Reform voters in West to dramatically increase its parliamentary representation.

Will enough Reform party supporters agree to lose most of their 'regional agenda' in exchange for a better long-term shot at a right-wing national government? A remaining commitment to tax cuts and fiscal conservatism plus social conservatism plus decentralization may be insufficient to retain all of the Alliance party's 2000 Western vote. Evidence from 1999 Angus Reid polls suggests that the creation of a new party with this de-regionalizing agenda was supported by less than one-quarter of Reform voters in British Columbia and Alberta. By contrast, a merger of Reform and the Conservatives—an option rejected by delegates at the 1999 United Alternative convention—was supported by close to half of these voters.[64]

There were also high-profile defections from the United Alternative bandwagon among Manning's federal caucus, and accusations from disaffected former party operatives of party attempts to 'rig' the membership vote[65] during the first stage of UA party formation.[66] Just before the January 2000 UA Convention and Reform Assembly, disgruntled MPs and activists complained that both meetings had been rigged to maximize positive exposure for the Alliance option, and virtually eliminate member opportunities to speak against it. A reading of the two meetings' agendas, or for that matter, of Preston Manning's 'Think Big' talk to Reform Assembly delegates,[67] makes this interpretation of the Reform party leadership's intentions hard to dispute.

Despite the best efforts of the leader, party whip Chuck Strahl,[68] the central party organization,[69] and the unofficial party magazines,[70] 40 per cent of the party's voting members rejected Manning's call for a supra-regional party in the first round of voting in 1999. Editorial opinion in the daily press suggested that a much stronger majority would be needed for Manning to stay on as Alliance leader and not hurt the new party's chances.[71]

Sixty per cent of voting members accepted Reform's transformation into the Canadian Alliance party in early 2000.[72] Nonetheless diehard regionalist activists may be lost to the Alliance as it searches more assiduously for ways of gaining a real foothold in Ontario. Disaffected Western regionalists appear to have mostly voted for the new party in 2000 as the only viable game in town. But the Alliance must now step up its efforts to deny real voice to Western regionalists. Following this, perhaps towards the end of the current Parliament, many Western regionalists may want to choose the 'exit' option via a 'Retro-Reform' party.

People choosing this option would not consider it a tragedy that their party will never hold national power. This was not their expectation or primary objective during their years inside Reform. They might move to accept Tom Flanagan's advice: continue to hold a principled place in the national political scene, securing policy influence even if not control of the reins of power.[73]

We should recall what Engelmann and Schwartz noted in their 1975 study of Canadian parties: compared to other regions, 'rejections of the governing party . . . are the norm in Western Canada.' Only once between 1921 and 1974, did 'the prairie provinces contribute a majority of their votes to the government, while British Columbia ha[d] come no closer than 49 per cent'.[74]

Historically, Westerners have not been easily convinced that their votes ought to aid the creation of national political coalitions. Many long-time Reformers are bitter veterans of the last instance of such a ploy, courtesy of Brian Mulroney's adroit but ultimately non-viable alliance between Western conservatives and Quebec nationalists. By the end of the Mulroney years, Western conservative regionalists had massively decided that without a clear commitment by the Mulroney government to western over central Canadian interests, keeping the Liberals from power was insufficient reason to support the Tories. This experience with 'betrayal' by the Mulroney Tories is still fresh in many long-time Reformers' minds.

Neither Joe Clark's Tories nor Alexa McDonough's NDP seem likely to attract large numbers of committed Western regionalists. Each party lost popular vote in the West in 2000. Evidently, a significant number of pre-1993 New Democratic voters from western Canada have continued to vote Liberal, for a party they do not much trust, so as to block the right-wing political agenda they most fear. Many past NDP supporters would see Alliance success on its own terms—broad interregional support for a combined agenda of fiscal and social conservatism—as the worst political outcome imaginable.

In summary, then, the Canadian Alliance faces a serious tradeoff between 'de-regionalizing' its appeal and retaining its Western vote. 'Going national' over the next Parliament could easily produce results that confirm the worst fears of party strategists. They may only unite the viscerally anti-statist, anglophone right, which is so thinly dispersed that in electoral terms, the party would become the 'NDP of the right'.

Most of the gamble inherent in the Alliance enterprise is being played on Ontario soil, and involves recruiting voters heretofore unwilling to support Reform. Is this likely?

Harvesting Ontario's Social and Fiscal Conservatives

Stripped of Reform's most prominent regionalist regalia, the Canadian Alliance must face a dilemma that Reform's regionalist identity spared it from having to confront for the past decade. For a party of the right wishing to move beyond third-party status, the dilemma emerges from the conjuncture of our single-member plurality electoral system, and the related brokerage party system. The Alliance must choose a strategy that allows it to harvest the vast majority of fiscal conservatives and social conservatives in any election.

If no such strategy exists, either because of the difficulties of combining the two conservative fields simultaneously, or because of other parties' abilities to harvest some of the crop, then the only real options left are variations on a third-party theme. Our electoral system almost guarantees that unless a new party can get away with running dramatically incompatible election campaigns in different regions, it will have great difficulty achieving convincing national party status. In this case, the dramatic incompatibility that the Canadian Alliance would have to sustain would be between a Western-oriented, central-Canada-bashing campaign west of Ontario, and a 'de-regionalized', less ideologically and personally aggressive campaign in Ontario. This seems a very tall order.

In the West, Reform attracted the clear majority of socially and fiscally conservative voters. But this 'invasion from the right' was facilitated by the gods of regionalism. What the gods of regionalism giveth, they can readily take away. Thus the Reform vote exaggerated the power of the social/fiscal conservatism tag-team by relying on electoral system distortions and regionalist cultural attractiveness. These same institutional and cultural factors punished Reform, and now the Alliance in Ontario, in terms of both seats and image. But until the spring of 2000, Reform primarily benefited from the gods of institutionalized regionalism.

In the 2000 federal election, three parties of the centre-right offered voters ample fiscal conservatism. Neither Liberals nor Tories offered as much as Reform or the flat-taxing Canadian Alliance did. But with the aid of hindsight, we can say that almost all anglophone voters strongly attracted to heavy doses of fiscal conservatism had already voted Reform. If they didn't vote for full fiscal conservatism, by choosing Reform, and more recently Alliance, why didn't they?

Some—especially in Ontario—were turned off by Reform and Alliance social conservatism, especially on matters of personal moral or 'lifestyle' choice. Fiscal conservatism has no necessary connection to social conservatism, except in the more philosophically demanding versions of conservative liberalism that enjoy little public support.[75] Non-religious-fundamentalist fiscal conservatives are likely to behave as models of rational-choice theory predict; religiously or philosophically inclined social conservatives are generally not. Many fiscal conservatives appear to accept Ralph Klein's advice to the 1999 United Alternative convention regarding the need for consistency between promotion of individual choice in the market and individual choice in 'moral compass' setting.

Social conservatives distrust consumer sovereignty over matters of morality and our 'social fabric'. Fiscal conservatives seem to know this. Why would they vote for negligible additional amounts of 'economic freedom', while accepting an attack on the lifestyle freedom, cultural pluralism, and other aspects of the liberal culture targeted by social conservatives? To keep Ontario's suburban, fiscally conservative voters happy, Mike Harris has prudently gone nowhere near the distance down this road proposed by many high-profile voices in Reform and now the Canadian Alliance.

Some fiscal conservatives in Ontario may not have voted for Reform in 1993 or 1997 because the party was too egregiously Western. But even when the Canadian Alliance jettisoned virtually all of Reform's Western themes for the 2000 federal campaign, very few additional voters voted Alliance who had not previously voted Reform. Alliance candidates collected 23.6 per cent of the Ontario vote in 2000, compared to 19.1 per cent voting for Reform in 1997. Even after a leadership and name change, the voices most readily identified with the Alliance were voices Ontarians associate with unfathomable expressions of anti-central-Canadian sentiment, in unnecessary third-party dress. Fiscal conservatives in Ontario appreciate

Reform and Alliance promotion of an agenda of fiscal conservatism over the past decade, but only a small proportion who had never voted Reform voted for Alliance candidates in 2000.

Having the two old parties compete with each other over tax cuts and program cuts under pressure from a new party of the right must seem a dream come true to these fiscal conservatives. But nothing in this scenario gives Ontario's fiscal conservatives substantial incentive to vote for the Alliance. They got much of what they wanted merely by having others in the West vote for Reform, or for the new Alliance. Jaded Westerners might wonder whether Ontario's élites will ever tire of free riding at Westerners' expense.

Reform and Alliance demands for decentralization of power in the federal polity and for equality among the provinces[76] do not resonate as strongly among Ontario's fiscal conservatives as they do for their Western counterparts. Ontarians easily translate this demand for provincial equality as a refusal to accommodate any of the demands Quebec's soft nationalists set as minimum conditions of Quebec's continued residence in the federal home. To Westerners' chagrin, conservative Ontarians do not appear increasingly likely to see this soft nationalism as an endless strategy for transferring resources to Quebec at the rest of Canada's expense.

The three recent federal Liberal sweeps in Ontario, as well as Reform's poor money-raising performance in the Ontario business community, suggest that ending one-party dominance in Ottawa has not been a decisive or sustained concern among Ontario's fiscal conservatives. It is true that Stockwell Day was endorsed by high-profile Ontario Conservative cabinet ministers and former members of Mulroney's inner circle during the Alliance leadership race, after Tom Long failed to make it to the second-round ballot. But it is also true that Tom Long was snubbed by Day's campaign team during the 2000 election, after having been promised a key role in the Alliance's Ontario campaign. And high-profile Long supporters in Mike Harris's government, like Robert Runciman, were quick to follow the November 2000 election with public criticism of Day's inability to extend Alliance appeal significantly beyond old Reform constituencies. With hindsight, we can say that Day's leadership of the Alliance did not pry enough extra Conservative voters away from their old party home to give the Alliance a promising base in Ontario.

Conclusion

In retrospect, the Reform party's successful 'invasion from the right' into the federal party system was best facilitated by a regionalist strategy. But entry into the system, and displacing all contenders on both the economic and social conservative fronts, are different matters. With the Canadian Alliance failing to convert Reform's *Blue Sheet* into a full-fledged conservative philosophy,[77] while shedding Reform's regionalist clothing, it is not substantially more electorally attractive than Reform. Large numbers of centre-right voters who never voted Reform did not see the flat-tax, program-cutting Alliance agenda as dramatically superior to the Liberals' fiscal policy and tax reductions. It seems unlikely that this situation will reverse in the near future, especially with the Alliance wracked with debate over their need to dump their own leader, and dropping in the polls.

Mildred Schwartz paved the way for Canadian political scientists' appreciation of how regionalism has generated some of the most intriguing irony in Canadian politics. In this chapter I have considered several dimensions of the regionalist irony conditioning and flowing from the experience of Canada's most electorally successful third party. I have argued that Reform's status as a party of the West needs to be placed in the context of its regionalism-trumping and often populism-trumping New Right ideology. The irony of regionalist populist rhetoric is that, while the language of 'special interests' and 'the people' can work well, it risks having its ideological foundations starkly revealed when key regional appeals are removed from the rhetorical package.

Since its inception, the Canadian Alliance party has been openly courting 'Bay Street' in ways that may soon give many Westerners pause. The irony of using a regionalist Trojan horse for an invasion from the right is that the grassroots can object when the horse is bridled to facilitate a second, Ontario-focused party system invasion. In the West, some of Reform's former supporters will become increasingly unhappy about letting the Canadian Alliance bury the historic Western campaign against central Canada, on whose rhetorical back Reform rode from 1987 to 2000.

Such are the perils of transition from regional party to national party status while attempting to marry Canada's two conservatisms.

NOTES

1. An earlier version of this paper was presented as a paper at the Regionalism and Party Politics in Canada Conference at the University of Calgary, March 1999. My thanks to the organizers, Lisa Young, Keith Archer, and Tom Langford, and to Mildred Schwartz for her inspiring address to the conference. Thanks as well to Lisa and Keith for allowing this essay to do double duty in my own book, *The New Right and Canadian Democracy: Understanding Reform and the Canadian Alliance* (Toronto: Oxford University Press, 2001).

2. For an elaboration of this point, see the chapter by Harry H. Hiller, 'Region as a Social Construction', in this volume.

3. For confirmation of this pattern, see Richard Johnston, 'Canadian Elections at the Millennium', *Choices: Strengthening Canadian Democracy*, 6, 6 (September 2000) Montreal: Institute for Research on Public Policy, 25.

4. See Thomas Flanagan, *Waiting for the Wave* (Toronto: Stoddart, 1995).

5. See Keith Archer and Faron Ellis, 'Opinion Structure of Party Activists: The Reform Party of Canada', *Canadian Journal of Political Science* 27, 2 (1994): 277–308; Flanagan, *Waiting for the Wave*; and Trevor Harrison, *Of Passionate Intensity: Right-Wing Populism and the Reform Party of Canada* (Toronto: University of Toronto Press, 1995).

6. See Roger Gibbins and Sonia Arrison, *Western Visions: Perspectives on the West in Canada* (Peterborough: Broadview Press, 1995); Elisabeth Gidengil, Neil Nevitte, et al., 'Making Sense of Regional Voting in the 1997 Federal Election: Liberal and Reform Support Outside

Quebec', paper at the annual meetings of the Canadian Political Science Association, University of Ottawa, June 1998; Harold Clarke et al., 'Not for Fame or Fortune: A Note on Membership and Activity in the Canadian Reform Party', *Party Politics* 7, 1 (2000); and Neil Nevitte et al., *Unsteady State: The 1997 Canadian Federal Election* (Toronto: Oxford University Press, 1999), chs 4 and 8.

7. See Nevitte et al., *Unsteady State*, ch. 4.

8. Joseph F. Fletcher and Paul Howe, 'Supreme Court Cases and Court Support: The State of Canadian Public Opinion', in *Choices: Public Opinion and the Courts*, 7, 3 (May 2000): fig. 4, 39, and table 4, 42.

9. Ibid., table 3, 41.

10. The Reform pParty's policy commitments are set out in its *Blue Sheet* and 1997 campaign document, *Fresh Start*. These were once available at the party's Web site at http://www.reform.ca.

11. The best account of this is still J.R. Mallory, *Social Credit and the Federal Power in Canada* (Toronto: University of Toronto Press, 1954).

12. This view is clearly articulated in the Aberhart government's submission to the Royal Commission on Dominion-Provincial Relations, *The Case for Alberta* (Edmonton: Government of Alberta, 1938).

13. See Archer and Ellis, 'Opinion Structure', esp. table 4, 292; Clarke et al., 'Not for fame or fortune'.

14. Fiscal conservatism was strenuously promoted in the early 1980s by the *Globe and Mail* and major Southam papers, in advance of its ad hoc, incoherent promotion by Grant Devine's Progressive Conservative government in Saskatchewan.

15. See Nevitte et al., *Unsteady State*, chs 4 and 8.

16. See Clarke et al., 'Not for fame or fortune'.

17. See Archer and Ellis, 'Opinion Structure'; *Unsteady State*, chs 4 and 8.

18. For regular demonstrations of the range of discomforts such Reformers feel about their society, see *BC Report* and *Alberta Report*, and since fall 1999, *The Report*, all published by the Byfield family.

19. This argument was initiated in Roger Gibbins, *Prairie Politics and Society: Regionalism in Decline* (Toronto: Butterworths, 1980). Current data confirming that Westerners are not more socially conservative than Ontarians can be found in Nevitte et al., *Unsteady State*, esp. 94–8. Concerning the sociological basis for a revival of Social Credit, Fred Engelmann and Mildred Schwartz opined that 'it is doubtful whether a defeated Alberta Social Credit Organization can find, in church or economy, anything on which to plant Aberhart-like seeds'. Fred Engelmann and Mildred A. Schwartz, *Canadian Political Parties: Origin, Character, Impact* (Scarborough, Ont.: Prentice Hall, 1975), 212.

20. See Mildred Schwartz, *Politics and Territory*, (Montreal: McGill-Queen's University Press, 1974), ch. 1.

21. In Clarke et al., 'Not for Fame or Fortune'. Table 6 shows that 82 per cent of Reform member survey respondents in 1993 believed that 'national referendums take power from politicians and give it to the people', 93 per cent endorsed a federal recall law, and 92 per cent supported legislation to enable 'citizens' initiatives'. Table 2 shows that Reform members and voters were well ahead of other party voters in holding negative evaluations of Canadian political parties.

22. In 1937, Aberhart quickly forced his government members to repeal existing recall legislation, after his constituents had collected enough signatures to force a recall vote. In municipal politics, of course, plebiscites have been regularly employed to approve major capital projects since World War I. Provincial use of direct legislation was considerably sparser. An interesting fact in the province-level picture concerns Alberta's 1913 *Direct Legislation Act*. It had fallen into disuse by the time of Aberhart's 1935 victory and was never employed under Social Credit rule. In 1958, Ernest Manning's government repealed the act following his deputy attorney general's suggestion that it might be found ultra vires by the courts if employed. See Kevin Steel, 'Take back the government', *Alberta Report* 22 March 1999, 11.

23. The questions read: 'Should voters be given the right, by legislation, to propose questions that the Government of British Columbia must submit to voters by referendum?' and 'Should voters be given the right, by legislation, to vote between elections for the removal of the Member of the Legislative Assembly?'

24. Klein has passed legislation requiring a referendum to introduce a provincial sales tax. This demagogic move should not be considered a serious concession to direct democracy.

25. However, Gary Filmon's Conservative government did enact a requirement for referendums on deficit budget legislation by Manitoba provincial governments, complete with fines for ministers of finance who fail to comply with the prohibition on deficits. In Ontario, Mike Harris preceded his 1999 summer election call with a promise to enact similar legislation (Bill 99) if re-elected.

26. For a suggestive account of this alienation, linked to the emergence of the phenomenon of 'cartel parties', see Peter Mair, 'Political Parties, Popular Legitimacy, and Public Privilege', *Western European Politics* 18, 3 (1995): 40–57.

27. See especially Nevitte et al., *Unsteady State*, ch. 8; Harold Clarke and Allan Kornberg, *Citizens and Community: Political Support in a Representative Democracy* (New York: Cambridge University Press, 1992); André Blais and Elisabeth Gidengil, *Making Representative Democracy Work: The Views of Canadians* Volume 17 of the research studies for the Royal Commission on Electoral Reform and Party Financing (Toronto: RCERPF and Dundurn Press, 1991); and Lisa Young, 'Value Clash: Parliament and Citizens after 150 Years of Responsible Government', in F. Leslie Seidle and Louis Massicotte, eds, *Taking Stock of 150 Years of Responsible Government in Canada* (Ottawa: Canadian Study of Parliament Group, 1999).

28. I discuss the major variants of these Western approaches to popular democracy in David Laycock, *Populism and Democratic Thought in the Canadian Prairies, 1910–1945* (Toronto: University of Toronto Press, 1990).

29. For a discussion of these, see Darin Barney 'Push-button Populism: The Reform Party and the Real World of Teledemocracy', *Canadian Journal of Communication* 21, 3 (1996): 381–413.

30. Resolutions can be found at http://www.unitedalt.org/convention/ resolutions.html.

31. 'Canadian Alliance Declaration of Policy', announced at the United Alternative meeting prior to the Reform Party Assembly, January 2000. Once at http://www.reform.ca/ca_policies; now see http://www.canadianalliance.ca/yourprinciples/policy-declare/index.html.

32. This support continues in the Canadian Alliance, although its relative importance to the overall Canadian Alliance agenda has declined, as symbolized by their being listed as numbers 72 and 73 in the 75-clause *Declaration of Policy*.

33. See chapters 5 and 6 in David Laycock, *The New Right and Democracy in Canada: Understanding Reform and the Canadian Alliance* (Toronto: Oxford University Press, 2001).

34. See Hugh Winsor, 'How the Liberals won again', *The Globe and Mail*, 12 February 2001, A4. Winsor discusses the Liberal pollster Michael Marzolini's report to Liberal activists on the value of this wedge issue to the latter half of the Liberal's campaign. According to Winsor's account of this report, once voters' minds were focused on the sense in which Alliance party moral values were inconsistent with those of the Canadian majority, the Alliance campaign began a 'steep slide and never recovered'.

35. The *Blue Sheet* discussion of political reform proposals, including direct democracy, was once available at http://www.reform.ca. There is no trace of these old policy statements on the current Canadian Alliance Web site.

36. See the preface to the *Blue Sheet*, as well as Preston Manning, *The New Canada* (Toronto: Macmillan, 1992).

37. Section 15.2 facilitates affirmative action programs in the name of equality under and equal benefit from the law.

38. See my discussion in David Laycock, 'Reforming Canadian Democracy? Institutions and Ideology in the Reform Party Project', *Canadian Journal of Political Science* 27, 2 (1994): 213–47. The primacy of the 'will of the constituents' over MPs' views and even party policy is affirmed in *Democratic Populism III Task Force Final Report* (Calgary: Reform Party of Canada, August 1999).

39. Flanagan, *Waiting for the Wave*.

40. This interpretation appears not to have changed since the publication of *Waiting for the Wave*. In late May 1999, Flanagan said of Manning's attempt to lead the party through a transformation to a United Alternative party that 'he doesn't really want to go down an ideological path'. 'Manning's big gamble', *The Globe and Mail*, 29 May 1999, A1.

41. Preston Manning, 'Uniting for the 21st Century', address to the United Alternative Convention, draft notes, once available at http://www.unitedalt.org.convention/manning.html.

42. The five resolutions, as amended by the founding convention, were found at http//www.unitedalt.org.

43. Under the congressional leadership of Newt Gingrich, Republicans orchestrated a remarkable showing in the 1994 Congressional elections. Republican candidates signed the 'Contract with America', a fiscally and socially conservative campaign manifesto.

44. See Nevitte et al., *Unsteady State*, Figure 4.1, 49. As illustrated, Reform supporters are well to the right of Liberal and Conservative voters on the political cynicism, moral traditionalism, support for free enterprise, opposition to Outgroups, sympathy for Quebec, and 'do more for women' scales constructed by the CES study team.

45. That it moved to the right, even between 1993 and 1997, is suggested in Nevitte et al., *Unsteady State*, Table 4.3, 53. Reform, Liberal, and Conservative supporters all moved significantly in the direction of greater moral traditionalism and greater support for unconstrained private enterprise between 1993 and 1997. What can't be proven through behavioural analysis, of course, is the degree to which the Reform party effected this shift.

46. Preston Manning and André Turcotte, 'Re-aligning Political Reality: A Formula for Renewing This Country's Political Discourse in the New Millennium', once found at http://www.unitedalt.org/whyua/whyre.html.

47. See Nevitte, et al., ch. 8, for a demonstration of two relevant facts here: that 1997 Conservative voters preferred Liberals and even the NDP to Reform as second-vote choice, and that one clear reason for this was that Reform and its leader were seen as 'too extreme' on matters of federalism, treatment of Quebec, and social policy for all other party voters.

48. See Clarke et al., 'Not for Fame or Fortune'. See Table 3: 'Reasons for becoming a member of the Reform Party'. Concern with moral principles in government was cited by 29 per cent of this survey's respondents as the most important reason for their joining Reform, and concern with the deficit and economic problems was cited by 31 per cent. Concern that Quebec is too powerful was cited by 17 per cent of respondents as the most important reason for joining Reform, while obtaining more equal provincial power and the Triple E-Senate was cited by 8 per cent and getting better regional representation in Ottawa was cited by 7 per cent. This adds up to 32 per cent who appeared to believe that 'the Tories appeared willing to accommodate Quebec and Ontario concerns prior to the West's', to use my language.

49. Once again, see Nevitte et al., *Unsteady State*, ch. 4, and Clarke et al., 'Not for fame or fortune'.

50. Among the organizations most prominent in support of Day's leadership bid were Focus on the Family Canada (led by Darrel Reid, once Manning's chief of staff), the Canadian Family Action Coalition, and the Campaign Life Coalition. See Peter O'Neill, 'Social Conservatives tell Day what they want', *Vancouver Sun*, 28 June 2000, A1, A6. A look at Day's catalogue of press releases during the leadership campaign reveals virtually no reference to such endorsements. Day tried hard to counteract the 'religious fundamentalist' image that emerged in press coverage of his campaign.

51. Hoeppner actually took the party to court over its attempts to cancel his party membership, but then dropped the suit following negotiations with then party Chairman Gee Tsang. See Hugh Winsor, 'Quixotic Reform MP chuckles in exile', *The Globe and Mail*, 14 January 2000, A4.

52. See, among others, Sid Noel, ed., *Revolution at Queen's Park* (Toronto: James Lorimer, 1997).

53. Alliance candidates picked up 15.7 per cent of 2000 vote in New Brunswick (13.1 per cent for Reform in 1997), 5.0 per cent of the vote in PEI (1.5 per cent for Reform in 1997), 9.6 per cent in Nova Scotia (19.6 per cent for Reform in 1997), and 3.8 per cent in Newfoundland (2.5 per cent for Reform in 1997).

54. 'Canadian Alliance Vote Results' (Table), *The Globe and Mail*, 26 June 2000, A6. This figure refers to normal votes, not 'tele-votes'.

55. Ibid.

56. Stockwell Day Media, 6/19/00 Press Release: 'Day Appeals to Bay Street and Main Street'.

57. Tom Flanagan and Stephen Harper, 'Conservative Politics in Canada: Past, Present and Future', in William D. Gairdner, *After Liberalism: Essays in Search of Freedom, Virtue and Order* (Toronto: Stoddart, 1998), 187.

58. For an analysis of the obstacles facing Reform efforts to expand into Ontario, see Nevitte et al., *Unsteady State*.

59. Day received 64 per cent of the 118,497 second-round ballots.

60. See, for example, Jeffrey Simpson 'Meanwhile, back at the Alliance ranch . . .', *The Globe and Mail*, 20 June 2000, A17.

61. The first round of voting occurred in May 1999. The 60.5 per cent 'Yes' vote was announced 10 June. Just under 50 per cent of the party membership cast ballots. The second round in March 2000, following various internal party consultations, produced a 92 per cent vote in favour of Reform party dissolution and Alliance formation.

62. Resolution #4, United Alternative Convention, as reported at http://www.unitedalt.org/convention/resolutions.html. (This site is no longer active.) In the January 2000 'Canadian Alliance Declaration of Policy', Senate reform involving an elected Senate and, vaguely, 'the distribution of Senate seats on an equal basis', is left to clause number 71 in a 75-clause policy list. In Reform *Blue Books* of old, Senate reform came as Principle Number 2, in the opening 'Statement of Principles'.

63. Manning, 'Uniting for the 21st Century'.

64. Respondents were asked: 'Delegates at the convention are going to be voting on three major options—create a new right-wing party, move toward merging the Reform and Progressive Conservative parties, or leaving things as they are now. If you were a delegate at this convention, which option would you vote for?' In Alberta, with n=273, 20 per cent favoured the first option, 48 per cent favoured the second, and 29 per cent favoured the third (*The Reid Report on Alberta*, January-March 1999, 37). In BC, with n=162, respondents were asked how they would have voted had they been a delegate at the convention held several weeks earlier. Twenty-three per cent favoured 'creating a completely new party', 46 per cent favoured moving toward merging the Reform and Progressive Conservative parties, and 27 per cent favoured leaving things as they are now. (*The Reid Report on British Columbia*, March 1999.) Thanks to Daniel Savas for supplying me with these two provincial *Reports*.

In the April 1999 national Angus Reid poll, 41 per cent of Reform party identifiers counseled the party to remain as it is, 40 per cent advocated a merger between the PC and Reform parties, and only 17 per cent saw creation of a 'new right-wing party' as the best option ('Voters icy to Reform-PC merger or new party of right, poll says', *The Globe and Mail*, 19 May 1999, A4).

65. Christine Whitaker, a former Reform party executive council member from Saskatchewan, denounced the party's attempt to sway its members in the first-stage referendum by including a party newsletter with the ballots mailed to members in early May 1999. Ms Whitaker was one of the early organizers of GUARD (Grassroots United Against Reform's Demise). See Tim Naumetz 'Anti-UA Reformers launch ad campaign denouncing proposal', *National Post* 8 May 1999, A8.

66. The first stage involved a full-membership mail-in ballot on the question, 'Do you want the Reform party of Canada to continue with the United Alternative process?' Like the Parti Québécois' first sovereignty referendum, this simply asked for permission to continue negotiations. A majority 'Yes' vote in first round led to party task forces, discussion of these task forces' recommendations at a spring 2000 Reform party convention, and a second referendum on party formation per se. See Will Gibson and Mike Byfield, 'Will Reform Reform?' *Alberta Report*, 19 April 1999, 10.

67. 'Think Big! Notes for Reform Assembly Speech', Ottawa, 29 January 2000, at *http://www.reform.ca/assembly/speech.html*. (This site is no longer active.)

68. Strahl circulated a letter to his caucus members in April 1999, denouncing the use of 'irresponsible, inflammatory, inaccurate fear-mongering' in Reform MPs' opposition to the UA 'new party' plan.

69. One clear indication of the organization's position came from a perusal of the party's Web site. Reading it yielded no evidence that there was any serious opposition to the 'new party' option. In fact, all one saw was an unqualified promotion of this option, including a twenty-page account of the United Alternative convention by Preston Manning to party members, and several of the items noted above under http://www.unitedalt.org. This latter site was, realistically, simply an extension of the Reform party Web site.

70. Both *Alberta Report* and *BC Report* gave enthusiastic support to the UA convention and campaign. Most of the coverage dismissed the idea that the move from Reform to 'United Alternative' might entail significant 'deregionalization'.

71. See *Vancouver Sun* and *The Globe and Mail* 11 and 12 June 1999.

72. I am not sure what to make of the fact that only 49.5 per cent of eligible Reform party voters cast mail-in ballots during the month of May 1999. All received a ballot in the mail. But all members also received, in the same package, a party newsletter rather clearly tilted in favour of a 'Yes' vote. This may have had a negative impact on referendum vote turnout, so the voting results may have under-reported the extent of grassroots party antagonism to the United Alternative plan.

73. Tom Flanagan, 'Re-founding the Reform Party', *The Globe and Mail*, 22 April 1999, A17. Flanagan suggests that the transformation of Reform into a United Alternative party

should go ahead, without Manning as leader. The 'retro-Reform' scenario I am sketching here involves this transformation begetting a second new party in reaction to the de-regionalizing thrust of the first new 'post-Reform' party.

74. Engelmann and Schwartz, *Canadian Political Parties*, 188.

75. Good examples of this blend of social and fiscal conservatism can be found in Gairdner, ed., *After Liberalism*.

76. Reform-style provincial equality has been accepted in the new Alliance's *Declaration of Policy*, Clause Number 62.

77. Flanagan, *Waiting for the Wave*.

Chapter 8

Has Ontario Become the Liberal Party's 'Solid Centre'?

Joseph Wearing

For more than half a century, the Democratic party enjoyed a considerable advantage in American national party politics because it dominated the Southern states, the so-called 'Solid South'. From 1880 until 1944, the Democratic presidential candidate carried virtually every Southern state and won eight of those elections. In three of them, Southern electoral votes provided the margin of victory.[1] In the 1993 Canadian election, and even more dramatically in 1997, the Liberal party clearly owed its victory to a virtually clean sweep of Ontario. That raises the question posed by this chapter: has Ontario become the Liberal party's 'Solid Centre' akin to the Democrats' 'Solid South'? (Even posing the question, however, reveals a short memory, since it was not so long ago that Quebec voters were blamed for keeping the Liberal party in power in Ottawa.) Regionalism has always had an impact on Canadian party politics. Like the Rockies or the Prairies, you can't miss it. But does it also *drive* Canadian politics and to the same extent everywhere? Has Ontario succumbed so thoroughly to the forces of regionalism that it has given the Liberals a monopoly on representing the province in Ottawa? The question posed in this chapter is thus partly a reflection on Mildred Schwartz's exploration of Canadian politics and regionalism, which forms the raison d'être for this book.

In her groundbreaking work, *Politics and Territory: The Sociology of Regional Persistence in Canada*,[2] published in 1974, Schwartz concluded that regionalism remained a predominant force 'in the political life of a country that otherwise bears all the characteristics of a modern state'.[3] Likewise, the 1997 Canadian Election Study found that, of all the socio-demographic variables, the sharpest cleavage was undoubtedly region.[4] Indeed, the Canadian party system now appears to be even more regionalized than it was in the 1960s, the period on which Schwartz's work was based.

Regional disaffection was first reflected in party politics in the decade after the first world war, when farm protest parties swept the Prairie provinces and even, for a short time, Ontario. Ontario quickly restored its allegiance to the two older parties, but regional protest politics of one form or another became a fixture throughout western Canada. Until the last decade of the twentieth century, the rest of the country remained wedded to the traditional two-party system. (A special case was Quebec, where the two older parties won most federal seats, while a quasi-regional, quasi-nationalist party, the Union Nationale, sometimes held power provincially but did not contest federal elections. Later it was succeeded by a separatist, nationalist party, the Parti Québécois, which also stayed out of federal elections.)

A good case can now be made for arguing that party politics have become increasingly regionalized in such a way that each region looks to one party to safeguard its interests. Reform, renamed the Canadian Alliance, is the party of western Canada; the Bloc Québécois (a sister party of the PQ) is the party of Quebec. Even the Liberal and New Democratic parties, formerly national parties, have been transformed into regional parties, according to this thesis. As Ontario MPs have become an increasingly larger segment of the whole Liberal caucus, there is a danger that voters in the rest of the country will tend to see the Liberal party as an Ontario party, accelerating the regionalization of the party system. The NDP, which once aspired to be the voice of the working class and trade unionists across the country, is now the voice of welfare-dependent Atlantic Canada and of the two poorer provinces of western Canada. In this regional game, the venerable Progressive Conservative party, with its long history as a nation-building party, is left with barely a toehold anywhere.

The case for increased regionalization of party politics can be challenged by raising a number of questions. Was the Liberal sweep related more to problems with the other parties than it was to Ontarians' love of the Liberal party? Will the current Liberal dominance of Ontario prove to be a passing phenomenon when some other party wins a goodly share of Ontario seats? Or have we, on the other hand, witnessed the birth of a new party system in which there are no longer national parties? In short, does the Liberals' dominance of Ontario and Ontario's dominance of the Liberal party indicate that, in the matter of regional politics, Ontario is a province just like the others?

In attempting to answer these questions, it must be noted first of all that the Ontario Liberal stronghold is both a recent and an incomplete phenomenon. The party that won virtually every seat in the federal elections of 1993, 1997, and 2000 failed even to win a plurality of Ontario seats in 6 of the 12 previous elections. Moreover, in the provincial arena, it held power for only five years in the second half of the twentieth century. At one point Harris's Conservatives had so polarized the province that, according to Mike Marzolini of the polling firm Pollara, there were really only two significant groups in the province: those who wanted a PC government and those who didn't. Another paradox: 40 per cent of provincial PC supporters would have voted Liberal in a federal election and only 35 per cent of provincial PCs supported the same party federally.[5]

In the political science literature, a predominant party system at the regional level tends to be the product of a relatively homogeneous, inward-looking society and manifests itself in both state and national politics. For example, in the United States, white Southern Democrats attempted to turn back the clock of history by disenfranchising blacks and maintaining an agricultural economy. The twin forces of voter registration and economic development led by migrating Northerners vanquished both Democratic ascendancy and the South's homogeneous society.[6] Today, the South is more Republican than Democratic. Other examples of predominant parties nurtured by a homogeneous political culture are the Christian Social Union (CSU), which has held power continuously in the Catholic, culturally distinctive German state of Bavaria since the foundation of the Federal Republic, and Social Credit, which ruled the fundamentalist Christian province of Alberta from 1935 to 1971.[7]

Ontario hardly meets the criterion of a homogenous society. Indeed, it is the country's most diverse province. Furthermore, true one-party dominance requires congruity between the region's legislature and its representation in the national legislature. There have been just two periods in Ontario's history when one party has dominated the provincial arena: the Liberals from 1871 to 1905 and the Conservatives from 1943 to 1985. However, in neither instance was provincial dominance transferred into the federal arena. In federal elections from 1878 to 1904, the Liberals never won more Ontario seats than the Conservatives; from 1945 to 1984, the Conservatives won a majority of Ontario seats in only five, mostly isolated, elections (that is, victories with defeats both before and after). Moreover, in the case of the CSU in Bavaria and Social Credit in Alberta, the voters see (or saw) the party primarily as a defender of regional interests—even if party élites sometimes yearned to take a leading role on the national stage. While Liberal Oliver Mowat, Ontario premier from 1872 to 1896, was a staunch defender of the province's interests (or more accurately, of provincial rights generally), his Conservative successors in the twentieth century often felt called upon to speak on behalf of the national interest.[8]

Appearance and Reality

While the Liberal sweep of Ontario in the 1993, 1997, and 2000 elections did make it appear that, at least for those three elections, the province had become the party's 'Deep Centre', the Liberal stranglehold is less convincing when one notes the vagaries of the electoral system and the dynamics of the 1997 campaign.

The Electoral System

Even though the Liberal vote in Ontario was down three percentage points from what it had been in 1993, the Liberals still won all but two seats in 1997, compared to all but one in 1993. For this, the Liberal party had to thank the electoral system. As Figure 8.1 shows clearly, the working of the electoral system almost always exaggerates the ebb and flow of the popular vote from one election to another. While the Liberals' popular vote in Ontario has usually ranged between roughly 30 per cent and 50 per cent, the party's share of federal Ontario seats has been as low as 15 per cent and as high as 99 per cent. In 1997, the party's popular vote was just 3 per cent higher than in 1953, but its share of Ontario's seats was 38 per cent greater. And what the electoral system gives, it can also take away, as the Liberal party found out in 1957, 1958, and 1984.

Figure 8.1: Liberal Votes and Seats in Ontario

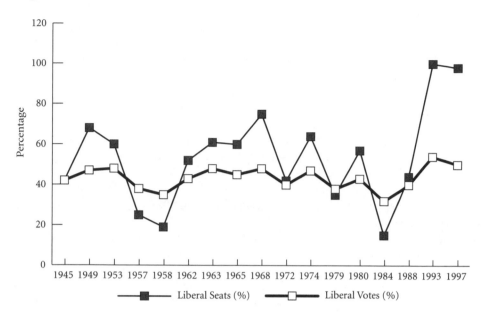

The 1997 Campaign

The dynamics of the 1997 campaign show that a Liberal sweep of Ontario was by no means assured. In the analyses of the 1997 Canadian Election Study data, Nevitte et al. have shown how voter intentions shifted during the campaign and especially following the televised leaders' debates.[9]

One factor that helped the Liberals was Ontarians' aversion to minority government. In that respect, they had not changed in the three decades between Mildred Schwartz's data from the 1965 election and Marzolini's data from 1997. 'Of all Canadians, those in Ontario were most consistently troubled by the absence of majority government,' said Schwartz in *Politics and Territory*.[10] In 1965, the country had had three years of minority government and could judge the results. In 1997, the situation was more complicated. Pollara's focus groups early in the campaign found that voters wanted a majority government and expected the Liberals to form one. This gave voters the luxury—or so they assumed—of casting a more egocentric vote for Reform or the NDP as a party that would 'best represent me'. The only uncertainty was which party would form the official Opposition. However, a Liberal majority was very dependent on the ebb and flow of party standings in the various regions and, with just nine days to go before the election, Pollara's tracking polls gave the Liberals only 127 seats—24 shy of a majority. Ontario was by no means solidly Liberal: Reform and the PCs were each close to winning half-a-dozen seats when a critical event occurred.

Reform ran its television ad attacking Quebec politicians and wondering whether it was now time for a prime minister from outside Quebec. The ad worked well in the West, but, when Jean Charest attacked it as 'bigotry', Ontario voters began to have second thoughts about Reform. With the largest number of visible minorities in the country, Ontario has become so culturally diverse that it backs away from any hint of racism or bigotry, according to Marzolini. In the eyes of Ontario's voters, Reform was playing with fire. The Liberals won those doubtful seats, not because of anything the party did, but because of the reaction to Charest's remark and to a growing perception that the election might not actually produce a majority government.[11] Although overall Liberal support was fairly steady in the month leading up to the election, Pollara's tracking showed much greater volatility in central Ontario, where Reform hoped to win some seats. A precipitous fall in support mid-month was followed by a sharp recovery in the last few days of the campaign, as shown in Figure 8.2. A gentler but even more decisive recovery also occurred in Metro Toronto and the surrounding suburban areas.

In the 2000 election, Ontarians' aversion to minority government again played into the hands of Liberal strategists. Liberal polling during the campaign showed the Alliance at 34 per cent and on the verge of a breakthrough. Days before the election, several media reports speculated on the possibility of a minority government. Fear of the Alliance became a prime motivating factor, strengthening the resolve of Ontario voters to stick with the Liberals on election day.[12]

Figure 8.2: 1997 Liberal Vote Tracking in Ontario

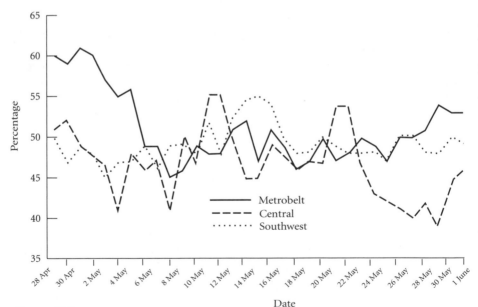

Source: Pollara

Jon Pammett, in his analysis of the 1997 campaign, also concluded that Reform's strategy of taking a tough stand on the Quebec question, while consolidating its position in the West, might 'have solidified the Liberal vote in the key province of Ontario'.[13]

An Unlevel Playing Field

While luck was a factor in the Liberals' 1997 grand slam of Ontario seats, it cannot be denied that the party also has some important longer-term advantages in the province. Those who identify themselves as Liberal supporters are a larger percentage of the electorate not only in Ontario but also in the other three regions of the country.[14] Ontarians' party loyalties appeared to be particularly affected by the economy's strong performance during the 1990s. The 1997 Election Study found that economic optimism was more of a factor in Ontario than elsewhere in accounting for Liberal voting.[15] Moreover, an association with the previous economic downturn hurt two of the Liberals' main opponents. The federal Conservatives and the Ontario NDP both had the misfortune to hold office during the recession of the early 1990s, which hit Ontario unusually hard. Both governments went down to crushing defeat in their respective elections of 1993 and 1995, and neither party has yet recovered. In a remarkably prophetic article written in 1992, Harold Clarke and Allan Kornberg showed that the electorate's gloomy evaluation of the economy at the end of 1990 was driving down support for the Conservative government across the country.[16] Public opinion in Ontario was even more alarmed. Canadian Gallup Poll data in Table 8.1 show that from March 1990 to February 1991 the percentage of Ontarians who thought the economy would worsen in the next six months was higher than for the country as a whole. At the same time, Mulroney's approval ratings sank below 20 per cent nationally and went even lower in Ontario. Also, beginning in August 1991, approval rating for Ontario's NDP premier headed for the basement.

The Reform party likewise faced a number of handicaps in its attempt to make a breakthrough in Ontario. Not only was its leader, Preston Manning, less popular in Ontario than in the West, but also the party was viewed generally as too extreme.[17] Although Reform received the second-largest number of votes in that province in both 1993 and 1997, it encountered the most resistance in attempting to win over new support. As shown in Table 8.2, when voters were asked whether they would ever consider voting Liberal, NDP, Conservative, or Reform, the percentage of Ontarians who would entertain the possibility of a Reform vote was much lower than those who would consider voting for the other three parties.

Broadening the Liberal Base

One reason for the Liberals' ability to keep Reform at bay may be found in the behaviour of the Ontario Liberal caucus during the thirty-fifth Parliament (1993–97). In previous Parliaments it had been largely an urban, left-of-centre group, but in 1993 the Liberals won Ontario ridings that had long been both socially and politically conservative, and their newly elected MPs reflected that conservative outlook. Even

Table 8.1: Economic Outlook and Approval Ratings of PM and Premier

Date	Economy Better		Economy Worse		Approve PM		Disapprove PM		Approve Premier	Disapprove Premier
	Ontario	National	Ontario	National	Ontario	National	Ontario	National	Ontario	National
Feb.–July 1986	38	32	31	34	37	42	NA	40	NA	NA
Sept.–Nov. 1987	30	31	37	30	29	30	NA	55	NA	NA
Mar.–Aug. 1988	32	31	26	30	34	35	NA	46	NA	NA
Oct.–Nov. 1989	NA	19	NA	46	26	28	63	55	NA	NA
Mar.–Apr. 1990	10	15	70	62	14	19	76	68	NA	NA
Oct. 1990–Feb. 1991	8	7	81	78	11	16	86	77	70	12
Aug.–Sept. 1991	43	44	34	34	12	15	83	76	40	42
Feb.–July 1992	42	39	35	38	8	11	87	81	28	60
Jan. 1993	NA	NA	NA	NA	20	17	75	76	25	64

Source: Gallup Canada Inc.

Questions: Do you think the economic situation in Canada during the next 6 months will get better or will get worse?
Do you approve or disapprove of the way Brian Mulroney is handling the job as prime minister?
Do you approve or disapprove of the way Bob Rae is handling his job as premier of Ontario?

Table 8.2: Regional Variations in Party Support

Whether would ever consider voting Liberal, by Region	Atlantic %	Quebec %	Ontario %	Man./Sask. %	Alberta %	BC %	Total %
Would consider voting for	66.8	59.5	75.4	65.6	61.1	70.7	68.1
Undecided	7.5	12.1	11.2	13.9	11.7	8.2	11.0
Would not consider voting for	25.6	28.4	13.4	20.5	27.1	21.1	20.9
Total	100.0	100.0	100.0	100.0	100.0	100.0	100.0

Whether would ever consider voting NDP, by Region	Atlantic %	Quebec %	Ontario %	Man./Sask. %	Alberta %	BC %	Total %
Would consider voting for	59.8	24.1	43.9	54.1	41.9	45.8	41.0
Undecided	10.2	14.5	13.3	16.6	10.0	8.0	12.6
Would not consider voting for	30.0	61.5	42.8	29.2	48.1	46.2	46.4
Total	100.0	100.0	100.0	100.0	100.0	100.0	100.0

Whether would ever consider voting Conservative, by Region	Atlantic %	Quebec %	Ontario %	Man./Sask. %	Alberta %	BC %	Total %
Would consider voting for	70.0	64.9	58.7	54.1	62.5	54.9	60.7
Undecided	9.6	12.4	13.8	15.7	12.5	10.5	12.7
Would not consider voting for	20.4	22.8	27.5	30.2	25.0	34.5	26.6
Total	100.0	100.0	100.0	100.0	100.0	100.0	100.0

Whether would ever consider voting Reform, by Region	Atlantic %	Quebec %	Ontario %	Man./Sask. %	Alberta %	BC %	Total %
Would consider voting for	29.6	12.2	34.2	40.8	62.0	51.6	33.3
Undecided	13.4	11.9	14.6	16.7	9.1	9.6	12.9
Would not consider voting for	57.0	75.9	51.2	42.5	28.9	38.8	53.8
Total	100.0	100.0	100.0	100.0	100.0	100.0	100.0

Source: Canadian Facts

Toronto elected some Liberals who took a conservative stance on certain social issues. The result was a much more diverse Ontario caucus than usual. Many of these new MPs, as well as their constituents, were profoundly uncomfortable with some of the government's social legislation, such as gun control, hate crime legislation, adding sexual orientation to the Canadian Human Rights Act, and reduced rights for denominational schools in Newfoundland. Although the Liberal party has the reputation of exercising tight discipline and being intolerant of dissent, the thirty-fifth Parliament actually witnessed a surprisingly high level of dissent on recorded divisions. In 16.1 per cent of the divisions, one or more Liberal MPs voted against the rest of their party, for a total of 1,310 dissenting votes. This was a higher level of dissent than that registered by the Reform party, where 259 dissenting votes were made in 7.9 per cent of the divisions. For both parties, the largest number of dissenting votes were in the relatively less sensitive area of private members' business, but 78 Liberal MPs voted against the government at the report stage and on third reading of government bills. On its amendments to the Human Rights Act, the government was forced to allow a free vote, in spite of earlier pledges to the contrary, because it realized that determined backbenchers were going to vote against the bill anyway.[18]

Reprisals were administered in a seemingly haphazard fashion. The most publicized dissenter was John Nunziata, who voted against the government on a money bill and was expelled from the Liberal caucus. In his case, retribution was final. Another was the veteran MP Warren Allmand, who voted against the government's budget and lost his position as chair of the House Justice Committee. However, a year later, all was apparently forgiven when Prime Minister Jean Chrétien rewarded him with a plum patronage position, the presidency of the International Centre for Human Rights and Democratic Development. The most frequent dissenter was Dan McTeague, who voted against his party 36 times and lost a committee position as a result. However within weeks, he was appointed to several other committees and had no trouble being renominated. Much as the party leadership pretended to discourage any show of dissent, it probably realized that individual MPs had to retain some credibility with constituents, who might otherwise have been tempted to vote Reform. Thus, by permitting a limited display of party dissent, the party was able to represent more adequately the diversity that is Ontario and to blunt the threat from Reform. But relaxing party discipline is not what one expects to see in the model of a regionally dominant party that jealously guards its right to represent its region.

The Prospects for a New Party System

If, in fact, the old system of national, brokerage parties has been replaced by a system of regional parties, then an Ontario-based Liberal party would be part of that unfolding schema. *Rebuilding Canadian Party Politics*, by Kenneth Carty, William Cross, and Lisa Young, contains a persuasive exposition of the new party system thesis.[19] One should exercise caution, however, in making definitive statements about the nature of contemporary party systems when one lacks the benefit of historical perspective. While voting behaviour certainly tends to follow an established pattern from one election to another, humans are also notorious for suddenly—or not so suddenly—changing their behaviour and diverging from patterns of apparently established party loyalties. It is not until several decades have passed that the political historian can more clearly see the larger design created by the shifting patterns of millions of ballots.

With that caveat, one can venture to make a few observations about the current party system in light of the 2000 federal election results. Certainly the refashioned Canadian Alliance looks to be an increasingly entrenched feature of the Canadian political scene. Although the partly failed to achieve its goal of a decisive breakthrough in Ontario, it did win two seats and came second in 80 of the remaining 101. The Bloc Québécois held on to a majority of the Quebec seats in spite of the failed referendum on independence in 1995. Both the NDP and the PC party held on to official party status in the House of Commons, if only barely, and with only three seats outside Atlantic Canada, the latter has a weakening claim to be considered a national party. Moreover, key provincial Conservatives in both Ontario and Alberta were drawn into the Alliance leadership campaign, and many have remained in the party.

But there is also evidence indicating that a regionally based party system is not developing. Reform changed its name and elected a new leader precisely in order to broaden its appeal and break out of its Western corral. Even Stockwell Day's overtures to Quebeckers, by making the case that he too believes in provincial autonomy, are the actions of a party leader who has more time for brokerage politics than his predecessor did. For its part, the Liberal party enjoys broad acceptance across the country. In Quebec it is more or less equally matched with the BQ and, according to the 1997 Election Study, '60 per cent of Canadians either voted Liberal or picked the Liberals as their second choice'.[20] In every region voters saw the Liberal party as the best one to represent national interests, if not necessarily regional interests.

Our evolving party system might just as easily turn out to be one in which a new party of the right faces an old party of the centre, egged on by a small, conscience party of the left and a dogged remnant of Quebec nationalism. That is not so very different from what we have had at times in the past. Significantly, in Canadian political history, it is the party of the right that has always had to reinvent itself: as the Liberal-Conservatives in 1854, as the Unionists in 1917, as the Progressive Conservatives in 1942, and (without a name change) under John Diefenbaker in 1956 and Brian Mulroney in 1983. It could be that future historians will regard the founding of the Canadian Alliance in 2000 as part of the same phenomenon.

Table 8.3: Voters' Choices to Represent Their Interests

| | Best Party to Represent Their Own Region's Interests | | | | | | |
	Liberal	PC	NDP	Reform	BQ	Other	Don't Know
Atlantic	29	24	32	5	–	2	9
Quebec	35	13	2	–	43	–	7
Ontario	58	12	8	10	–	1	11
Prairies	20	9	15	48	–	1	7
BC	19	3	21	47	–	1	8

| | Best Party to Represent National Interests | | | | | | |
	Liberal	PC	NDP	Reform	BQ	Other	Don't Know
Atlantic	45	19	15	6	–	1	14
Quebec	53	19	5	2	10	1	10
Ontario	56	11	5	14	–	2	12
Prairies	43	10	7	27	–	1	12
BC	49	6	10	23	–	2	10

Source: Marzolini, 'Regionalization of Canadian Electoral Politics', 195–6

Conclusion

While regionalism has always been an extremely important factor in Canadian politics and elections, there is a sense in which regionally based parties go against the grain of Canadian political history. As Denis Smith demonstrated in his 1950s thesis on Western protest parties, none of these parties saw themselves as parties of regional protest and, when that is what they became, none was particularly happy to stay with that role.[21] The Progressives, the CCF, and Social Credit each longed to escape from their limiting regional bases, just as the Canadian Alliance does today. Even the Bloc Québécois wants to be a national party. It simply defines 'nation' in a different way!

Nor should we overlook the role of our often-maligned electoral system in fuelling the nationalizing impetus. While Alan Cairns and others have shown how the system benefits parties with pronounced regional strengths,[22] we need to remember that the same electoral system doomed Reform to perpetual opposition status with all its 'wasted' votes in Ontario as long as it was unable to break out of its Western base. Its successor desperately wants to avoid being seen as a party of Western protest and strives to be perceived by Ontario voters as a national party.

Earlier we looked at various models of one-party dominance, none of which seemed to have much relevance for the situation in Ontario. A different and perhaps disturbing model is provided by contemporary India. Sudha Pai, writing on the transformation of the Indian party system after the 1996 Lok Sabha elections, has found that the breakdown of a one-party dominant system is being replaced by a gradual transition to a new 'region-based multiparty system'.[23] Besides the three all-India parties, each of which has a base in certain regions, there are also seven regional parties of significant size. Although the complexities of the party system in the world's most populous democracy make Canadian party politics look simple by comparison, it is a sobering indication of where Canada might be headed if Canada's parties should find themselves driven further into their regional strongholds and if the Liberals' luck in squeezing majority governments from the electoral system should happen to run out.

If Canada is to retain a system of competing national parties rather than moving to a regionalized system on the Indian model, Ontario is the key. Regional defensiveness—taking the form of lopsided allegiance to one party—has never been a feature of Ontario's political history. Ontario is the most diverse province in the country and elections there have always been keenly competitive. It is an unlikely candidate to become the Liberals' 'Solid Centre'. It would be more in keeping with Ontario's history to theorize that it is waiting to be wooed by whichever opposition party can convince the province's voters that it is a genuine national party and an alternative government to the Liberals.

NOTES

1. Congressional Quarterly, *Presidential Elections, 1789–1992* (Washington, DC: Congressional Quarterly, 1995).

2. Mildred A. Schwartz, *Politics and Territory: The Sociology of Regional Persistence in Canada* (Montreal: McGill-Queen's University Press, 1974).

3. Ibid., 313.

4. André Blais, Elisabeth Gidengil, Richard Nadeau, and Neil Nevitte, 'Accounting for the Vote in the 1997 Canadian Election', a paper presented at the annual meeting of the Canadian Political Science Association, Ottawa, 1998.

5. Interview with Michael Marzolini, 17 February 1999.

6. The classic analysis of political change in the South is Kevin B. Phillips, *The Emerging Republican Majority* (New York: Doubleday, 1970), ch. 3.

7. On predominant party systems, see Alan Ware, *Political Parties and Party Systems* (Oxford: Oxford University Press, 1996), 158–60. For the CSU, see Stephen Padgett and Tony Burkett, *Political Parties and Elections in West Germany* (London: Hurst, 1986), 115–26. For Social Credit, see J.A. Irving, *The Social Credit Movement in Alberta* (Toronto: University of Toronto Press, 1959); C.B. Macpherson, *Democracy in Alberta: The Theory and Practice of a Quasi-party System* (Toronto: University of Toronto Press, 1953).

8. See, for example, A.K. McDougall, *John P. Robarts: His Life and Government* (Toronto: University of Toronto Press, 1986), chs 12–14.

9. Neil Nevitte, André Blais, Elisabeth Gidengil, and Richard Nadeau, *Unsteady State: The 1997 Canadian Federal Election* (Toronto: Oxford University Press, 2000), 17, 19.

10. Schwartz, *Politics and Territory*, 253.

11. Interview with Marzolini.

12. *The Globe and Mail*, 12 February 2001.

13. Jon H. Pammett 'The Voters Decide' in Alan Frizzell and Jon H. Pammett, eds, *The Canadian General Election of 1997* (Toronto: Dundurn Press, 1997), 241.

14. Nevitte et al., *Unsteady State*, 69–70.

15. Elisabeth Gidengil, André Blais, Richard Nadeau, and Neil Nevitte, 'Making Sense of Regional Voting in the 1997 Canadian Federal Election: Liberal and Reform Support Outside Quebec', *Canadian Journal of Political Science* 32, 2 (1999): 262.

16. Harold D. Clarke and Allan Kornberg, 'Support for the Canadian Federal Progressive Conservative Party since 1988: The Impact of Economic Evaluations and Economic Issues', *Canadian Journal of Political Science* 25, 1 (1992): 29–53.

17. Nevitte et al., *Unsteady State*, 95–6.

18. Joseph Wearing, 'Guns, Gays, and Gadflies: Party Dissent in the House of Commons under Mulroney and Chrétien', a paper presented at the annual meeting of the Canadian Political Science Association, Ottawa, 1998.

19. R. Kenneth Carty, William Cross, and Lisa Young, *Rebuilding Canadian Party Politics* (Vancouver: University of British Columbia Press, 2000), ch. 10. An earlier attempt to discern different periods of party competition is in Joseph Wearing, *Strained Relations: Canadian Parties and Voters* (Toronto: McClelland & Stewart, 1988), 39–46.

20. Nevitte et al., *Unsteady State,* 134.

21. The conclusion of the thesis is contained in Denis Smith, 'Prairie Revolt, Federalism and the Party System', H.G. Thorburn, ed., *Party Politics in Canada,* 1st edn (Toronto: Prentice Hall, 1963), 126–37.

22. Alan C. Cairns, 'The Electoral System and the Party System in Canada, 1921–1965', *Canadian Journal of Political Science* (1968): 55–80.

23. Sudha Pai, 'Transformation of the Indian Party System: The 1996 Lok Sabha Elections', *Asian Survey* 36, 12 (1996): 1170–83.

Chapter 9

Political Realignment in Atlantic Canada?

David K. Stewart

Discussions of political realignment in Canada are controversial. Many believe that 'partisan ties in Canada are flexible for a majority of the electorate, and those voters make up their minds *de novo* at each election which party to support'.[1] From this perspective, the Canadian electorate is fundamentally 'dealigned', and the notion of a realignment of partisan support is problematic. This view has been challenged in recent election studies that have critiqued the way partisan ties were historically measured. As Richard Johnston et al. argue, 'we claim that many Canadians do indeed have abiding party commitments; the challenge is to measure them correctly'.[2]

Students of party politics in the Atlantic region have rarely engaged in this debate. Instead, portrayals of party politics in Atlantic Canada have focused on the stability that encompasses political competition at both the federal and provincial levels. As Rand Dyck explained, 'All four provinces have been characterized by a traditional two-party system, Liberals and Conservatives. . . . There has also been a close integration of federal and provincial parties in the region. Third parties have been notoriously unsuccessful, in spite of the fact that the economic situation might be expected to encourage their development'.[3]

This perspective on Atlantic Canada remained dominant through the 1993 federal election. In their introduction to the *Almanac of Canadian Politics*,[4] Munroe Eagles et al. observed that 'the Atlantic Provinces are the one region in which the traditional two-party system remains intact. . . . Conservatives continue to be the alternative to the governing Liberals both federally and provincially.'

Such comments could not preface an introduction to an almanac of 1997 election results. Strange things have happened in Atlantic Canada. In that year, the combined vote for the federal Liberal and Conservative parties fell to all-time lows in three of the four Atlantic provinces. Almost 40 per cent of the federal NDP caucus represented Atlantic Canadian constituencies and the party held seats in each provincial legislature. (Indeed, in Nova Scotia, the NDP formed the official opposition after the 1998 provincial election and won the second largest vote share in the 1999 election.)

This chapter explores the unprecedented results of the 1997 election in Atlantic Canada. It begins by noting some of the distinctive features that underlie the region's politics. This is followed by a brief review of trends in Conservative and Liberal support in the region during the third-party system, from 1963–88.[5] Consideration then turns to the NDP's success in the 1997 federal election, as well as the most recent provincial elections. The paper concludes by presenting data on regional party identification and voting taken from the 1997 Canadian Election Study (CES). Two broad conclusions follow from this analysis. The first is that party support in the Atlantic region has neither realigned nor dealigned. The second highlights the difficulties involved in speaking of the Atlantic region: electoral results from the four provinces can be summed only at the cost of disguising important provincial peculiarities. With respect to Atlantic Canada, Donald Smiley's[6] request that studies focus on provinces rather than regions is a useful one.

Conservative and Liberal Dominance

It has been simple to distinguish Atlantic Canada from the rest of the country in political terms. The region's unwavering rejection of third parties is unmatched anywhere else. Often explanations for third-party failure have been linked to political culture, building on the path-breaking work on political cultures by Richard Simeon and David Elkins.[7] More recently, political cultural explanations have waned as it appeared that the region's political culture had grown closer to that of other regions.[8] Nonetheless, there remain a number of important characteristics that distinguish Atlantic Canada from the rest of the country. In Ian Stewart's words: 'With respect to the distribution of religious beliefs, of family incomes, of ethnic backgrounds, and of community size . . . the Maritime provinces are easily distinguishable from those in the rest of Canada. Specifically, Maritimers are especially likely to be Protestant, to be poor, to be of British descent, and to live in rural, but not farming, communities.'[9] Other distinctive characteristics include high levels of church membership and attendance, an extensive tradition of out-migration, and the absence of recent immigration. These features, combined with a relatively high tolerance for patronage and a desire to support parties likely to form a federal government, provide a basis for understanding Liberal and Conservative dominance.

This dominance is impressive. Only the Conservatives and Liberals have governed in Atlantic Canada, and these parties have virtually monopolized federal representation. As Table 9.1 indicates, between 1963 and 1988 the combined support for the federal Liberals and Conservatives was extremely high. On only 2 of 36 occasions did support for the traditional parties dip below 80 per cent, while on 22 occasions the support was at least at the 90 per cent level. However, there were some differences between the island provinces of Newfoundland and Prince Edward Island, on the one hand, and Nova Scotia and New Brunswick on the other. In the mainland provinces, support for the older two parties did not reach the 90 per cent plateau after 1968, while in the rest of the region it continued to exceed that level more often than not in Newfoundland and without exception in PEI.

The relatively high and consistent level of support for the two parties disguised variations in support during the third-party system. As Table 9.2 shows, the range in

Table 9.1: Combined Federal Liberal–PC Popular Vote (%), 1963–1997

	1963	1965	1968	1972	1974	1979	1980	1984	1988	1993	1997
Nfld	95	97	95	94	91	69	83	93	87	94	75
PEI	98	98	97	92	95	93	93	93	91	92	83
NS	94	91	93	87	89	81	79	84	88	76	59
NB	87	90	94	88	80	85	83	86	85	84	68

Source: Tony J. Coulson, 'Statistical Appendices: Canadian Election Results, 1925–1993' (Appendix B) in A. Brian Tanguay and Alain-G. Gagnon, eds, *Canadian Parties in Transition* (Toronto: Nelson Canada, 1996); 1997 results from Elections Canada, *1997 Offical Voting Results: Synopsis.*

Table 9.2: Third-Party System, 1963–1988: Federal Popular Vote Range (%) and Mean

	Liberal Range	Mean	PC Range	Mean	NDP Range	Mean
Nfld	36–65	48	30–57	42	1–31	10
PEI	41–50	45	41–54	50	2–7	5
NS	33–47	40	39–55	48	6–21	12
NB	32–50	45	33–53	42	4–16	10

Source: Coulson, ('Statistical Appendices', Appendix B).

popular vote for each party was by no means narrow. The failure to elect many New Democrats did not indicate a static electorate unwilling to transfer their support from one party to another, since there were significant variations in the success rates of the Liberals and Conservatives.

The 1997 Election

The 1993 election, with its repudiation of a Conservative government, marked a sharp departure from the patterns of support evident throughout the third-party system. Between 1963 and 1988, all federal elections were dominated by the Liberals and Conservatives. In none of these elections did the vote share of these parties fall as low as the highest vote share obtained by the NDP. When the Liberals formed the government, the Conservatives were the official opposition, and when the Tories were in government, the Liberals held official opposition status. The New Democrats were the only other party to consistently receive representation in the House of Commons, but their vote share never surpassed 20 per cent. Although the third-party system was marked by regional differences in support patterns, in Atlantic Canada, support for the Liberals, Conservatives, and New Democrats essentially reflected the general pattern. The one exception was that the overall level of NDP support in the region was somewhat lower than it was in the rest of the country.[10] In 1993 the Conservative vote in the Atlantic region, as in all of Canada, fell to all-time lows, and the Tories elected only one member. Nonetheless, they remained the main regional competitor for the Liberals.

In Atlantic Canada, the 1997 election marked an even sharper departure from the norms of this system as the NDP surpassed its previous popular vote highs in three provinces, thereby producing record lows in the combined Liberal and Conservative vote. Although the Conservatives enjoyed the advantage of a popular leader, Jean Charest, and a Liberal government whose changes to the unemployment insurance program and emphasis on deficit reduction had left it unpopular in the region, the Tory vote remained below their third-party system low in PEI and Nova Scotia, and below previous mean levels of support in the rest of the region.

These results continued a period of electoral volatility which had commenced in 1984, as shown in Table 9.3. During this relatively brief period, support for the Conservative party ranged from a high of 58 per cent, in Newfoundland in 1984, to a low of 24 per cent, in Nova Scotia in 1993. Similarly, Liberal support peaked at 67 per cent, in Newfoundland in 1993, and in 1997 bottomed out at 28 per cent, in Nova Scotia. For the NDP, while the 1997 election results were clearly the best of times, their 1993 results were equally clearly the worst of times. In 1993, the NDP won only 5.3 per cent of the popular vote in Atlantic Canada, but in 1997 their share climbed to an unprecedented 23.7 per cent.[11] (All results calculated from Elections Canada, *Official Voting Results: Synopsis* for 1993 and 1997).

Despite movements in votes, the most dramatic changes were in the partisan composition of the region's parliamentary caucus. In 1997, for the first time, no party was able to win a majority of the region's seats. The NDP, with a quarter of the region's seats, managed to double the number of seats it had won in the entire third-party system up to that time. Strange things, indeed, had been happening in Atlantic Canada.

How are we to make sense of this? Had partisan support in Atlantic Canada realigned, or did the recent electoral volatility indicate a stable state of de-alignment? In an attempt to answer these questions, let us scrutinize the NDP's 1997 'Atlantic Breakthrough',[12] as Alan Whitehorn called it, along with recent provincial election results and voter surveys from the 1997 Canadian Election Study, which can be used to consider voting and party identification at the individual level.

A careful examination of the 1997 results reveals that euphoria over the unprecedented NDP breakthrough needed to be restrained. Although the party finally demonstrated an ability to win seats in the region, it remained third in regional preferences and seats. All of the eight seats won by the NDP were in Nova Scotia and New

Table 9.3: Popular Vote by Party (%), 1984–1997

	Liberal				PC				NDP				Reform	
---	84	88	93	97	84	88	93	97	84	88	93	97	93	97
Nfld	36	45	67	38	58	42	27	37	6	12	4	22	1	3
PEI	41	50	60	45	54	42	32	38	6	8	5	15	1	2
NS	34	47	52	28	51	41	24	31	15	11	7	30	13	10
NB	32	45	56	33	54	40	28	35	14	9	5	18	9	13

Brunswick, and seven of the eight wins occurred in areas that the party has previously represented in provincial legislatures. Aside from these seats, New Democratic support in Atlantic Canada was limited. In 18 of the 32 constituencies in the region, the NDP attracted less than a fifth of the vote, while in 12 of those ridings, its candidate did not even win the 15 per cent of the popular vote necessary to recover the deposit. The party owed its moderate success to its selection of Alexa McDonough as leader, the unpopularity of the Liberal government, and the competitive weakness of the Conservative party.

Six of the NDP victories were in Nova Scotia or, more specifically, in Cape Breton and Metropolitan Halifax. Historically, the core of CCF-NDP support in Atlantic Canada has been in Cape Breton. As recently as 1979, the party held one of the area's federal seats and four in the provincial legislature. Since 1980, the party has increased its support in Metro Halifax and has consistently secured representation in the provincial legislature. The party has not, however, been as successful on the rural mainland, a trend which persisted in 1997. The New Democrats swept the Metro Halifax and Cape Breton seats but could not record even a second-place result in the rest of the province. The election results in Nova Scotia point out the relevance of intra-provincial regionalism (see Table 9.4). Support for the NDP ranged from 46 per cent in Cape Breton to 37 per cent in Metro Halifax and just 19 per cent in the rest of the province. The Tories dominated the rural mainland with support levels twice that of the New Democrats and with the Liberals serving as the main opponent.

Support for Reform aided the New Democrats in Nova Scotia. Despite advocating policies that many commentators felt were hostile to Atlantic Canada, Reform took 14 per cent of the rural mainland vote and 10 per cent of the Halifax vote. Indeed, in two of the four Halifax ridings the combined PC-Reform vote exceeded that of the victorious NDP. This suggests that the NDP victories in Metro Halifax benefited from a Tory-Reform vote split.

In these Metro Halifax ridings, the personal impact of Alexa McDonough was undoubtedly strong. McDonough, who had represented a Halifax riding provincially for more than a decade, took 49 per cent of the votes in her riding, but none of her fellow Halifax New Democrats surpassed 35 per cent. With such close results, it seems reasonable to conclude that McDonough's personal popularity and the Tory-Reform vote split were important factors in the Atlantic breakthrough, at least in Nova Scotia.

The New Brunswick results at first glance appear more significant. The party overcame its traditional weakness among francophone voters by recording victories in two

Table 9.4: Nova Scotia Mean Popular Vote, by Region, 1997

	Metro Halifax	Cape Breton	Rural Mainland
Liberal	27	32	28
PC	26	22	38
NDP	37	46	19
Reform	10	—	14

ridings with francophone majorities. And only one of these victories came in an area where they had experienced earlier electoral success.[13] However, in the other ridings with a substantial proportion of francophone voters, their share of the popular vote did not reach the 20 per cent level, and the party finished a distant third. As in Nova Scotia, regional voting patterns were obvious, and the New Democrats were not competitive in all regions. In the five ridings in the predominantly English-speaking portion of the province, the New Democrats trailed even Reform (see Table 9.5).[14] A discussion of political change in the Atlantic region must note the demonstrated ability of Reform to attract votes in southern New Brunswick, where the party garnered more than 20 per cent of the vote in four of five ridings. These areas have also provided disproportionate support to the Confederation of Regions (COR) Party in provincial elections.[15]

Interpretations of NDP victories in Cape Breton and New Brunswick must address the possibility that these results were intended to express dissatisfaction with the Liberal government. Although New Democrats had enjoyed some provincial success in these areas, the four seats were considered among the safest federal Liberal seats not just in the region, but in the country. The two Cape Breton seats remained Liberal even during the 1984 Tory sweep, and in 1993 each of the incumbent Liberals was returned with more than 60 per cent of the votes cast. The Beausejour seat in New Brunswick was similarly safe. It was the only New Brunswick seat not to succumb to the Tory tide of 1984 and was sufficiently secure that Jean Chrétien chose it as the site for his return to Parliament after winning the Liberal leadership in 1990.[16] The remaining New Brunswick seat, Acadie Bathurst, covered an area that had failed to return a Liberal only once in the previous century[17] and was represented by the province's only cabinet minister.[18] New Democratic success in traditionally safe Liberal seats, two of which were held by powerful cabinet ministers, may well indicate a desire to send a message of dissatisfaction to the Liberal government rather than substantial political change.

Changes in the Provincial Party Systems

In a discussion of party organization in Canada, Rand Dyck[19] explained that linkages and co-operation between the federal and provincial parties have traditionally been stronger in the Atlantic region than elsewhere in the country. Similarly, R.K. Carty's study of constituency-level party activities revealed the greater propensity of Atlantic Canadian activists to pursue activities at both the federal and provincial level.[20] Given

Table 9.5: New Brunswick Mean Popular Vote North vs. South, 1997

	North of Diagonal	South of Diagonal
Liberal	39	26
PC	29	43
NDP	24	10
Reform	7	21

the close linkages between federal and provincial parties in Atlantic Canada, any comprehensive assessment of political realignment needs to examine provincial election results. Change at both levels would provide stronger evidence that partisanship in the region has been transformed. Indeed, recent provincial elections (as shown in Table 9.6) have provided mixed messages, giving further support to the contention that a regional focus downplays the provincial peculiarities.

This is most obvious in Nova Scotia, where the 1998 and 1999 elections provided an indication that patterns of popular support had shifted and that the beneficiary of this shift was the New Democratic Party. In both of these elections the New Democrats received higher vote shares than they had in previous elections. Indeed, in 1998 the NDP vote was greater than that of the Tories, while in 1999 it exceeded the Liberal total. Nonetheless, the party was not able to completely replicate its federal success. In both elections, the party did very well in Metro Halifax, winning most of that region's seats. However, the Liberals recovered sufficiently from the 1997 federal debacle to remain the dominant party in Cape Breton. The Tories dominated the rural mainland and, in 1999, received sufficient support in Metro Halifax to form a majority government. The New Democrats had hoped that their strong showings in the 1997 federal election and the 1998 provincial election would lead them into government in 1999. This did not happen, however, as Nova Scotians unhappy with the Liberal government bypassed the NDP and elected the Tories.[21]

The results in Halifax suggest that the federal NDP's success there was based on more than vote splits and a 'native daughter' effect. The provincial results in 1998 and 1999 confirmed that the NDP had made substantial inroads in that part of the province, even without the popular Alexa McDonough leading the party. Recent seat redistributions, which had given the city its proportionate share of provincial seats, have also given the party a very valuable base in Halifax. NDP support in that region seems unlikely to dissipate, and the party should remain competitive in both federal and provincial elections.

The Cape Breton results suggested more complexity. With a Cape Bretoner as leader, the provincial Liberals recovered from their weak federal showing to carry the region in both 1998 and 1999. Although the New Democrats remained competitive, the party will likely experience difficulties in holding Cape Breton and Metro Halifax simultaneously. As Agar Adamson and Ian Stewart have pointed out, 'enmity between the two major geographic regions of Nova Scotia continues to the present day'.[22] The

Table 9.6: Popular Vote in Provincial Elections (%)

	Liberal	PC	NDP
Nfld (Feb. 1999)	50	41	8
PEI (Nov. 1996)	34	58	8
NS (July 1999)	30	38	31
NS (Mar. 1998)	35	30	35
NB (June 1999)	37	53	9

federal decision in 1999 to close mines on Cape Breton illustrates some of the difficulties involved here. It is quite possible that the provincial Liberals will suffer some
of the wrath that should be directed at the federal Liberal party for the job losses that
will ensue from mine closures. On the other hand, it has been suggested that these
closings might have been averted if the region had re-elected Cape Breton cabinet
minister David Dingwall in 1997. Island voters may believe that the loss of representation in the federal cabinet may have had very negative consequences for both the
island and the province. Such a belief is unlikely to increase the number of future
federal NDP votes.

In contrast to the Nova Scotian results, the 1999 Newfoundland provincial election
provided little evidence for a consolidation of NDP support. While the party attracted
22 per cent of the 1997 federal vote, its share of the provincial vote was only 8 per cent.
Admittedly, this was up almost 4 percentage points from the previous provincial election, and the party increased its legislative presence from one to two. Nonetheless, the
lesson of the 1999 provincial election is that, in Newfoundland, government remains
a choice between Liberals and Conservatives.

Essentially the same inference may be drawn from both the 1999 New Brunswick
election and the 2000 PEI election. In New Brunswick, despite the collapse of the COR
party, the NDP share of the popular vote fell slightly from its share in 1995. The party
garnered less than 9 per cent of the vote and elected only one member. As of 2000,
there were as many elected New Democrats in the House of Commons as there were
in the Provincial legislature. Clearly, the federal success did not spill over into provincial politics. In Prince Edward Island, the NDP secured its first legislative seat in 1996,
but in 2000 the member was unable to hold his seat and the party's share of the popular vote remained a paltry 8 per cent. It appears that the vote increases the NDP
received in the 1997 federal election were not indicative of a general movement
towards that party.

Our analysis of the aggregate federal and provincial election results suggest that the
NDP breakthrough in 1997 must be interpreted cautiously. Although partisan politics
in Nova Scotia has been transformed, the province's regional divisions remained
important and the NDP was not on the verge of domination. In the Atlantic region at
large, aside from Metro Halifax and Cape Breton, the Liberals and Conservatives
retained a huge advantage. At present only three of the 130 legislative seats in
Newfoundland, PEI, and New Brunswick are occupied by New Democrats.

Party Identification and Voting Behaviour

Individual-level data provided by the 1997 CES lend further support to the contention
that the NDP's Atlantic breakthrough did not constitute political realignment.[23] At the
most basic level, the 1997 CES provided no indication that identification with the NDP
was growing in Atlantic Canada. (See Table 9.7 for a presentation of federal party
identification figures for 1988, 1993, and 1997.)[24]

Identification with the Conservative party was down only slightly from 1988 (when
there were no Reform candidates in Atlantic Canada), while identification with the

Table 9.7: Federal Party Identification in Atlantic Canada (weighted)

	Liberal	PC	NDP	Reform	None	N
1988	28	32	5	—	35	n=273
1993	45	21	6	2	25	n=264
1997	31	25	5	3	36	n=260

Source: 1988 results from Richard Johnston, André Blais, Henry E. Brady, and Jean Crête, *Letting the People Decide: Dynamics of a Canadian Election* (Montreal and Kingston: McGill-Queen's University Press, 1992); 1993 CES, 1997 CES.

Liberal party was greater than in 1988, when the party won 20 of the region's seats. Overall, the proportion of Atlantic Canadians identifying with one of the two major parties remained relatively stable at 60 per cent in 1988, 65 per cent in 1993, and 56 per cent in 1997, and there was no significant increase in the number of Atlantic Canadians not identifying with any party.

The regional differences apparent in the aggregate results in Nova Scotia and New Brunswick provided a hint that, despite 1997's unprecedented results, the social bases of partisan support in the region had not undergone a dramatic break from traditional patterns.[25] This impression is strengthened by the individual-level data, which reveals that religion remained significantly associated with voting in Atlantic Canada. Sixty-one per cent of the Liberal voters in the region were Catholic, while 63 per cent of Conservatives and 82 per cent of Reformers were Protestant. Despite their victories in New Brunswick, the New Democrats drew only 40 per cent of their support from Catholics. The Liberal party continued to enjoy disproportionate support from French-speaking Atlantic Canadians, and the New Democratic support from non-union households remained relatively low (see Table 9.8).

Realignment or Dealignment?

It thus appears that the 1997 election results do not justify the contention that a substantial realignment in partisan identification occurred in Atlantic Canada. Russell Dalton et al. explained that there are 'three general types of electoral periods—stable

Table 9.8: 1997 Vote by Religion, Language Spoken at Home, and Union Household (%)

	Liberal	PC	NDP	Reform	N
No religion	24	21	43	12	n=11
Protestant	15	43	24	17	n=101
Catholic	37	31	26	3	n=76
French-speaking	39	20	30	—	n=25
English-speaking	23	40	25	13	n=166
Union household	26	29	33	8	n=71
Non-union household	25	42	20	13	n=115

Source: 1997 CES (weighted).

alignments, realignments, and dealignments. . . . What is different about periods of stability is that the coalitional basis of long-term support for the respective parties remains unaltered. Inter-election differences represent only momentary defections from enduring partisan loyalties.'[26] Although NDP support grew substantially between 1993 and 1997, that electoral period is best described as one of stable alignment. There was no direct evidence of realignment among individual voters.[27] There were some indications of dealignment. As Table 9.3 indicated, there was much volatility in regional vote patterns over the 1984–97 period, and it is also true that the proportion of the electorate that declined to vote rose.[28] But according to Dalton et al., 'dealignment is a period during which the party-affiliated portion of the electorate shrinks as the traditional party coalition dissolves'.[29] This does not accurately depict the state of federal partisanship in Atlantic Canada.

Short-Term Factors

The surprising 1997 results grew from the inability of the Liberal party both to attract votes from those who did not identify with any party and to limit the defection of its own identifiers. Among Atlantic Canadians who claimed no party identification, Liberal support trailed that of the New Democrats (who won plurality backing), the Conservatives, and Reform. Even more importantly, more than two-fifths of Liberal identifiers defected to other parties, with 22 per cent voting NDP and 18 per cent opting for the Tories (see Table 9.9). More than a quarter of the votes cast for New Democratic candidates came from Liberal identifiers.

Atlantic Canadians expected more from a Liberal government. After all, the Atlantic region was the only one to reward the Liberals with majority support in the important 1988 election. Furthermore, no region was stronger in support for the Liberals in 1993. Traditionally, the government caucus from the Atlantic region was able to 'act as a lobby for regional needs and the conduit for regional benefits'.[30] Support for governing parties was based in part on the assumption that this would continue to be effective and thus 'the traditional parties were the only ones in the game, with the idea of voting for a third party seen by most to be either nonsensical or to be inviting potentially punitive ramifications'.[31] The actions of the Liberal government in reforming the Employment Insurance program and reducing the level of spending on social programs raised serious questions about this assumption. The

Table 9.9: 1997 Vote by Party Identification (%)

	Liberal Vote	PC Vote	NDP Vote	Reform Vote	N
None	12	32	37	18	n=62
Liberal	59	18	22	1	n=58
PC	4	75	11	9	n=44
NDP	—	34	66	—	n=9
Reform	15	—	—	85	n=6

Source: 1997 CES (weighted).

large 1993 caucus proved ineffective in protecting regional 'entitlements'[32] and the Liberals seemed unresponsive to regional concerns. Both the Conservatives and New Democrats believed that Atlantic Canadians were unimpressed with the Liberal record. As Peter Woolstencroft explained in his analysis of the Tory campaign, the party believed that 'there was a strong anti-government sentiment in Atlantic Canada that could only redound to their advantage ... driven by the Liberal failure to produce jobs for the region and exacerbated by resentment over the harmonization of the GST and provincial sales taxes'.[33] Similarly, Alan Whitehorn maintained that 'the Atlantic region, with Canada's highest rate of unemployment, had been hit hard by the Liberal government's cuts to the UI program',[34] and Geoff Martin suggested that this was especially true of francophone and coastal New Brunswickers.[35]

The 1997 CES revealed the depth of this dissatisfaction with the Liberal record. More than three-fifths of Atlantic Canadians believed that the cuts implemented by the Chrétien government were 'unfair'. The Liberals were able to attract only 11 per cent of the vote from individuals with this opinion.[36] More strikingly, 43 per cent of Liberal identifiers held this position. Thus, even people predisposed to support the party were unhappy with its record.

Atlantic dissatisfaction with a Liberal party traditionally meant a migration of voters to the Conservatives. Certainly in the past, as Bickerton noted, 'the region seemingly has had valid reason to reject the traditional parties, if one accepts that relative economic deprivation or inequality is often a cause of, or an ingredient in political protest'.[37] Nonetheless, these valid reasons did not translate into third-party support. The 1997 results showed that in that election, the New Democrats were the primary beneficiaries of such dissatisfaction. Part of the explanation for this rests with the changed competitive position of the Conservatives. In previous elections, there had been a reasonable expectation that shifting votes from the Liberals to the Conservatives could produce a change in government without jeopardizing a strong regional voice within the government caucus. In 1997, however, Atlantic Canadians did not believe that the Conservatives were likely to form a government, so considerations of this sort were not relevant.[38]

The competitive weakness of the Progressive Conservative party was obviously influenced by the existence of the Reform party. The strong Reform base in western Canada undoubtedly contributed to the Atlantic perception that the Conservatives could not win the election, and the presence of a Reform candidate on the ballot likely cost the Conservatives victory in a handful of Atlantic ridings. Reform's existence also influenced the kind of campaign the Conservatives were able to run. The party was unable to run a national campaign. As William Cross pointed out, 'More than any other party, the Conservatives came the closest to offering different electorates contradictory messages'.[39] They focused on health care and social policy in Atlantic Canada while stressing tax cuts in voter-rich Ontario. Despite this (or perhaps because of this) the Conservatives displayed the strong base they possessed in the Atlantic region by attracting the largest regional vote share and winning a plurality of the region's seats. In any analysis of the 1997 election results in the region it is important not to lose sight of the fact that the Progressive Conservatives party, which had elected only one Atlantic MP in 1993 and garnered less than a third of the regional vote, in essence, won the 'Atlantic election'.

The competitive position of the New Democrats was improved by both the relative weakness of the Tories and the unpopularity of the Liberal government. Additionally, the NDP had helped to position itself as a legitimate voice for regional discontent by selecting Alexa McDonough as leader. For the first time in its history, the party was led by an Atlantic Canadian, and Whitehorn maintains that 'the new MPs from Atlantic Canada owe a great deal to her profile and performance.'[40]

Voter surveys lend some support to this contention. Atlantic Canadians felt most warmly towards Charest, but McDonough was rated more highly than Chrétien. More importantly, in Nova Scotia, where the NDP received more than half of its regional votes, McDonough was rated more favourably than both Charest and Chrétien, and the NDP surpassed the Conservatives in positive feelings (see Table 9.10). Other survey evidence presented by Marzoli indicates that a plurality of Atlantic Canadians believed the NDP was the best party to represent the region's interests and viewed McDonough 'as the most regionally sensitive of the leaders and as their "native daughter"'.[41]

An unpopular provincial Liberal government compounded the party's problems in Nova Scotia. Both Liberal Premier John Savage and his Tory predecessor Donald Cameron had taken controversial steps towards reducing the use of patronage in provincial politics. As Adamson and Stewart explained, 'The selection of Donald Cameron in 1992 by the PCs marked a clear change in Nova Scotia politics. . . . John Savage is his logical successor when it comes to reform.'[42] These attempts to reduce patronage had two effects. First, a reduction in patronage removed one of the historic impediments to voting NDP.[43] Second, many Tories and Liberals were angry at the changes their leaders had instituted and were less willing to work for their party in an election campaign.[44] These reforms appear to have weakened both the Liberals and Conservatives and therefore worked to the advantage of the NDP.

In none of the other provinces were incumbent governments as unpopular or were premiers as intent on eradicating patronage. Thus, not surprisingly, the evidence of partisan change is largely limited to Nova Scotia. Two other pieces of evidence support this contention. First, outside Nova Scotia, the Liberals and Conservatives remained

Table 9.10: Party and Leader Mean Thermometer Ratings, 1997

	Charest	Chrétien	McDonough	Liberal	PC	NDP
Region	54.7	51.0	53.5	50.8	48.1	47.1
Nfld	52.1	46.6	49.1	45.9	47.1	45.3
PEI	53.2	56.3	51.0	55.2	50.9	44.7
NS	52.2	54.2	55.9	49.7	46.8	48.6
NB	56.5	51.1	52.2	49.4	53.1	46.2

Source: 1997 CES (Data for region weighted).

well in front of the NDP in the popular vote. Second, 1997 party identification patterns differed significantly by province, with Nova Scotians less likely to identify with the Liberals and more likely to claim no partisan identification (see Table 9.11).

In Newfoundland, Prince Edward Island, and New Brunswick, more than 60 per cent of the electorate continued to identify themselves as Liberal or Conservative, while in Nova Scotia only 46 per cent of the electorate made such an identification, and 45 per cent of Nova Scotians indicated that they had no party identification. This does not mean that the NDP breakthrough represented a partisan realignment even in Nova Scotia, but it does mean that the party did not have to confront an electoral majority identifying with its opponents.

Conclusion

This chapter has argued that the unprecedented election results of 1997 did not indicate major changes in regional partisanship. Rather, the relative Liberal and Conservative weakness and the concomitant NDP strength stemmed from the confluence of a number of short-term factors. These included a popular NDP leader from Atlantic Canada, a federal Liberal government whose cuts were perceived as unfair by more than three-fifths of the region's voters, and a right-wing alternative party that drew support from the Conservative party, forcing it to mount a campaign that varied by region and made it less likely that Atlantic voters would perceive the Tories as an alternative government. In Nova Scotia, these factors were compounded by an unpopular provincial government and the controversial efforts of both Conservative and Liberal governments to eliminate patronage. Partisanship in Nova Scotia may well have changed in ways that have not yet occurred in the rest of the region. Indeed, the overall regional picture has partially obscured both the changes in Nova Scotia and Reform's base in New Brunswick.

Political realignment did not occur in 1997, and in 2000 the New Democrats lost ground in both votes and seats. Nonetheless, federal election results display a substantial degree of volatility, and the current period may be transitional. In the long run, the proximate causes of an electoral breakthrough are less important than how parties respond to the new electoral challenges. The actions of the Mulroney and the first-term Chrétien governments clearly suggested a lack of concern about the possibility of losing support in the Atlantic region. This is not overly surprising, since the region has only 10 per cent of the seats in the House of Commons and history told the

Table 9.11: Provincial Variations in Federal Party Identification (%)

	Liberal	PC	NDP	Reform	NONE	N
Nfld	40	24	6	—	30	n=90
PEI	34	26	6	—	34	n=88
NS	29	17	7	2	45	n=87
NB	29	32	3	6	30	n=87

Source: 1997 CES.

Liberals and Conservatives that they could take for granted support in the Atlantic region. In 1988, an unpopular Conservative government held on to 12 of the region's seats and in 1997 an even less popular Liberal government won 11.

The 2000 election indicated that the Liberals and Tories were placing a somewhat greater emphasis on the Atlantic region. The Liberals were hoping that an increase in seats in the Atlantic region could offset potential losses elsewhere, while the Tories needed Atlantic seats to retain official party status. By responding to some of the region's concerns, the Liberals increased their seats in the region to 19, and the New Democrats lost half of the eight seats they won in 1997. Equally troubling for the notion of an electoral realignment was the fact that the Conservatives more than doubled the NDP in regional seats.

The New Democrats remain a third party in Atlantic Canada, albeit one that has demonstrated a regional base within the region. Although there has not been a general political realignment, the New Democrats have become a major player in the Metro Halifax region. In 2000, the party won three of the four federal seats in Metro Halifax, and of the 14 provincial seats it holds in Atlantic Canada, 10 are in the Halifax area. Finally, the party has a secure regional beachhead.

NOTES

1. Jon H. Pammett, 'Tracking the Votes' in Alan Frizzell, Jon H. Pammett, and Anthony Westell, eds, *The Canadian General Election of 1993* (Ottawa: Carleton University Press, 1994), 143.

2. Richard Johnston, André Blais, Henry E. Brady, and Jean Créte, *Letting the People Decide: Dynamics of a Canadian Election* (Montreal and Kingston: McGill-Queen's University Press, 1992).

3. Rand Dyck, *Provincial Politics in Canada* (Scarborough, Ont.: Prentice Hall, 1986), 29–30.

4. Munroe Eagles, James P. Bickerton, Alain-G. Gagnon, and Patrick J. Smith, *The Almanac of Canadian Politics* (Toronto: Oxford University Press, 1995).

5. R.K. Carty, 'Three Canadian Party Systems' in George Perlin, ed., *Party Democracy in Canada* (Scarborough, Ont.: Prentice Hall, 1988).

6. Donald Smiley, *The Federal Condition in Canada* (Toronto: McGraw Hill Ryerson, 1987).

7. Richard Simeon and David J. Elkins, 'Provincial Political Cultures in Canada' in David J. Elkins and Richard Simeon, eds, *Small Worlds: Provinces and Parties in Canadian Political Life* (Toronto: Methuen, 1980).

8. Ian Stewart, *Roasting Chestnuts: The Mythology of Maritime Political Culture* (Vancouver: University of British Columbia Press, 1994).

9. Ibid., 43.

10. See Carty, 'Three Canadian Party Systems' for a full discussion of the third-party system, as well as the party systems which preceded it.

11. Another indication of the unprecedented NDP strength in Atlantic Canada in 1997 can be seen by comparing the percentage of the party's total vote coming from the region in 1993

and 1997. In 1993 Atlantic Canada contributed only 6.5 per cent of the NDP vote; in 1997 the region accounted for 23.7 per cent. All results calculated from the Elections Canada *Official Results: Synopsis* for 1993 and 1997.

12. Alan Whitehorn, 'Alexa McDonough and the Atlantic Breakthrough for the New Democratic Party' in Alan Frizzell and Jon Pammett, eds, *The Canadian General Election of 1997* (Toronto: Dundurn Press, 1997).

13. The first NDP victory in New Brunswick came provincially in the Tantramar riding, which lies within the federal riding of Beausejour.

14. Patrick Fitzpatrick, in his account of New Brunswick politics, indicated that a diagonal could be 'drawn from Grand Falls in the north west to Sackville in the south east: north of this diagonal all districts are either French or mixed . . . south of the diagonal the population is predominantly English'. See Patrick Fitzpatrick, 'New Brunswick: The Politics of Pragmatism' in Martin Robin, ed., *Canadian Provincial Politics* (Scarborough, Ont.: Prentice Hall, 1972).

15. The Confederation of Regions party (COR) is a right-of-centre party often associated with its opposition to official bilingualism. It formed the official opposition in New Brunswick from 1991 to 1995. For a discussion of COR and its rise and fall see Martin (1998). Although Martin describes the 'fall' of COR in the 1995 provincial election, COR outpolled the NDP in 20 of 36 ridings and in the cities of Fredericton and Moncton. It fell to less than 1 per cent of the vote in the 1999 provincial election. See Geoffrey Martin, 'We've Seen It All Before: the Rise and Fall of the COR Party of New Brunswick, 1988-1995', *Journal of Canadian Studies* (1998).

16. In the Beausejour riding there were some discussions even within the NDP's Election Planning Committee about the desire of local voters to defeat the Liberals. As Geoffrey Martin explains, 'One member of the EPC argued during the campaign that we should ask people to "Vote Angela" rather than "Elect Angela". He based this on the view that, had people thought Angela Vautour would win, they might not have voted for her, given that many people, the argument goes, just wanted to throw a scare into the Liberals by making it a close contest.' See Geoffrey Martin, 'Anatomy of an Upset: The Angela Vautour-NDP Coalition in Beasejour-Petitcodiac', a paper presented at the annual meeting of the Atlantic Provinces Political Science Association, Sydney, Nova Scotia, 1997. Vautour's personal commitment to the NDP was demonstrated in September 1999 when she crossed the floor to sit as a Tory.

17. Eagles et al., *Almanac.*

18. Rand Dyck, 'Links Between Federal and Provincial Parties and Party Systems' in Herman Bakvis, ed., *Representation, Integration and Political Parties in Canada* (Toronto: Dundurn Press, 1991).

19. See R.K. Carty, *Canadian Political Parties in the Constituencies* (Toronto: Dundurn Press, 1991), 50.

20. Support for the NDP declined by 4 percentage points in the 1999 election and the party lost 8 of its 19 seats.

21. Agar Adamson and Ian Stewart, 'Party Politics in the Not So Mysterious East' in Hugh Thorburn, ed., *Party Politics in Canada* (Scarborough, Ont.: Prentice Hall, 1996), 506.

22. Data from the 1997 Canadian Election Study were provided by the Institute for Social Research, York University. The survey was funded by the Social Sciences and Humanities Research Council of Canada (SSHRC), grant number 412–96–007, and was completed for the 1997 Canadian election team of André Blais (Université de Montréal), Elisabeth Gidengil (McGill University), Richard Nadeau (Université de Montréal), and Neil Nevitte (University of Toronto). The Institute for Social Research, SSHRC, and the Canadian Election Survey Team are not responsible for the analyses and interpretations presented here.

24. Ironically, its highest level of identification came in 1993, when the party received its lowest level of popular support.

25. Johnston et al. argue that one must look beyond the overall numbers in understanding party identification because also 'central is how the parties fit into the social structure'. See Richard Johnston et al., *Letting the People Decide*.

26. Russell J. Dalton, Paul Allen Beck, and Scott C. Flanagan, 'Electoral Change in Advanced Industrial Democracies' in Russell J. Dalton, Scott C. Flanagan, and Paul Allen Beck, eds, *Electoral Change in Advanced Industrial Democracies: Realignment or Dealignment?* (Princeton: Princeton University Press, 1984), 11.

27. It is important to remember that these conclusions are not based on panel data.

28. In both 1993 and 1997 the turnout in all four provinces was below the mean for the third party system.

29. Dalton, 'Electoral Change', 14.

30. James Bickerton, 'Parties and Regions: Alternative Models of Representation' in Brian Tanguay and James Bickerton, eds, *Canadian Parties in Transition* (Toronto: Nelson, 1996), 503.

31. Ibid., 505.

32. Michael Marzolini, 'The Regionalization of Canadian Politics' in Frizzell and Pammett, eds, *The Canadian General Election of 1997*, 200.

33. Peter Woolstencroft, 'On the Ropes Again? The Campaign of the Progressive Conservative Party in the 1997 Federal Election' in Frizzell and Pammett, eds, *The Canadian General Election of 1997*, 80–1.

34. Alan Whitehorn, 'Alexa McDonough and the Atlantic Breakthrough', 106.

35. Martin, 'Anatomy of an Upset', 4.

36. Among voters who believed the cuts were unfair, the vote share was PC 42 per cent, NDP 32 per cent, Reform 13 per cent, and Liberal 11 per cent. The Liberals were supported by 45 per cent of those who believed the cuts were fair while the Tories gained the support of 30 per cent, the NDP 16 per cent, and Reform 8 per cent.

37. Bickerton, 'Parties and Regions', 503.

38. The Conservatives received majority support from the minority of voters who felt the party had a better than even chance of winning the election.

39. William Cross, 'The Increasing Importance of Region to Canadian Election Campaigns', in this volume.

40. Whitehorn, 'Alexa McDonough and the Atlantic Breakthrough', 106.

41. Ibid., 203.

42. Adamson and Stewart, 'Party Politics', 525.

43. See Bickerton, 'Parties and Regions'.

44. Adamson and Stewart, 'Party Politics'.

Part 4

Comparative Perspectives on Regionalism

Introduction

Regionalism is not a uniquely Canadian phenomenon. The final chapters in this volume enrich the discussion of regionalism's importance in political systems by providing comparative accounts and by exploring the interaction between regionalism and globalization. The chapters suggest that regionalism and sub-national loyalties remain an important variable in the study of party systems, political institutions, and political cultures in this age of globalization. As chapters by Hudson Meadwell and Anthony Sayers show, there is already a high degree of complexity in the interaction between regionalism and political institutions at the domestic level. The question that Livianna Tossutti addresses is how to understand regionalism and persistent sub-national loyalties in light of the apparent impact of globalization on states, political systems, and political cultures. Not surprisingly, one of her most important conclusions is that new technologies and world views influence the behaviour of citizens, groups, and parties, thereby increasing the complexity of contemporary political systems.

Hudson Meadwell's chapter analyzes secessionist movements in contemporary democracies. Secession, or exit, is the ultimate manifestation of regionalism and emerges almost exclusively in regions with distinctive ethnic majorities. Meadwell observes that the most powerful movement for independence among industrialized democracies is found in Quebec. He attributes the success of this movement to the institutional design of the Canadian state, which he terms 'consociational federalism'. This institutional design, according to Meadwell, encourages secessionist challenges as it shapes political identities, the political feasibility of secession, and the opportunity structures of movement activists and entrepreneurs.

In Chapter 11, Anthony Sayers compares the impact of regionalism on political institutions in Canada and Australia—countries that share common cultural traditions and federal and parliamentary institutions. He argues that regionalism interacts with institutional characteristics, such as the appointed Senate and first-past-the-post electoral system in Canada, to produce particular kinds of political parties and relationships in Parliament between the Cabinet and the legislature.

Of course, the influence of region is not just at the level of institutions but also outcomes, and Sayers argues that in the current institutional environment, 'no political party can hope to provide an integrative vision of the country for all Canadians'. Instead, parties must compete in an environment of electoral volatility. The electoral system rewards parties for strong provincial bases of support and the capacity to create alliances amongst these bases, rather than for attempting to promote grand integrative visions. The result is a politically powerful Cabinet that assumes the task of representation and accommodation of diverse interests at the highest level, 'unshackled by detailed party platforms, clear ideologies, or the need to explain themselves at length to party members or to the Parliament'. The cost of doing political business this way can come in the area of democratic governance. The strength of regionalism in the political life of the country thus helps to account both for powerful executives and for the 'provincialization of Canadian politics over the last forty years'.

In Chapter 12, Livianna Tossutti provides an empirical analysis of the persistence of sub-national political identities in the age of globalization. In particular, she tests one of the central tenets of globalization theory: that the 'localism' impulse in globalization should be understood in terms of post-modern values—cosmopolitanism, pluralism—rather than pre-modern values of parochialism or modern values that emphasize standardization and conformity. Tossutti creates a comparative profile of the membership of the Lega Nord in Italy and the Bloc Québécois in Canada—two autonomist parties defined by their ethnic and territorial identities—to test the 'globalist-localist' theory, where 'renewed interest in territorial identification can be seen as the product of a global interconnectedness and possibilities for individual autonomy and group distinctiveness'.

Based on analysis of socio-demographic characteristics, issue opinions, and lifestyles, Tossutti finds that there are many explanations for the persistence of sub-national loyalties. Indeed, the post-modern profile fits only about 25 per cent of the Lega Nord members, and it is difficult to decipher a clear post-modern profile in the membership of the BQ. Tossutti finds strong support for her argument that there is a 'need to undertake a nuanced analysis of the "new" localism, rather than to accept unsubstantiated theories, including the modernization theory about the "inevitable decline of territorial and ethnic identities" or a simple theory of globalization and assumptions that localist impulses will reflect the postmodern characteristics of cosmopolitanism and openness to diversity".

Chapter 10

When Voice Encourages Exit[1]

HUDSON MEADWELL

The purpose of this chapter is to put the case of Quebec nationalism in a comparative cross-national context. Of course, this is not to underplay the importance of comparisons across provinces in Canada. It is to emphasize, however, the most striking feature of Quebec politics since the 1960s—the continuing importance of demands for independence. This is not a fleeting feature of Quebec politics. Nationalism and the demand for independence are solidly entrenched. In its politics, Quebec is not just like other provinces. Thus a cross-national perspective may add some value to the study of Quebec and, indeed, Canada. Yet, as I hope to show in this chapter, Quebec is also not quite like other sub-state nations in the advanced industrial world.

This discussion provides an opportunity to examine a piece of folk wisdom in the social sciences, commonly expressed in the saying 'voice discourages exit'. When applied to the politics of nationalism, this claim implies that the more a sub-state nation is accommodated politically, the lower will be the likelihood of its secession. On the contrary, I will argue, voice can encourage exit.

An analysis of the case of Quebec will provide some support for one generalization that is relevant to the arguments of this chapter: Support for separation varies with the degree of political institutional capacity that sub-state nations control. A corollary proposition is also considered: that support for separation increases after sub-state nations win local legislatures. Some of the political dynamics of Scotland, Catalonia, and the linguistic communities of Belgium are considered in light of this proposition. Evidence in support of this proposition is more mixed because of the political strategies of nationalist activists and the net effects of the European Union. All of the changes to territorial politics in these cases are relatively recent, however, and it is too early to conclude that separation is a dead issue in western Europe. Clearly it is not dead in North America.

Nothing is foreordained in any of the cases of sub-state nations within the advanced industrial world, including Quebec, but Quebec has advanced the farthest. It has the most powerful movement for independence. And no other sub-state nation, save perhaps the Flemish, yet has access to local political institutions as powerful as the political institutions of the Quebec provincial government. Nationalist activists and entrepreneurs in Quebec have been able to effectively organize and mobilize support for independence by using these institutions. As other sub-state nations achieve political innovations that decentralize territorial politics, will they converge toward the Quebec pattern? Or will there be, at least in the near and medium term, continuing differences?

The Case of Quebec

Within a 15-year period, two referendums were held in Quebec, in 1980 and 1995.[2] The last referendum was virtually a dead heat. Among francophones, the support for the 'Yes' side increased by almost 20 per cent from its 40 per cent in 1980. Three provincial governments since 1976 have been controlled by a party that supports significant change to the territorial status quo. Failure in constitutional negotiations also had the effect of notching up the level of support for sovereignty, although these effects may have declined with time. Despite the sensitivity of survey results to the wording of questions, there is consistent support for independence in various polls and surveys.[3] In no other case in the developed western world is there this combination of political leadership and organization, popular support, and referendum results. Other movements lag behind Quebec. It is instructive to consider why this case leads other sub-state nations and regions.

The explanation advanced in this chapter has two components: first, the institutional design of the Canadian state encourages sub-state nationalist mobilization, and second, there are no overarching supranational political institutions in North America that might compensate for the centrifugal tendencies of territorially decentralized power sharing in Canada. The design of the Canadian state encourages secessionist challenges in some parts of its territory, and is not nested in a larger design that could encourage cohesion. The institutional design of the Canadian state can be described as 'consociational federalism'.[4]

In the remainder of this section, alternative explanations of secession are considered and those properties of consociational federalism that increase the likelihood of secession are specified.

Some Explanations of Secession

Two arguments about *facilitating conditions* and two arguments about *proximate causes* of support for secession will be explored here. We shall then look at an institutional explanation of variations for support for secession that emphasizes the effects of political inclusion on demands for radical change.

1. *Supra-national political integration encourages territorial fragmentation.* This proposition suggests that supra-national integration creates new institutions that weaken constitutent states and strengthen the position of sub-state nationalists. According to this proposition, Quebec should lag behind other regions and sub-state nations in Europe because there is much more supra-national political integration in Europe than in North America. But this is clearly not the

case: Quebec is closer to separation than any sub-state unit in Europe, and there is no supra-national political integration in North America.[5]

2. *Economic integration encourages territorial fragmentation.* Freer trade in a regional trading system lowers economic dependence on the national economy, lowers the transition costs of independence, and contributes to economic viability when independence is achieved.[6] These effects should make the political mobilization of support for secession easier. However, economic interdependence and regional economic integration are features of the environments of all sub-state nationalist movements in the developed western world. While it is true that the European Community has entrenched a deeper form of economic integration than NAFTA, interdependence and integration are nevertheless characteristic of both Europe and North America. Thus it is not obvious that economic integration can account for the comparative strength of the secessionist option in Quebec.

It should be added here that most observers of the European Union did not and do not foresee support for separation increasing within sub-state nations. Some emphasize a pattern of mixed and overlapping sovereignties within the Union. Political nationalism that seeks to make state and nation congruent is not consistent with these emergent features of the Union, and these observers believe that it will not be very important as a result. Instead actors in sub-state nations will manoeuvre to insert themselves in the interstices of these multiple arrangements.[7] If there are institutional barriers to separation within the Union, according to this point of view, they have little to do with a true supra-national European constitution. The latter implies a pattern of sovereignty that is incompatible with the variable geometry they believe will continue to characterize the Union. From this perspective, the Union is a new form of political association and full-blown political nationalism merely a relic of the past. States are atavistic survivals from an earlier age, and members of sub-state nations are far too advanced to want one of their own.

Indeed, it has been claimed that members of sub-state nations are 'post-nationalists' (a claim made about Scotland)[8] or, if they are civic nationalists, they are so civic-minded as to be hardly nationalists at all. Certainly, from this point of view, members of sub-state nations are not expected to support secession, which is associated with ethnic rather than civic nationalism.[9] Despite the ways in which economic integration increases the range of feasible opportunities for members of sub-state nations, by lowering the transition costs of new state-formation—zones of peace and economic interdependence modify economic and military economies of scale—members of sub-state nations are not expected to have an interest in independence.

According to a second point of view, support for separation will not increase, not because of changing patterns of sovereignty, but because states will continue to dominate European politics. The barriers to separation that will be invoked are not associated with a European constitution because, from this point of view, such a constitution is unlikely to emerge. Rather, the barriers to secession will be unit-level and related to the hierarchical structures and institutions of states. In other words, state institutions will continue to dominate—both within the Union and within their territorial borders. So intergovernmental relations will continue to be more important than supranational relations and sub-state nations will be constrained by the hierarchical ordering principles of territorial states. If members of sub-state nations have an interest in independence, they will be unable to express it in political institutions.

The argument of this chapter is different from both of these positions. Sub-state political nationalism that seeks statehood is not yet dead in industrial democracies, since it clearly is alive in North America and is not yet a thing of the past within the European Union, either. Accommodation in the form of self-government is likely to encourage rather than restrain or satisfy members of sub-state nations.

3. *Unique economic specialization contributes to secession.* Specialization in production creates common interests among people.[10] Leaving aside the relationship between common interests and secession (a gap that is often addressed through a version of proposition four, specified below), the Quebec economy should be highly specialized, particularly in those activities occupied by francophones, if this proposition is true. But the timing of nationalist mobilization in Quebec, and the introduction of demands for independence in the late 1960s, strongly suggests that these changes occurred in a period of declining economic specialization.[11]

4. *Nationalist identity-formation contributes to secession.* Political nationalists are motivated to make the national and political congruent.[12] The stronger the sense of nationhood in stateless nations, the easier it is to mobilize support for secession. I accept this proposition, but point out that identity-formation is sensitive to prevailing institutional arrangements. Nationalists in Quebec have deliberately used the institutions of the provincial government to influence the formation of identities. The institutional design of the Canadian state has provided the infrastructure to shape the sub-state identities that contribute to a sense of national difference, and makes it easier also to politicize these differences. The processes of identity-formation facilitated by consociational federalism should increase the likelihood that the baseline level of support for nationalism will be higher than in circumstances where either this design is not present or no substitutes exist for it. The same institutional design also provides political entrepreneurs and activists with the opportunity to mobilize a greater degree of support for independence for any given level of nationalism than could be mobilized if this design were absent.

5. *Increased voice lowers the likelihood of exit.* Increased inclusion weakens political radicalism. Conversely, according to the usual argument, political exclusion should increase the likelihood of radical political challenge. In the case of political nationalism, according to this argument, exclusion should increase the

likelihood of secession and inclusion should lower it. One version of this argument makes an analogy between the inclusion of classes, particularly the working class, and the political inclusion of sub-state nations.

Nationalism is not about winning inclusion in the political institutions of another nation, however. The basic reason is that sub-state nationalism has an important territorial dimension. Sub-state nationalists do not seek to capture the state or change the regime while holding constant the boundaries of the state. Political accommodation is a second-best outcome for political nationalists. Differences between secession and revolution undermine the analogy. Socialists could and did hold out the hope of a peaceful transition to socialism through inclusion in political institutions, access to political power in the centre, and the transformation of economic relations through the instruments of political power. By contrast, sub-state nationalists do not hold out the hope of a peaceful transition to independence via equivalent participation in political institutions. So the analogy fails.

There is no other way within nationalism to achieve nationalist goals except to preserve differences; nationalists are committed to separateness and autonomy. Political inclusion modelled on class inclusion would not recognize these differences. Separateness and autonomy are precisely what communitarian socialists gave up when they decided to participate in democratic political institutions.[13] There is no equivalent in patterns of class inclusion to consociational federalism. Put differently, the inclusion of classes is a form of assimilation; the accommodation of stateless nations is, virtually by definition, non-assimilationist.

Recall as well that there is actually something conservative about political nationalism, which further weakens the analogy between class inclusion and the inclusion of sub-state nations. The goal of political nationalists—to have a state of their own—does not challenge the prevailing organizational principle of international society, unlike socialism which seeks deep economic and political transformation. A socialist world has always been more difficult to imagine than a world that has been modified only by the number of states. As a consequence, the politics of class inclusion should be more stable. This stability is produced primarily by the uncertainties associated with a transition to socialism. Political radicalism is more likely to be self-limiting, given these uncertainties. While there are certainly costs associated with a transition to independence, they are not of the same magnitude. In general, then, it should be more difficult to deter a transition to independence than to socialism.

Consociational federalism supplies a distinctive type of political inclusion. The Québécois nation is not excluded; indeed, it has a substantial jurisdictional presence in the Canadian federation through provincial institutions, as well as political weight in federal governments and institutions. Sovereignists were even the official opposition in the last federal Parliament and continue to dominate the representation of

Quebec in the Canadian House of Commons. For 28 of the last 30-odd years, the Canadian prime minister has been from the province of Quebec, and for more than 20 of those years, the prime minister has been francophone. Despite this inclusion, the likelihood of secession is higher in Quebec than in any other part of the developed western world. Institutional design is the explanation for this inversion of the socio-logical truism. The case of Quebec makes nonsense of the claim that 'secession is caused in largest part by the desire to escape from empire; the desire for exit is bred by the denial of voice'.[14]

Consociational federalism is a deep form of territorially decentralized power-sharing among sub-state nations. It is an unusual design among advanced industrial states.[15] Aside from Switzerland and Germany, European states have tended to be unitary. Consociational arrangements, moreover, were not implemented to accom-modate nations per se, but more specific subcultures. Switzerland, for example, is multilingual rather than multinational. The Dutch *zuilen*, the classic model of consociationalism, were not nations. In European society, the use of federal decen-tralization to accommodate the demands of sub-state nations is both relatively recent and limited. In the late 1970s, Spain began to move towards asymmetric internal arrangements that recognized the historic nations of Catalonia and the Basque country. Belgium implemented a complicated process of federal decentral-ization in 1993. Westminster authorized referendums on the creation of local legis-latures in Scotland and Wales in 1997. The latter changes did not create federal institutions.

Yet in Canada, federal institutions have been used to accommodate French and English from Confederation onwards. The design of the Canadian state has been distinctive. It has been described as consociational federalism.[16] Without accepting Lijphart's theory of consociational democracy, Canadian consociationalism has two core features of consociational politics: power-sharing among corporate groups and internal subgroup autonomy.[17] These features are nested within federal institutions and parliamentary government, however. Unlike Belgium, for example, Canada was federal from the start. Consociationalism and federalism did not cross-cut, and the transition from religion to language as markers of national community among fran-cophones occurred differently.

Further, there is little intrastate federalism in Canada because there is no effective elected upper legislature. As a result, interstate mechanisms of negotiation and bargaining among the executives of the governments within the federation ('executive federalism') dominate intrastate institutions. Research by Doreen Barrie and Roger Gibbins has been consistent with this point: Parliament has served less and less as a vehicle through which provincial political élites are drawn into national politics. As they put it, 'Political ambitions in Canada do not knit elected offices into a hierarchi-cal, national structure.' Provincial office serves as an alternative to—rather than as a stepping stone towards—national office.[18] The result of this combination of some features of consociationalism and a federal polity that lacks integrating institutions is a relatively deep form of decentralized power-sharing.

The Incentive Structures of Consociational Federalism

Consociational federalism preserves differences and encourages sub-state national-ism, while providing nationalists with an embyronic state. It increases the political feasibility of secession and, at the same time, its institutional arrangements help to resolve problems of co-ordination and free-riding in nationalist collective action. Let us examine here two results that are associated with feasibility, in order to flesh out how the institutions of self-government in Quebec have shaped nationalist collective action.

This section builds on the following intuition: There is a distinction to be made between 'strategic' and 'sincere' supporters of secession. Some individuals support secession in order to strengthen their bargaining position with the central govern-ment. They do not really want to secede because, if secession were to occur, they would lose access to this bargaining relationship and the resources it provides. Such individuals are *strategic* secessionists: they threaten to secede in order to extract resources. Other secessionists, however, have a *sincere* desire to leave. While some of this group of supporters of secession may be more sensitive to the costs of leaving (transition costs) than are other sincere supporters, they do not support secession in order to extract resources.[19] Hence their 'sincerity'.

State agents would dearly love to know which is which in a given population. However, distinguishing the two types of support can be difficult precisely because strategic secessionists are disguising or misrepresenting their preferences. It turns out that the very condition that produces sincere secessionists also makes the threat to secede more credible, and thus should encourage strategic support for secession. This condition is, of course, the feasibility of secession, as considered earlier in the chapter, and feasibility is influenced by how political institutions are designed. That is to say, threats to secede are unlikely to be credible when the feasibility of independence is very low and they should be more credible as the feasibility of independence increases. However, as the feasibility of independence increases, sincere support for indepen-dence should also increase.

Hence the importance of what I have called consociational federalism. This is a design that increases feasibility and thus influences nationalist collective action. Feasibility, first, should increase sincere support for secession. Why should a sub-state nationalist not take advantage of the feasibility of secession and pursue indepen-dence? Second, feasibility should also increase insincere or strategic support for seces-sion. Why, for example, should political entrepreneurs in one group demand less, when they judge that they can achieve more by threatening to secede? These results are consistent with the proposition that, as feasibility increases, agreements produced through power-sharing are less likely to be self-enforcing and political radicalism less likely to be self-limiting.[20]

I mentioned above that agents of the government who are interested in preserving the interests of the state would like to be able to distinguish sincere from strategic supporters of secession. They want to devise optimal strategies to deal with support for secession, and different types of support might demand different strategies.

However, they are forced to devise these strategies under institutional constraints. The basic problem, I believe, is that consociational federalism encourages sincere support for secession and, further, that the institutions of consociational federalism are difficult to change.

Such a design should produce a larger proportion of sincere secessionists than within other institutional designs in the developed western world because, first, the more feasible is withdrawal, the larger—all else being equal—will be the number of individuals whose sincere preference is withdrawal; and, second, the political feasibility of withdrawal varies with institutional design. Consociational federalism encourages sincere support for secession. This support is not a result of strategic misrepresentation of preferences. When support for secession is sincere, secession is not used as a threat; rather, secession is a means to a desired goal. Moreover, sincere supporters of secession do not understate their demand for the collective goal of independence in order to free-ride on the active support of others in the group. This is true by virtue of the technical meaning of free-riding which, by definition, is a case of strategic misrepresentation of preferences.

This does not mean that sincere support for secession is insensitive to the political costs of transition. In a consociational federation, however, these costs should be relatively lower. Individuals are habituated to a central state whose agents have not established a reputation for toughness.[21] Furthermore, the barriers to transition should be lower than in other designs, such as in Europe, which may include different political institutions that shape political agendas and forms of political organization, and also produce a predisposition for policies that deter challenges to the territorial state.

For the purposes of this discussion, it is assumed that there are two subsets of sincere supporters of secession, as long as preference-formation and public expressions of preferences are not determined completely by community norms and identity and political institutions. These subsets are distinguished by significant differences in sensitivities to increasing transition costs. In both subsets, it is assumed, sincere support for secession falls as transition costs increase but, in one subset, it declines substantially more for every unit increase in transition costs than it does in the other subset. The 'stickiness' of the second subset is a dynamic effect of consociational federalism, absent in other designs, which is related to the organizational capacity that sub-state nations are endowed with inside its institutional arrangements. Individual preference-formation is less likely to be completely determined by changes in transition costs within a consociational federation, compared with other designs that do not provide equivalent forms of territorially defined communities and state-like political institutions that help to solve problems of co-ordination and free-riding. So, in a consociational federation, there may continue to be sincere supporters of secession, even if transition costs increase. Not all support for secession is strategic. In other words, sensitivity to transition costs can be consistent with sincere preference representation, and the choice dynamics of a cost-sensitive actor with sincere preferences are different from the dynamics associated with preference misrepresentation. It therefore should be remembered that a strategy-proof mechanism designed to eliminate insincere support for secession would not eliminate all support for secession.

But it is a plausible hypothesis that not all support for secession is sincere. There is, therefore, another result of consociational federalism. It can permit the strategic misrepresentation of preferences. Consociational federalism is a 'non-dictatorial' institutional design, and this means that it is susceptible to manipulation by 'misrepresented' (that is, insincere or strategic) preferences.[22] Its infrastructure encourages sincere support for secession, as was argued above, but insincere or strategic support for secession can be present at the same time. Indeed, credible threats to secede, which are one important form of strategic behaviour in these cases, are also associated with the presence of sincere support for secession.

The existence of strategic secessionists indicates that there are incentives to mimic the public attitudes and behaviour of sincere secessionists. This is just what makes the threats of strategic secessionists credible. There are sophisticated strategies that can be played by political entrepreneurs who use exit as a threat. Voters can vote tactically and misrepresent their preferences. Strategic supporters of secession are in effect free-riding on the institutional status quo, purposely overstating their interest in secession in order to extract resources from the state. Threats of withdrawal need to be credible to be useful, however. What increases the credibility of such a threat? As I proposed earlier, when the act of withdrawal is more feasible politically, threats to withdraw are more credible. Threats are less credible if withdrawal is less feasible.

Supporters of secession, whether sincere or strategic, must interact with the state. After all, this is their primary political foil. Agents of the state would prefer to be able to reliably distinguish between sincere and strategic supporters of secession. From the point of view of a state agent, interested in preserving the territorial integrity of the state, the key is not to 'strategy-proof' institutions (which might eliminate strategic support for secession) but to lower the number of *sincere* supporters of secession. A move that successfully lowered the number of sincere supporters would also have indirect effects on those actors who threaten secession. It would make their threats less credible, because credibility should co-vary with the number of sincere supporters, given that both insincere and strategic support is influenced by the feasibility of independence. By contrast, eliminating strategic support for secession will not necessarily have any effects on sincere support.

Although state agents may not have complete information about the structure of support for independence (if they did, they could distinguish sincere and strategic supporters), they can take advantage of the relationship between 'real' preferences and the feasible set of alternatives in the following way. If they can narrow the boundaries of the feasible set or change the weights of alternatives within it, they can force actors to rethink their prior decisions. There are two ways in which the feasible set may be modified. One is through institutional redesign; the other is through more informal commitments about the future behaviour of state agents. The political problem for state agents is that institutional redesign is difficult without the agreement of those sub-state nations protected by the institutional arrangements of consociational federalism. Institutional redesign may be preferable in the long run because it should induce more fundamental change in preference over the longer term. Yet, while institutional innovation is preferable, it is hard to achieve and the fallback position is to attempt to establish credible commitments that will deter secession in the future. The difficulties are compounded because the informal commitments about behaviour in the future must be credible. If institutional innovation could be accomplished, such threats would not be needed.

The intention of either redesign or commitment is to make an institutional design less vulnerable to fundamental challenge by, in effect, introducing de jure or de facto restrictions on choices available to actors. These moves may not completely eliminate sincere support for secession but, to the extent that such responses do have effects on sincere supporters, it is by changing sincere support for secession into constrained support for some state of affairs that stops short of new state formation.

Agents of the state who can credibly manipulate the boundaries of the feasible set by narrowing the range of alternatives within the set might be able to separate sincere secessionists from strategic secessionists. If it is credibly communicated that resistance by the central state will increase the costs of transition to independence, and that such resistance is planned if the need arises, a threat to secede loses some of its efficacy.

State agents, moreover, can benefit from another feature of the situation of strategic secessionists. Strategic secessionists have private information unavailable to state agents. They know that their public preferences for independence are insincere. They can, in certain circumstances, have an interest in revealing this information. Generally, if the costs of strategic behaviour become too onerous to bear, actors will be inclined to forgo it. These individuals must ensure, for example, that sincere secessionists, for whom independence is more than a bargaining position, do not control the political agenda within the group. They will not want to be dragged along toward independence by sincere secessionists. The situation of strategic secessionists is volatile. Their success is associated with a narrow range of sincere support for secession. Too few sincere supporters of secession within the group means that threats to secede are not credible; too many sincere supporters of secession may make threats to secede privately unbearable. For threats of secession to continue to be credible *and* bearable, a policy of tougher commitments from the state has to reveal a level of sincere support that falls within this range. Hence the volatility of strategic supporters. Their optimal level of sincere support must be high enough to make threat behaviour publicly credible, but low enough to make threat behaviour privately bearable.

The real problem that state agents face in a consociational federation may not be threat behaviour but the possibility that the institutions of consociational federalism have shaped the structure of sincere support for secession in such a way that the subset of 'sticky' support is much larger than the subset of insincere support, and also larger than the subset of cost-sensitive sincere support. And the longer the institutions of consociational federalism have been in place, the greater the communal and political encapsulation of the group and thus the higher the likelihood that sincere support for secession will be sticky; that is, more insensitive to transition costs than it would be within other institutional designs. The general problem is that consociational federalism is very decentralized and that, past some threshold point (difficult to specify *a priori*), the tendency toward fragmentation can be irreversible.

However, a central government that can credibly communicate its commitment to increasing transition costs will face a less serious threat to the territorial integrity of the state. There will be fewer sincere supporters of secession and less strategic misrepresentation of preferences. A central government that has no credible reputation for toughness, on the other hand, will likely confront a larger number of sincere supporters of secession, and will find it difficult late in the game to take up a hardline policy that might work to distinguish sincere and strategic supporters of secession. A hardline policy, in this context, represents a change in a longer pattern of accommodation and may not be believed and thus not change behaviour until it is too late. Or it may be so surprising, when set against the prior pattern, that it is interpreted as a potential remaking of the institutional design that fostered accommodation. A tougher stance that comes too late also may be counterproductive, if it increases the intensity of sincere support for secession. The best way to deter secession is through designing institutions rather than through more informal commitments about the future, but in a consociational federation that type of institutional innovation is difficult to achieve on a consensual basis.[23] There are too many interests vested in those very arrangements that need to be modified. Without institutions that tend to limit sincere and strategic support for secession, sub-state nationalists and state agents will become engaged in a threat game, as they have in Canada.

There is currently no constitutional solution that can win acceptance simultaneously amongst francophones in Quebec and the rest of Canada. In the absence of a constitutional solution, and without a reputation for toughness, the federal government has moved toward making credible its commitment to defend the territorial integrity of Canada. It has done so by situating the issue of secession within the rule of law, thereby redrawing the rules of the game for a future referendum.

Institutional Innovation at the State Level in Europe

I have argued that accommodation in the form of self-government should encourage rather than restrain or satisfy sub-state nationalists. In this section, I consider some of the recent changes to territorial politics in Spain, Britain, and Belgium in light of this argument. In these cases, I argue, territorial change will fuel demands for more change. Scotland is one instance where this dynamic will emerge. The historic nations of Spain, particularly Catalonia, are perhaps another example, since the choices of Catalan nationalists were time-dependent during the democratic transition. In Catalonia, nationalists can demand more now than they did during the transition because the political regime is well consolidated. The more consolidated the regime in Spain, the more likely that support for further autonomy will increase. Moreover, as the other regions of Spain also demand more, the historic nations (including Catalonia, Galicia, and the Basque Country) can also bargain for more, as well—in order, they will argue, to preserve the principle of asymmetry in territorial politics.[24]

The national question wrecked the transition from dictatorship to democracy in Spain in the early 1930s and opened the door to Franco. In the second attempt, in the late twentieth century, to make the transition to democracy, Catalan nationalists sought to avoid a similar debacle. They judged that it was better in the short term to contribute to the consolidation of a Spanish liberal democratic regime and to use democratic institutions, made available as the regime became consolidated, to advance their cause. They preferred this option, rather than to threaten the transition by playing a radical nationalist card and risk the return of some form of authoritarianism.

Scotland has been granted a Scottish Parliament. In contrast to Catalonia, the creation of a local parliament in Scotland immediately precipitated demands for more power and institutionalized support for independence. The reason is that liberal democracy has a long history in Britain and is fully consolidated. Demands for more power would not threaten liberal democracy.

The United Kingdom has been historically a composite, but still a unitary state. It was internally differentiated, but there has been one centre of political sovereignty: the sovereign-in-Parliament. Scotland retained distinctive institutions in education, law, and religion after the Union of 1707, but gave up its legislature and accepted the Hanoverian succession.

In September 1997, a referendum called by the British government was held in Scotland on the creation of a Scottish legislature with law-making and taxing powers over strictly domestic matters. This referendum was called by a government in which Scots held central Cabinet posts: the chancellor of the exchequer (Gordon Brown), foreign secretary (Robin Cook), minister of defence (George Robertson), and the minister for social security (Alistair Darling). It passed easily and elections to this legislature were held in May 1999. This initiative, a part of a larger New Labour plan to reorganize territorial politics in Northern Ireland, Wales, and England, was intended to weaken the Scottish National Party (SNP).

New Labour expected that this version of home rule would kill off the nationalist movement and the SNP. It is more likely that the Scottish Parliament will provide an arena of contestation and a locus of power for nationalists, that they will move to enlarge its competences once they control it, and that they will use referendums as a bargaining tool. The SNP went on record that a referendum on independence was possible during its mandate if elected, and the party quickly demanded increased powers for the legislature, including a foreign ministry. As one SNP candidate put it in late 1998: 'They thought that people would be so grateful, but when we got a taste of power, it only made us want more.'

Opinion polls had indicated that the SNP had led Labour in terms of voting intentions at several points in the long run-up to the 6 May election, although Labour won a plurality of seats. Labour formed a coalition government with the Liberal Democrats, while the SNP formed the opposition. One might hold out to Labour the consoling thought that support for independence might decline in the future, despite the fact that the SNP is in a far stronger position in the Scottish legislature than it could ever hope to be in the British House of Commons. The central conclusion to draw about a case such as Scotland, however, is that it is not the immediate results of the election that matter, so much as the enduring changes to Scottish politics that will result from institutional change. The SNP has a new institutional home and, at some point, it will govern, whether alone or in coalition.

In the cases of Scotland and Catalonia, institutional innovations have stopped well short of the degree of power-sharing characteristic of relations between the federal government and the government of Quebec. These versions of local government in Catalonia and Scotland are still embedded in domestic political institutions that are more hierarchical than the institutions of the Canadian state. It is very likely, however, that these initial innovations will increase rather than dampen demands for further change.

Recent constitutional changes have moved Belgium toward a deep form of territorially decentralized power-sharing. These changes have transformed a unitary state into a federal state, and the innovations also recognize the overriding importance of linguistic differences in contemporary Belgian politics. National power-sharing between religious groups has been replaced by territorial power-sharing between linguistic groups that have increasingly defined themselves as nations. But this transition in self-definition from language community to nationhood has not been complete. And the old system of consociational power-sharing among the three political 'families' (Liberals, Social Christians, and Socialists) has not been completely replaced by sub-state nationalism.

The three 'families' were dominant in different regions: the Socialists in Wallonia, the Social Christians in Flanders, and the Liberals to a lesser extent in Brussels. While they all fragmented (in 1978, 1968, and 1972 respectively) along linguistic lines, these parties were able to use federal reform to secure local dominance. The demand for federal reform was initiated by nationalist or linguistic parties in Flanders, Wallonia, and Brussels, but it was the traditional parties of consociationalism that turned these demands to their own ends. They endorsed federal reform because they calculated that they could control the local jurisdictions that it created. Federalism would strengthen sub-national governments and 'would expand their [the traditional parties'] powers at the regional and communal levels and once again make them an indispensable coalition dominator at the national level'.[25] As a result, 'the Flemish region has come to be dominated by the CVP [Social Christians] and the Walloon region by the PS [Parti socialiste]'.[26]

These parties are not, strictly speaking, nationalist parties. They have less interest in independence than nationalist parties in historic nations. Further, these parties may be better off working within the Belgian state within the European Union. Officials from the regions and communities now can represent Belgium in the Council of Ministers on selected issues related to their competences as assigned in the Constitution, thus controlling all of the votes that Belgium has on the Council, and they can bind Belgium as a whole to the outputs of the Council. They would control fewer votes as a completely independent state. Nor as an independent state could they bind those other parts of Belgium that they now can bind to Union directives.[27]

There appear to be effects of consociationalism that continue to be relevant, and that cut across the potentially centrifugal effects of territorial decentralization. These effects have been reinforced by political change at the European level, since the domestic changes have occurred at the same time as the European Community was deepened. Supra-national integration could modify the incentive structures of this type of consociational federalism. It is difficult to tell, at this stage, whether the Belgian pattern is stable.

Power-sharing among nations within a single state is not likely to be self-enforcing. Political radicalism will be less likely to be self-limiting as the feasibility of independence increases. Whether Quebec is the future of Europe remains to be seen, of course. But to the extent that there are no countervailing institutions to compensate for the centrifugal effects of consociational federalism, territorial politics in Europe will increasingly resemble contemporary politics in Canada and Quebec. A great deal depends on the evolution of the political institutions of the European Union.

Conclusion

Politics are different in Quebec. It is not a province just like the others. Nor is it like other sub-state nations in western Europe. There are two important differences between North American and European society. Federalism has not often been used in Europe to accommodate ethnic groups or nations. In contrast, there is a relatively deep form of territorial power-sharing in Canada. There is economic integration without political integration in North America, unlike Europe, where the piecemeal and incremental pooling of sovereignties has created an important supra-national political framework.

To these differences, one can add this observation: The most powerful movement for independence in the developed western world is the nationalist movement in Quebec. Its success is related to these features of Canadian politics and North American society identified above. The institutional design of the Canadian state encourages secessionist challenges. Economic integration lowers the transition costs of independence. The absence of supra-national political institutions means that there is no extra-state institutional avenue by which to bypass the Canadian state. Finally, as discussion of the case of Quebec demonstrates, the political theory that increased voice lowers the likelihood of exit in sub-state nations is underdeveloped theoretically, empirically unsubstantiated, and, if it is an expectation that drives public policy, remarkably foolish.

Notes

1. The author thanks Roger Gibbins, Patrick James, Michael Lusztig, Chris Manfredi, Alan Patten, and Rick Schultz for comments and the SSHRC for financial support. An earlier version of this chapter was presented at the American Political Science Association Convention, September 1998. I thank Henry Hale for organizing the panel.

2. The 1980 question asked for a mandate to negotiate 'sovereignty association' that 'would enable Quebec to acquire the exclusive power to make its laws, administer its taxes, and establish relations abroad—in other words, sovereignty—and, at the same time, to maintain with Canada an economic association including a common currency. Any change in political status resulting from these negotiations will be submitted to the people through referendum'. The 1995 question was, 'Do you agree that Quebec should become sovereign, after having made a formal offer for a new economic and political partnership, within the scope of the Bill respecting the Future of Quebec and of the agreement signed on 12 June 1995.' The reference to the Bill designates legislation passed in the Quebec National Assembly in the summer of 1995. The June agreement was an accord signed by three party leaders (Bouchard, Parizeau, and Dumont) that committed the *souverainistes* to a formal offer of partnership after a referendum, rather than a unilateral declaration of independence. There is now evidence that Parizeau did not plan to honour the commitment. See Jacques Parizeau, *Pour un Québec souverain* (Montreal: VLB Editeur, 1997), 283–8.

3. For example, Edouard Cloutier, Jean H. Guay, and Daniel Latouche, *L'évolution de l'opinion publique au Québec depuis 1960, ou comment le Québec est devenu souverainiste* (Montreal: Québec/Amérique, 1992); Richard Nadeau, 'Le virage souverainiste des québécois', *Recherches Sociographiques* 33 (1992): 9–49; Pierre Martin, 'Générations politiques, rationalité économique et appui à la souveraineté au Québec', *Revue canadienne de science politique* 27 (1994): 345–59.

4. In using the concept of consociation, I am not committed to the theory of consociational democracy. For effective criticisms of the political theory of consociational democracy, see Ian S. Lustick, 'Lijphart, Lakatos and Consociationalism', *World Politics* 50 (1997): 88–117 and David D. Laitin, 'South Africa: Violence, Myths and Democratic Reform', *World Politics* 39 (1987): 258–79.

5. Stéphane Dion, 'Why is Secession Difficult in Well-Established Democracies? Lessons from Quebec', *British Journal of Political Science* 29 (1996): 269–83; Saul Newman, *Ethnoregional Conflict in Democracies* (Westport, Conn,: Greenwood Press, 1996).

6. Hudson Meadwell, 'Ethnic Nationalism and Collective Choice Theory', *Comparative Political Studies* 22 (1989): 139–54.

7. Gary Marks, François Nielsen, Leonard Ray, and Jane E. Salk, 'Competencies, Cracks and Conflicts: Regional Mobilization in the European Union', *Comparative Political Studies* 29 (1996): 164–92; Michael Keating, *Nations Against the State* (London: Macmillan, 1996).

8. For example, David McCrone, *Understanding Scotland: The Sociology of a Stateless Nation* (London: Routledge, 1992), 215–21.

9. Keating, *Nations Against the State*.

10. Michael Hechter, 'The Dynamics of Secession' *Acta Sociologica* 35 (1992): 267–83.

11. Hudson Meadwell, 'The Politics of Nationalism in Quebec', *World Politics* 45 (1993): 203–42.

12. Ernest Gellner, *Nations and Nationalism* (Ithaca, NY: Cornell University Press, 1983).

13. Adam Przeworski, *Capitalism and Social Democracy* (Cambridge: Cambridge University Press, 1985).

14. John A. Hall and T.V. Paul, 'The State and the Future of World Politics' in *International Order and the Future of World Politics*, T.V. Paul and John A. Hall, eds (Cambridge and New York: Cambridge University Press, 1999), 403–4. This claim draws on the theoretical language of Albert O. Hirschman, *Exit, Voice and Loyalty* (Cambridge, Mass: Harvard University Press, 1970). Hirschman, however, now concedes that his original argument was 'primitive'. See his article 'Exit, Voice and the Fate of the German Democratic Republic: An Essay in Conceptual history', *World Politics* 45 (1993): 176. He acknowledges that the basic 'hydraulic' model of exit and voice is not universally valid. Exit and voice need not undermine each other; indeed, they can work 'hand in glove'. Hirschman no longer provides independent theoretical support for the claim that increased political voice lowers the likelihood of exit, since he now admits that voice and exit can increase jointly.

15. For some discussion of how state formation and consolidation differed in North American society, see Hudson Meadwell, 'Secession, States and International Society', *Review of International Studies* 25 (1999): 371–87 and Hudson Meadwell, 'Institutional Design and State Breaking in North American Society' in David Carment, Frank Harvey, and John F. Stack Jr, eds, *The International Politics of Quebec Secession: State Making and State Breaking in North America* (New York: Praeger, 2001).

16. Samuel LaSelva, *The Moral Foundations of Canadian Federalism* (Montreal: McGill-Queen's University Press, 1996); S.J.R. Noel, 'Canadian Responses to Ethnic Conflict' in John McGarry and Brendan O'Leary, eds, *The Politics of Ethnic Conflict Regulation* (London: Routledge, 1993); S.J.R. Noel, 'Consociational Democracy and Canadian Federalism' in Kenneth McRae, ed., *Consociational Democracy* (Toronto: McClelland and Stewart, 1987); Arend Lijphart, 'Non-Majoritarian Democracy: A Comparison of Federal and Consociational Theories', *Publius* 15 (Spring 1985): 3–16; Herman Bakvis, 'Alternative Models of Governance: Federalism, Consociationalism and Corporatism' in Herman Bakvis and William M. Chandler, eds, *Federalism and the Role of the State* (Toronto: University of Toronto Press, 1987).

17. Arend Lijphart, *Democracy in Plural Societies: A Comparative Exploration* (New Haven: Yale University Press, 1977); Arend Lijphard, *The Politics of Accommodation* (Berkeley: University of California Press, 1968).

18. Doreen Barrie and Roger Gibbins, 'Parliamentary Careers in the Canadian Federal State', *Canadian Journal of Political Science* 22 (1989): 137–45.

19. For a theoretical argument that support for secession is always strategic, see Daniel S. Treisman, 'Russia's "ethnic revival": The Separatist Activism of Regional Leaders in a Postcommunist Order', *World Politics* 49 (1997): 212–49. His claim seems to be general, and not limited to the postcommunist world.

20. For further discussion see Hudson Meadwell, 'Stateless Nations and the Emerging International Order' in T.V. Paul and John A. Hall, eds, *International Order in the Twenty-first Century* (Cambridge: Cambridge University Press, 1999).

21. On investments in reputation, see David Kreps and Robert Wilson, 'Reputations and Imperfect Information', *Journal of Economic Theory* 27 (August 1982): 253–79. For another argument, drawn from work on public good provision and deterrence theory, see Hugh Ward, 'The Risks of a Reputation for Toughness: Strategy in Public Goods Provision Modelled by Chicken Supergames', *British Journal of Political Science* 17 (1987): 23–52. For an application of this literature to Canadian politics, see Patrick James, 'The Chain Store Paradox and Constitutional Politics in Canada', *Journal of Theoretical Politics* 11 (1999): 5–36.

22. Peter C. Ordeshook, *Game Theory and Political Theory* (Cambridge: Cambridge University Press, 1986), 82–9, 235ff.

23. Christopher Manfredi and Michael Lusztig, 'Why Do Formal Amendments Fail? An Institutional Design Analysis', *World Politics* 50 (1998): 377–400.

24. The same competitive process produced by asymmetrical territorial arrangements can also be anticipated in Great Britain, given the differences in territorial political institutions introduced in Scotland, Wales, and England.

25. Saul Newman, *Ethnoregional Conflict in Democracies* (Westport, Conn.: Greenwood Press, 1996), 93.

26. Ibid., 98.

27. Bert Kerremans and Jan Beyers, 'Belgium: The Dilemma Between Cohesion and Autonomy' in Keneth Hanf and Ben Soetendorp, eds, *Adapting to European Integration* (London: Longman, 1998).

Chapter 11

Regionalism, Political Parties, and Parliamentary Politics in Canada and Australia

Anthony M. Sayers

While regional political homogeneity is often overstated in descriptions of Australian politics,[1] Canadian regionalism in its many forms is more acute, and underpins a number of the distinctive qualities of the Canadian polity. There is the relative organizational looseness of Canadian political parties in comparison with their Australian counterparts, reflecting attempts by Canadian political parties to accommodate social and regional diversity. The more 'cadre' form of Canadian parties, with their strengthened role for local constituency organizations and the party leadership but 'hollow' centres, contrasts with the more 'mass' nature of Australian parties, with their permanent organizational and policy committees, arguably less powerful leaders, and relatively weaker local branches. In Canada, unlike Australia, links between national parties and their regional namesakes are weak or non-existent. Furthermore, Canadian regional party systems often bear little resemblance to each other or to the national partisan competition.

Compared with their Australian counterparts, Canadian constituency associations have a greater say in nominating candidates to run for election and enjoy greater autonomy in organizing local campaigns. In contrast, the focus of political activism within Australian parties is usually above the level of the constituency, in the often-permanent secretariats that parties use to select candidates, discuss policy, and make other collective decisions. There are few permanent institutions in which activists could seek membership, at any level of most Canadian parties. Rather, constituency associations, with their often cyclical existence, define the organizational life of parties, and set the terms on which party activists gain access to parties and the political system more generally.

Another set of contrasts can be found if we consider parties in their parliamentary setting. The degree to which governing parties dominate parliamentary politics is exaggerated in Canada, mainly because of the use of first-past-the-post electoral systems, but also because of unicameralism or nascent unicameralism at the national and provincial levels. Powerful upper houses and a mix of electoral systems have complicated the task of parties in Australian parliaments, limiting their capacity for dominance. Similarly, the domination of Parliament by the executive appears greater in Canada, where parties and politics more generally are increasingly understood in terms of leaders.[2] The selection of party leaders by the non-parliamentary party in Canada has strengthened their hand over their parliamentary colleagues.[3] The domination of parties by leaders, and Parliament by parties, ensures that the executive has a good deal of control over the legislative process. In Australia, leadership selection is by parliamentary caucus, with ordinary party members excluded from the process. Party leaders must be wary of the way in which they treat their fellow parliamentarians, and can be punished if perceived by colleagues to be high-handed or an electoral liability. Moreover, they must invariably negotiate with upper houses controlled by non-government parties, further limiting executive dominance.

There is at least anecdotal evidence of the relative difficulty encountered by opposition parties in Canadian parliaments as they pursue the government. During 1998 and 1999, attempts by the Reform party (now the Canadian Alliance) to embarrass the prime minister and other ministers over a range of issues, including the APEC inquiry and government grants, were markedly less successful than the Australian Labor party's pursuit of Coalition government ministers over travel allowances. In the latter situation, a number of ministers were forced to resign. This suggests that the Alliance is less well organized and the government perhaps better insulated than in the Australian case. While the shorter electoral cycle in Australia, in which lower house elections occur every two to four years,[4] may account for some of this, other dynamics such as electoral systems, the character of parliament, and the relative size and resources available to opposition parties may also play a role in determining the character of parliamentary debate.

Perhaps the most remarkable contrast between parliaments in the two countries is that control of Canada's House of Commons can only be achieved with a particular constellation of regional support that for most of the last century has been the preserve of the Liberal party. Consequently, and in sharp contrast to the Australian case, where a number of possible geographic and social electoral coalitions produce governments, there is an institutionalized regional cleavage between Government and Opposition that has spurred the development of new oppositional parties. The Bloc Québécois and the Canadian Alliance are the most recent manifestation of this logic. The centralization of power at the national level has further encouraged this regionalization of Canadian politics. In searching out regional electoral support, powerful cabinets and prime ministers broker complex political deals along regional lines with their equally powerful provincial counterparts, guaranteeing that political discourse remains embedded in the language of region.

The greater regionalization of Canadian society helps explain how two countries that share a common Westminster heritage can have such distinctive parties and parliamentary experiences. The retention of a cadre style of organization, with strong local constituency associations and powerful leadership, has helped Canadian parties deal with a deeply divided society. Parties attempt to integrate diverse regional and ethnolinguistic interests within a strongly majoritarian institutional framework that forces governing parties to bear much of the burden of transmitting societal demands to the state. In comparison, parliamentary institutions in Australia mix majoritarian and consensus logics, providing multiple access points for social demands and reducing the integrative burden on governing parties. A loose organizational structure, with few links between national and provincial levels of the party and avoidance of the permanent policy secretariats found in mass parties, has proved an effective vehicle for dealing with this task in Canada.

It is this lack of cohesiveness that helps support the twin power centres of Canadian parties: local associations and parliamentary leadership. Such an arrangement maximizes the power and freedom of the leadership or executive to accommodate complex, competing political demands, while leaving local constituency associations free to respond to local political circumstances. This freedom is further enhanced by parliamentary dynamics. As leaders dominate their parties, so too do governing parties dominate Parliament. Often reduced to very small numbers with limited resources, opposition parties are unlikely to be able to support grand extra-parliamentary organizations. This limits their capacity to oversee the executive and reinforces the cyclical character of parties. We see this in the nature of executive federalism in Canada, where first ministers make agreements knowing that they will be endorsed routinely with little if any party or parliamentary debate. The drawback of this (perhaps efficient) form of policy making is a reduction in the openness and democratic credentials of Parliament and the policy process.

Voter Volatility, Regionalism, and Party Organization

The loose organizational style of Canadian parties is related to high levels of voter volatility and competitiveness at the constituency level (that is, narrow margins of victory in many seats. These conditions produce a high turnover rate of MPs that distinguishes Canada from other Anglo-American democracies.[5] The same electoral volatility is evident if one compares Canadian provinces and Australian states (see Tables 11.1 and 11.2). As a result of this volatility, constituency associations regularly conduct contested nominations, highlighting their central role in Canadian political parties.

Volatility also gives local party organizations more autonomy in running local campaigns, as it works to limit the capacity of the central party to direct campaigning. The regionalized nature of this volatility means that there are always parts of the country where national parties struggle to win seats. They may hold nearly all the seats in one province, and nearly none in the next. This may also be true in the same province across time, from one election to the next. Maintaining a constant presence or even attempting to ensure central control of what little party activity there is would be an expensive and futile exercise. Dramatic changes in electoral performances favour the cyclical existence and loose organizational form of cadre-style parties that do not attempt to maintain elaborate local organizations between elections. It is arguably cheaper and easier for parties if their associations are all but moribund between elections.

Table 11.1: Vote and Seat Volatility Canadian Provinces, 1945–1990

Parliament	Mean Party Support Change (%)	
	Votes	Seats
Newfoundland	6.0	15.4
Prince Edward Island	3.6	20.0
Nova Scotia	4.0	15.3
New Brunswick	4.9	20.3
Quebec	7.1	16.6
Ontario	4.2	10.5
Manitoba	6.1	11.0
Saskatchewan	8.9	19.9
Alberta	7.6	8.0
British Columbia	4.5	9.7
Averages	**6.4**	**12.6**

Source: David Stewart, 'Comparing Party Systems in the Canadian Provinces and Australian States' in Campbell Sharman, ed., *Parties and Federalism in Australia and Canada* (Canberra: Federalism Research Centre, ANU, 1994), Table 9.3.

Table 11.2: Vote and Seat Volatility Australian States, 1945–1990

Parliament	Mean Party Support Change (%)	
	Votes	Seats
New South Wales	2.7	3.9
Queensland	3.6	5.0
South Australia	3.3	3.8
Tasmania	3.9	4.7
Victoria	3.3	6.5
Western Australia	3.7	3.9
Averages	**3.4**	**4.6**

Source: Campbell Sharman, 'The Party System of the Australian States: Patterns of Partisan Competition, 1945–1986' *Publius* 21 (1990), 96.

The regionalization of the party system, which limits relations between many provincial and national branches of the same party, removes provincial party organizations as possible links between national and local party branches and as conduits for the imposition of national imperatives at the provincial or local levels. Attempts by the NDP to work against these tendencies have met with only modest success, while the construction of the Canadian Alliance is an attempt by the Reform party to address the underlying logic of a highly regionalized country.[6] The strength of provincial sources of voter volatility[7] suggests that Canadian political parties need to be able to adjust to varying provincial circumstances. But they lack key institutional linkages with provincial organizations that might help in this regard. Only local campaigns are in a position to respond to the exigencies of local and provincial volatility. Moreover, predicting the set of winnable seats is very difficult for Canadian parties, and limits the capacity of parties to run centralized campaigns. Therefore, parties that seek government are beholden to their local affiliates.

Political Parties and State-Society Relations

We have already seen that the inability of political parties to adequately integrate ethnolinguistic and regional diversity helps explain their loose organizational style. But there are other incentives for parties to maintain relatively few links between their national offices and provincial or local party organizations, and to eschew the powerful extra-parliamentary policy-making bodies found in parties in most other Westminster-derived systems. Sartori noted that parties connect the rigid political institutions of the state and the wider, always mobile, society.[8] It is arguable that the political demands thrown up by a more divided Canadian society are likely to be harder to reconcile than those emanating from Australian society.

Using Lijphart's distinction between majoritarian and consensus forms of politics, Canadian political institutions can be seen as heavily majoritarian in nature. While the Charter of Rights and Freedoms and some aspects of executive federalism might be seen as requiring consensus politics, Canadian parliaments are executive-dominated. As well, first-past-the-post voting in Canada favours parties with strong regional support rather than non-territorial-based backing, and reduces the likelihood of minority or coalition government. The use of preferential (alternative) voting in most lower houses in Australia favours coalition building, while the use of proportional representation in most upper houses has encouraged greater diversity of representation in these chambers. In the Commonwealth Parliament, this has allowed even small national parties to gain seats by collecting together nation-wide electoral support. Proportional representation has also worked to ensure that governments rarely have control of both houses of parliament, forcing them to compromise with a differently constituted and powerful upper house, reducing the dominance of the executive.

In this sense, Australian parliamentary institutions offer many more access points to societal demands, at both the Commonwealth and state levels, than their Canadian counterparts. There are also more parties, representing different constituencies (some national, some local, and some regional) with access to powerful upper and lower chambers not as dominated by executives. Yet it is arguable that Canadian governments face a much more complex mix of policy demands than do their Australian cousins. Moreover, the dominance of parties by leaders, of parliaments by governing parties, and, therefore, of parliaments by the executive, means that effective policy-making input has one main conduit. This means that political parties, and the governing party in particular in Canada, carry a much heavier burden in terms of transmitting societal demands to the state than their Australian counterparts. Again, the loose, cadre organization adopted by most successful Canadian parties has benefits in this regard.

Just as Canadian parties rarely maintain permanent local organizations and links with their provincial counterparts, neither do they have permanent or powerful extra-parliamentary policy-making bodies. This is useful, because the parliamentary wing of the party, and in particular, the leader, can formulate policy with fewer internal party or external political constraints. It allows leaders to respond to the diversity and volatility of Canadian politics in innovative ways. They are not tied to a particular policy, nor are sensitive or national issues such as the Quebec question regularly debated by the party in open forums. Given the emotions attached to such issues, and their at least perceived intractability, avoiding such debates and the need to come to a policy position or 'solution' allows greater flexibility and avoids potentially divisive debate. Avoiding the need to manage these relationships, both organizationally and in terms of trying to maintain a cohesive policy outlook, releases parties from a heavy burden and allows them to be more flexible and responsive. What they forgo is the capacity to internalize policy debate and generate strong party platforms. The result is a relatively closed, executive-dominated policy process that is not particularly democratic.

Richard Katz and Peter Mair have suggested that political parties can best be understood by considering how they operate in three arenas: the constituency, the head office, and the legislature.[9] At the constituency level, cadre style Liberal and Conservative associations have a cyclical existence, but are important and powerful as a result of their control of the nomination process and campaigning. In this way, they allow parties to remain responsive to changes in local political conditions over time. Even the NDP, which attempts to retain persistent party organizations between elections, struggles to do so. It is local responsiveness that allows Lawson to claim that Canadian parties have a decidedly representative hue.[10] At the national level, these parties have head offices and parliamentary organizations that persist between elections and are designed to deal with the disciplining logic of the House of Commons. That is, they are designed not so much to be representative, but to aggregate and integrate public opinion so that they may present a unified, coherent policy agenda in the Commons. This is more consistent with the dynamics of mass parties, or what Lawson calls participatory parties, suggesting a disjunction between the national and local levels of Canadian parties. This tension between representativeness and participatory politics is distinctive, and it sets Canadian parties apart from those in other industrialized nations.

While allowing for responsiveness at the margins and coherence at the centre, this structure leaves a vacuum at the intermediary level. That is, there are few permanent bodies that can offer party members a role in policy development, and that can limit or direct the policies adopted by the parliamentary wing. In addition, there are few links between the national and provincial party of the same name. This gap may be essential if party élites are to integrate the diverse opinions and forces present at the margins, since it allows them to avoid direct confrontation between incompatible objectives and policies as well as debate on the well-known but intractable problems of Canadian politics. That is, this hollow centre allows Canadian parties to balance the representativeness of local associations with the majoritarian cohesiveness of the party in the legislature, and even the head office. The resulting structure has been described by Allan Kornberg et al. as 'a short, truncated pyramid'.[11]

Given this, it is useful to add a fourth aspect of party structure to those suggested by Katz and Mair: namely, the nature of intermediary structures designed to develop policies and link various levels of a party in a federation.[12] The strength of these structures in comparison with the party in the legislature and head office, and with the party in the constituency, provides an indication of the locus of power and policy making within a party. Parties lacking these structures are likely to be pursuing catch-all strategies that eschew member-driven policy development. Those that maintain intermediary bodies are, at least rhetorically, more like mass parties, willing to promote policy discussion and formulation amongst their membership.

Political Parties and Parliamentary Dynamics

When one compares electoral and parliamentary politics in the two countries, other contrasts are evident. Whereas electoral volatility, measured in terms of party vote and turnover of MPs, is greater (and usually very much so) in Canada,[13] parliamentary volatility, measured in terms of government turnover, is very similar in the two countries. This is true at both the regional and national levels. Tables 11.1 and 11.2 provide evidence of greater electoral volatility at the provincial level in Canada compared with the Australian states. If we use seat volatility as a surrogate measure for the turnover of MPs, it would seem that the relatively high rates found at the national level in Canada are likely to be reproduced at the provincial level. Such different outcomes likely reflect the use of preferential and proportional voting in the mostly bicameral Australian legislatures and first-past-the-post voting in Canada. Australian voters have a range of ways in which to express any desire for change, and to some degree, preferential voting encourages more moderate outcomes in the way it constructs majorities. Certainly in Canada, first-past-the-post has the capacity to promote minor parties to major roles (as happened with Reform) and demote major players such as the Tories to bit roles, in a way that is less likely to occur in Australia.

All things being equal, one might expect higher levels of volatility to translate into more rapid turnover of governing regimes in Canada. This, however, is not the case. Between 1945 and 1990, the party in government changed on average 3.5 times in the Canadian provinces (ranging from once in Alberta to seven times in Manitoba), and 4.3 times in the Australian states (ranging from three times in Queensland and New South Wales to six times in Western Australia).[14] Allowing for the greater number of elections in Australia (an average of 15.5 as compared with 12.2), Canadian and Australian parliaments are very similar in this regard. The national parliaments of each country experienced similar levels of stability over the same period.[15]

What is striking about the combination of electoral volatility and regime stability in Canada is the image it presents of parties thrashing about, winning and losing large numbers of seats, while the main game remains largely unchanged. A high rate of turnover is consistent with the perceived importance of constituency organizations and local campaigns, since there is enough turnover to keep them involved in nominating candidates and running competitive campaigns. In parliaments, high turnover suggests larger numbers of amateur parliamentarians. On the government side, this means backbenchers with less experience in questioning their own party leaders or using parliamentary procedures to achieve some preferred legislative outcome. Similarly, volatility suggests opposition members with relatively little experience in using parliament to question and embarrass the government.

In addition to an unusual combination of volatility at the level of individual MPs with regime stability, there is another factor that affects the working of Canadian parliaments: one-party dominance.[16] Stewart has described the much greater degree of one-party dominance, particularly in legislatures, found in Canada in comparison with Australia.[17] The exception is the consistency with which the Australian Labor Party remains the largest electoral party in most contests, a dominance that is not translated into the legislature because of coalitional politics amongst the non-Labor parties. Another way of considering partisan dominance of legislatures is presented for Canada and Australia in Tables 11.3 and 11.4. These tables attempt to give a sense of the 'relative' dominance of the largest party in Canadian and Australian legislatures over their nearest rival. What these tables suggest is that the largest (and usually, though not always, governing) party is in Australia not quite twice as large as its opposition.[18] In Canada, the largest party is over six times bigger on average. This figure is skewed by the exceptional case of Alberta, where opposition parties have been unusually small. Even when Alberta is removed from the calculation, however, the largest party is three-and-a-half times larger than the opposition. Once again, electoral systems play a role in this outcome. But what does this mean for parliamentary politics?

One can easily imagine that high turnover rates and small numbers of opposition MPs would only strengthen the executive in Canadian parliaments. The 'presidentialization' of the role of Canadian first ministers may be one manifestation of this. A relatively few, poorly resourced, inexperienced, opposition MPs facing the usually

Table 11.3: Government and Opposition in Canadian Parliaments, 1945–1990

| | Seat Difference | | Index of |
Parliament	Raw Average	Percentage Average	Parliamentary Dominance Average (Gov/Opp)
Canadian	80.2	29.9	2.5
Newfoundland	22.4	56.1	5.2
Prince Edward Island	14.9	48.5	3.6
Nova Scotia	19.3	47.1	4.6
New Brunswick	20.5	38.9	3.0
Quebec	45.1	44.6	4.2
Ontario	42.9	43.5	3.8
Manitoba	13.0	22.9	2.0
Saskatchewan	24.1	42.4	3.2
Alberta	52.4	78.0	32.9
British Columbia	18.7	35.5	2.6
Averages	**32.1**	**44.3**	**6.2 (3.5 W/O Alberta)**

Table 11.4: Government and Opposition in Australian Parliaments, 1945–1990

Parliament	Seat Difference Raw Raw Average	Percentage Average	Index of Parliamentary Dominance Average (Gov/Opp)
Commonwealth	16.8	16.1	1.9
New South Wales	19.2	20.2	1.9
Queensland	17.4	24.0	1.9
South Australia	7.7	17.4	1.4
Tasmania	4.3	12.9	1.9
Victoria	17.0	23.0	1.9
Western Australia	9.5	18.7	1.7
Averages	**13.1**	**18.9**	**1.8**

most experienced government MPs—the Cabinet—suggests an important imbalance in the workings of Parliament. Moreover, it must be disheartening for opposition MPs to daily have to confront the large difference in seats that separates them from government. It is no wonder that many discover that Parliament is not the place to engage the government in a duel over policy. Perhaps this is one reason why the Commonwealth Parliament of Australia has more of an edge to it than its Canadian equivalent: the opposition is relatively well resourced, experienced, and can imagine winning government much more easily than its Canadian counterpart.

Once again, the institutional forces in the Canadian Parliament reinforce the dominance of the executive and work to limit access to alternative points of view. There are other implications as well. When there is a change of governing regime, by definition, the new government must bring many new or at least inexperienced members to Parliament. The lack of ministers with previous experience suggests a period of learning in which mistakes are likely to be made. Perhaps the Mulroney government was the best recent example of this.

There is another lesson to be drawn from this comparison. With respect to the sorts of regional alliances that are cobbled together by political parties in winning elections, Canadian parties by necessity pursue provincially based coalitions, whereas Australian parties may pursue a range of possible coalitions. An opposition party looking 'up' at the mountain of seats that separates it from government must naturally turn to thoughts of how best to ascend to the summit.

In the Australian case, and consistent with its topography, the mountain is a modest one. As we have seen, governments enjoy smaller seat advantages over their opposition than do Canadian governments. Moreover, there are various routes to the summit. For example, popular wisdom concerning the two most recent Australian national elections credits an alliance of rural and regional Australia, working against the major metropolitan centres (particularly of the east) as having allowed the Coalition to win and maintain office. This rural coalition is just one of a range of winning arrangements open to Australian parties. Historically, mobilizing voters along class lines has provided another route to power.

Canadian parties do not have access to a range of alternative coalition strategies in their pursuit of power: provincially described regional politics remain the only means of cobbling together a winning number of seats. In the Canadian case, the mountain to be scaled is, appropriately, right out of the Rockies: governments tend to enjoy large seat advantages over their opposition. And, as the Reform party/Canadian Alliance knows all too well, there is but one route to the top. This route involves a provincially based regional strategy that, taking account of the number of MPs they send to Ottawa, must include one or both of Ontario and Quebec. Given the strength of provincial patterns of voting and the electoral system, it is very unlikely that anything other than a province-based alliance will get the required numbers.

Conclusion

Canada and Australia share a number of important political features. The lack of a revolutionary break with Britain, the grafting of federalism onto a Westminster tradition, and the size of the two countries are shared characteristics that make comparison worthwhile. Of course, Australia has no equivalent to Quebec, and many of the differences between the two countries can be seen to result from this fact. Thus, a finding of greater regionalism in Canada subsumes the impact of this ethnolinguistic divide. Still, being able to compare how similar institutions operate in different contexts provides a powerful heuristic tool for analyzing the dynamics of Canadian politics.

What we have found is that regionalism has helped to fix in place the loose, cadre form of Canadian parties. This despite the fact that the Canadian Parliament is strongly majoritarian in character, a factor that has been identified as a key mechanism for encouraging mass parties in other Westminster-derived parliamentary systems.[19] An unelected Senate and an electoral system that produces dominant governing parties reinforce the majoritarian tendencies of Parliament. This domination further entrenches the supremacy of the executive against the legislature and the party leadership against its MPs.

It appears that just because the parliament is so majoritarian and the society so diverse, no political party can hope to offer an integrative vision of the country for all Canadians—the funnel is too wide at one end and too narrow at the other. Or to put it differently, the gradients of integration and representation are too steep, given the current institutional arrangements. Success has flowed to those parties that have managed to avoid offering such a vision, but rather, have left the difficult job of accommodating diverse interests to the handful of people who constitute the Cabinet. There, unshackled by detailed party platforms, clear ideologies, or the need to explain themselves at length to party members or Parliament, ministers have been able to pursue pragmatic deal making.

Canadian political parties have also needed local organizations capable of responding to very different circumstances from one riding or province to the next, and also capable of running effective local campaigns without strong unifying platforms and central party control. By leaving important functions such as the nomination of candidates and local campaigning in the hands of ordinary party members, successful Canadian parties have managed to provide a distinctive set of incentives for members to remain involved in the party at the riding level. This is very different from the incentives offered to members of tightly organized parties, which for the most committed, invariably focus on permanent, intermediary party organizations. Local autonomy allows constituency organizations in Canada to reflect the society in which they operate, and one assumes, to select candidates in tune with local conditions. While the dominance of the party leadership may limit the policy input of these members, their presence in the party room (plus that of senators) provides an opportunity for party leaders to see and hear the state of the nation.

While perhaps effective, such executive dominance is not easily defended on democratic grounds. No doubt this dynamic, along with the domination of the federal Parliament by one party, has underpinned the symbiotic relationship between interest groups and the executive that has become a feature of Canadian politics, and which itself has been criticized as being less than democratic. Untested by strong parliamentary debate, executives must look outside Parliament to know what the people are thinking. Not surprisingly, governments develop complex relations with various interest groups in order to gather information need to run the country effectively.

With only one route available to parties that wish to form the national government, while others are left with relatively few legislative seats, strong opposition is not likely to be a feature of Parliament. This leaves executives free to dominate the legislative process and encourages them to engage in deal making to protect their provincially based support. Somewhat ironically, then, this highly centralized bargaining game has been crucial in promoting the provincialization of Canadian politics over the last 40 years.

NOTES

1. Campbell Sharman and Anthony Sayers, 'Swings and Roundabouts? Patterns of Voting for the Australian Labor Party at State and Commonwealth Lower House Elections, 1901–1996', *Australian Journal of Political Science* 33, 3 (1998): 339–54.

2. Patrick Weller, *First Among Equals: Prime Ministers in Westminster Systems* (Sydney: Allen and Unwin, 1985).

3. John Courtney, *Do Conventions Really Matter? Choosing National Party Leaders in Canada* (Montreal and Kingston: McGill-Queen's University Press, 1995), 49–53, Table 3.3.

4. The House of Representatives at the Commonwealth level has a maximum term of three years and the state lower houses have maximum terms of four years.

5. Richard Johnston, 'The 1993 Canadian General Election: Realignment, Dealignment, or Something Else?', a paper presented at the 1996 annual meeting of the Canadian Political Science Association; Donald Blake, 'Party Competition and Electoral Voting: Canada in

Comparative Perspective' in Herman Bakvis, ed., *Representation, Integration and Political Parties in Canada*, vol. 14 of the research studies for the Royal Commission on Electoral Reform and Party Financing, (Ottawa and Toronto: RCERPF/Dundurn Press, 1991).

6. Anthony Sayers, *Parties, Candidates and Constituency Campaigns in Canadian Elections* (Vancouver: University of British Columbia Press, 1999), ch. 10.

7. Christian Leithner, 'Electoral Nationalisation, the Focus of Representation and Party Cohesion: A Five-Nation Anglo-American Analysis' in *Australian Political Studies* (1997) vol. 2 of Proceedings of the 1997 Annual Conference, Australasian Political Studies Association, 509–37, Table 1.

8. Giovanni Sartori, *Parties and Party Systems: A Framework for Analysis* (Cambridge: Cambridge University Press, 1976), xi.

9. Richard S. Katz and Peter Mair, 'The Evolution of Party Organizations in Europe: Three Faces of Party Organization' in William Crotty, ed., *Political Parties in a Changing Age*. Special issue of the *American Review of Politics* 14 (1994): 593–617.

10. Kay Lawson, 'When Linkages Fail' in Kay Lawson and Peter Merkl, eds, *When Parties Fail: Emerging Alternative Organizations* (Princeton: Princeton University Press, 1988).

11. Allan Kornberg, Joel Smith, and Harold D. Clark, *Citizen Politicians—Canada* (Durham, NC: Carolina Academic Press, 1979).

12. Richard S. Katz and Peter Mair, eds, *How Parties Organize: Change and Adaptation in Party Organization in Western Democracies* (London: Sage Publications, 1996).

13. Blake, 'Party Competition'.

14. Jeremy Moon and Michael Lusztig, 'Post War Patterns in Incumbency in the Australian States and Canadian Provinces' in Campbell Sharman, ed., *Parties and Federalism in Australia and Canada* (Canberra: Federalism Research Centre ANU, 1994), 212–14; David Stewart 'Comparing Party Systems in the Canadian Provinces and Australian States' in Sharman, ed., *Parties and Federalism*, Table 9.5.

15. Moon and Lusztig, 'Post War Patterns', 212. The duration and extent of Liberal dominance of Parliament may have played a role in the institutionalization of relations between the Liberals and various societal groups and is reminiscent of the relationship between the long-serving Liberal Democratic government of Japan and business cartels in that country. See Leslie A. Pal, *Interests of State: The Politics of Language, Multiculturalism and Feminism in Canada* (Montreal: McGill-Queen's University Press, 1993); Will Kymlicka, *Multicultural Citizenship: A Liberal Theory of Minority Rights* (New York: Oxford University Press 1995); and Chalmers Johnson, *MITI and the Japanese Miracle: The Growth of Industrial Policy 1929–1975* (Palo Alto, Calif.: Stanford University Press, 1982).

16. Maurice Pinard, *The Rise of a Third Party: A Study in Crisis Politics* (Scarborough, Ont.: Prentice Hall, 1971).

17. Stewart, 'Comparing Party Systems', Table 9.2.

18. Coalitional politics complicates my use of this measure, which assumes that the largest party is the governing party. In the case of the Commonwealth Parliament in Australia,

treating the non-Labor coalition as a single party when it wins elections, but not when it is in opposition, raises the index by about 0.3 for the period. Treating the coalition as a single party for all elections brings it back to nearly its original level.

19. Samuel H. Beer, *British Politics in the Collectivist Age* (New York: Alfred A. Knopf, 1967).

Chapter 12

Regionalism in an Age of Globalization

Livianna Tossutti

The emergence of 197 new ethnic, regional, and religious parties in 21 advanced capitalist societies since 1945 is a powerful testimonial to the contemporary relevance of sub-state loyalties.[1] The resurgence of spatial and cultural identities in affluent Western democracies has defied the expectations of modernization theorists, who predicted that 'parochial' regional and ethnic identities would diminish in importance in the modern age. The growth of these parties raises the question of whether sub-state loyalties are linked to contemporary processes of globalization and post-industrialization. In this chapter, an analysis of survey data on the demographic characteristics, issue orientations, and lifestyles of supporters of the separatist Bloc Québécois in Canada and the Lega Nord in Italy tests whether ethnic and regional loyalties reflect the outcomes of increased international interdependence and economic restructuring.

The Traditional View: Integration and Convergence

Traditionally, political scientists and sociologists expected that modernization would erode sub-state political identities. Convergence theorists argued that economic concentration, mass enfranchisement, scientific and technological advancements, mass communications, population mobility, and the expansion of social welfare programs would strengthen the legitimacy of the state and weaken citizen ties to ethnicity, race, language, and territory.[2] State building, modernization, and the erosion of sub-national loyalties were held to be interdependent and inevitable. Tendencies to preserve distinct cultural or territorial characteristics were expected to wane in the face of strong pressures in the modern state to assimilate.[3]

During the 1960s and 1970s, ethnic and territorial protest in Canada, Belgium, the United Kingdom, and other Western countries illustrated that economic and political modernization had paradoxically generated decentralist demands for neighbourhood councils, power devolution to sub-state governments, and the revival of ethnic nationalism.[4] There is a growing literature that now links the post-war revival of nationalism and regionalism to increased international interdependence and post-industrial restructuring. The so-called 'new localism' is distinguished from earlier ethnocultural revivals in that it is held to be 'cosmopolitan' (familiar with many countries, sophisticated, free from national prejudice)[5] rather than 'parochial' (provincial, narrow) and insulated from international forces.[6]

Globalization and the 'New Localism'

Writers of the globalist-localist school argue that the new localism, which refers to the resurgence of ethnic and regional movements, the decentralization of economic production, environmentalism, and a renewed interest in living in smaller cities, represents a postmodern escape from the 'alienation and identity loss' engendered by modernization. Modernization is driven by instrumental rationality, an emphasis on material values of production and consumption, the concentration of power in the central state, hierarchical relationships, cultural assimilation, territorial sovereignty, and inter-state differentiation.[7] Postmodernity refers to a climate of rebellion against rationalism, and against a belief in the superiority of Western values and the existence of one religious or political centre.[8]

Before considering the potential links between international interdependence, economic restructuring, and the new localism, the terms 'globalization' and 'post-industrial' must be defined. Globalization refers to a set of processes by which links across state boundaries grow stronger. Robertson views globalization as a 'compression of the world and the intensification of consciousness of the world as a whole'.[9] Signs of the accelerated pace of globalization include the growth of supra-national institutions or accords such as the European Union and the North American Free Trade Agreement, the spread of multinational corporations, international capital mobility, and advancements in computerized technology and transportation that have facilitated rapid flows of information and people across state frontiers. It is argued that these transformations in the international environment have eroded the classic functions and legitimacy of the state, and have reinforced citizen attachments to sub-state institutions and identities.[10]

While few would argue that states are becoming redundant, there is a widespread acknowledgement that globalization has reduced centralized political control by providing opportunities for policy to be negotiated by sub-national actors. European Union institutions have become arenas where ethnocultural groups lobby for the protection of minority languages and human rights, and where regional and local governments contribute towards policy development in the fields of public health, education, culture, and the economy.[11]

Continental market integration and capital mobility have also provided new incentives for ethnoregional parties in Quebec, Flanders, Catalonia, and Scotland to abandon economic protectionism and seek political independence. Supporters of international free trade argue that capital mobility would reduce the costs of political separation by allowing smaller regions to 'exploit their comparative advantage of low cost to attract investment'.[12] Opponents of accords like the North American Free Trade Agreement perceive that international convergence in trade policy has the potential to erode the sovereignty, identity, and policy independence of individual states.

In addition to the expansion of supra-national organizations and regional free trade areas, globalist-localist scholars contend that the resurgence of the new localism is linked to the spread of computerized technology and faster modes of transportation.[13] The gradual erosion of spatial and temporal barriers between countries tests the capacity of central governments to monitor and control international population movements and the exchange of ideas. Access to personal computers, faxes, the Internet, cell phones, and affordable air travel permits individuals, firms, and sub-national governments to bypass state agencies and communicate directly with their counterparts abroad. Advances in science and technology have also led to economic decentralization. Technological developments have made the territorial dispersion of production possible, since companies are now less dependent on proximity to natural resources or traditional transportation networks such as roads and waterways.[14] Employees can work from home, and firms can relocate to peripheral areas where land and labour costs are more affordable. Technology has also facilitated the transition from Fordist to post-Fordist production models, where there has been a shift from mass production in big plants to production and specialization in smaller firms that can adapt to the rapidly changing demands of world markets.

More frequent contacts between people from different countries can reinforce the importance of preserving and promoting local identities. Although the new technology has the potential to help dominant cultures overwhelm minority traditions (the prevalence of English-backed software serves as an example), sub-state actors can use the same technology to defend their interests. Ethnic and regional political parties, as well as sub-national governments, often develop multilingual Web sites in order to communicate their messages or promote distinctive local products to global audiences. As Mlinar has argued, the same scientific breakthroughs that have shrunk the world have also given people and sub-national governments the incentive and means to detach from the political centre.[15]

Globalist-localists also contend that fundamental changes in the workplace have reinforced sub-state political identities. One of these changes involves the post-industrial restructuring of economic production, where there has been a shift away from the provision of raw materials and manufactured goods in all Western societies towards tertiary employment, production, and consumption modes requiring a skilled and specialized workforce.[16] These trends are held to sustain each other because workers in manufacturing and processing industries operate in a hierarchical system that requires conformity to decisions handed down from above, while employees in the service and information economy work in relatively decentralized decision-structures that encourage innovation.[17] The emergence of a highly educated workforce and a less hierarchical work environment has made it more likely that educated workers in tertiary activities will challenge central authorities and call for decentralized political arrangements.[18]

Thus, the theoretical literature offers two dominant explanations of contemporary ethnoregional parties: they may be parochial remnants of a premodern era, as the convergence theorists argue, or cosmopolitan reflections of globalization and post-industrialization in a postmodern era.

The Quebec and Northern Italian Cases

One way of assessing the nature of ethnic and regional appeals is to examine the attitudes, lifestyles, and sociological composition of supporters of electorally successful sub-state parties. The Bloc and Lega are ideal choices for this study, since the former party attained Official Opposition status in the Canadian Parliament, and the latter participated in a coalition government.

The Lega's roots can be traced to the early 1980s in the Veneto region of northeastern Italy, when the first regional league was formed to promote cultural protection, and later, the decentralization of powers to the regions and provinces. As these leagues spread to northwestern and central Italy, they criticized the corruption and inefficiency of the Italian bureaucracy, taxation and investment policies that were perceived to penalize the north and favour the south, and questionable development strategies that had failed to reduce regional economic disparities. The League also opposed immigration from North Africa, the Middle East, and eastern Europe.[19] In 1991, the regional leagues formed the Lega Nord to advocate the federalization of unitary Italy. Since 1996, the Lega had campaigned for the creation of an independent Padania that would include northern Italy and parts of central Italy, but dropped this demand in 2000 in favour of devalution.

The Lega's electoral support grew from 8.7 to 10.1 per cent between the 1992 and 1996 general elections. In many northern provinces, its share of support for the proportional quota of seats in the Chamber of Deputies ranges between 20 and 40 per cent.[20] Following the spring 1994 election, the Lega participated briefly in a centre-right coalition government. Since 1996, its support has stagnated in subsequent administrative, regional, and European ballots. In April 2000, the Lega rejoined a political alliance that captured 8 out of 15 presidencies in regional elections. The most recent national election, held in May 2001, saw the Lega and its centre-right allies defeat the centre-left coalition.

In 1990, the Bloc Québécois (BQ) was formed in response to the defeat of the Meech Lake Constitutional Accord. The constitutional amendment had been drafted to meet Quebec's conditions for signing the Constitution Act, which had been patriated from London in 1982. Canada's fundamental law was then reformed to include a Charter of Rights and Freedoms and an amending formula, without conceding new powers to the provinces. Many Quebeckers attributed the demise of Meech to provincial resentment at a clause recognizing Quebec as a 'distinct society'. These events led frustrated Liberal and Conservative MPs from Quebec to create the BQ. In the 1993 federal election, the Bloc won 54 of the 75 Quebec seats in the House of Commons to become the Official Opposition. In late 1995, the Quebec government held a referendum on sovereignty, which the federalist opposition barely won with 50.6 per cent of the popular vote. In the two federal elections held since then, the Bloc's popular support in Quebec dropped and stabilized at between 38 and 40 per cent.

Hypotheses: Premodern versus Postmodern Regionalism

The proposed links between globalization, post-industrialization, and the new localism suggest several hypotheses about the potential socio-demographic characteristics of Lega and Bloc supporters (Table 12.1). If the globalist-localist perspective can shed light on the appeal of the Lega and Bloc, then their members are likely to be young, relatively affluent, highly educated individuals. They would work in small, post-Fordist firms and would be employed in tertiary activities. They would also tend to live in the smaller communities whose appeal is part of the revival of the new localism.

The behavioural literature offers several reasons for these expectations. Ecological analyses of Lega support in Veneto and Lombardia between 1985 and 1989 found that the leagues developed in small and mid-sized towns dominated by small industry, as well as in provinces characterized by higher levels of disposable income and home ownership.[21] Similar patterns characterize the support base for other European regional parties. For instance, the Flemish nationalist Volksunie has achieved its best results in Belgian cantons where a high percentage of people work in tertiary and upper-income occupations. Individual level analyses of support for the Volksunie and

Table 12.1: Indicators of Premodern and Postmodern Localism

Indicator	Premodern	Postmodern
Socio-demographic	Older Not highly educated Resides in smaller centres Not affluent Employed in small firms	Young Highly educated Resides in smaller centres Affluent Employed in small, tertiary sector firms
Issue orientations	Materialist, domestic (unemployment, debt, inflation, crime, defence) Opposes assimilation Supports lower immigration levels	Post-materialist, international (environment, immigration) Opposes assimilation Opposes lower immigration levels
Geographic attachment	Local strongest; national and international weak	Local and international strongest; national weakest

Lifestyle patterns	Low individuation:
	• parochial
	• low geographic mobility
	• low class mobility
	• resides in culturally homogeneous
	  neighbourhood
	• little travel
	• infrequent technology use
	• unilingual
	• little interest in foreign news
		High individuation:
		• cosmopolitan
		• high geographic mobility
		• high class mobility
		• resides in multicultural
		  neighbourhood
		• frequent travel
		• frequent technology use
		• speaks other languages
		• interest in foreign news

the Catalan Convergence and Union have revealed that they appeal to the young, the well-educated, and the managerial and professional classes.[22] Studies of the Bloc electorate have also shown that it draws disproportionate support from young people aged between 18 and 29.[23]

Globalist-localist theorists argue that global tendencies have brought new issues to the forefront of citizen consciousness. As Strassoldo has argued, the two new elements of twentieth-century globalization processes are the ecological world view and aspirations for a 'pluralist, non-hierarchical, de-centred world-society'.[24] If transnational issues underpin the issue priorities of the respondents, then subjects such as the environment and immigration should figure in their identification of important concerns. Likewise, domestic topics such as unemployment, debt reduction, and crime should not dominate their priorities.

Contemporary globalization is held to reject a conception of world unity based on one set of values and the dominance of a core area, and to favour pluralism.[25] In order to gauge the openness of regional party supporters to cultural diversity, the respondents were asked to express their opinions on immigrant assimilation and quotas. An individual who accepts pluralism would be expected to oppose assimilation and limited immigration. Agreement with either of these propositions would entail some resistence to global cultural diversity. Where people choose to reside is another indicator of intense, daily exposure to multicultural influences. Therefore, it is proposed that if the party members reflect cosmopolitan tendencies, they will be more likely to indicate that they live in multicultural neighbourhoods.

The territorial attachments of the respondents were also probed in the survey. Rosenau has argued that the coexistence of supra-nationalism and localism is not paradoxical, but rather the expected product of rapid change in the international political environment. Where modernization and state building were supposed to redirect citizen loyalties to countries, accelerated international interdependence, the relative decline of state power, and the transference of competences to lower-order governments are held to promote dual attachments to local and international geographic areas.[26] A 1992–93 survey conducted in four provinces of Lombardy and Veneto found that Lega sympathizers were more likely to feel closer to their province-region, Europe, and northern Italy (in that order), than were supporters of non-secessionist parties, who cited the province-region and Italy as the areas to which they felt closest.[27] Therefore, if the globalist-localist thesis can shed light on regionalism, then party members will be more likely to express weak attachments to Canada or Italy and strong feelings for local/intermediate *and* continental spaces.

Advancements in computer technology, transportation, and educational attainment have increased the possibilities for individuals to escape lifestyles that were once predetermined by geography and social class. The result has been an increase in intergenerational spatial and social mobility.[28] If the parties attract individuals who reflect these transformations, then they will have lived or attended school in areas other than their birth region, and will belong to a different socio-economic class from that of their parents.

The interdependence of events and people in different locales is another feature of globalization. As McLuhan has argued, the electronic age has made the world a village where people are increasingly involved in each others' lives.[29] New technologies have destroyed both temporal and spatial discontinuities: computers, faxes, and other technologies link people in different time zones and allow them to work around the clock.[30] Therefore, if the globalist-localist perspective is accurate, individuals who are receptive to global influences are likely to be connected to people and events around the world through frequent foreign travel, technology usage, a knowledge of several languages, and a strong interest in foreign news.

Research Design

This study is based on an analysis of original survey data on Bloc and Lega members, and on a secondary analysis of Italian and Canadian voters from across the political spectrum. Since surveys do not generally focus on globalization themes, Italian- and French-language surveys were developed to probe the issue orientations, lifestyle patterns, cultural interests, and socio-demographic characteristics of the Lega and Bloc members. The self-administered questionnaires were distributed to members of the Bloc across Quebec, and to their Lega counterparts in five provinces of Piemonte, a region in northwestern Italy, where the party won between 15 and 23 per cent of popular support in proportional elections to the Chamber of Deputies during the 1990s.

Since party officials did not permit access to confidential membership lists, non-random, snowball sampling techniques were employed to locate current members.[31] Due to the reliance on non-probabilistic sampling techniques, the results were cross-checked against previous literature and comparable items in the 1995 International Social Survey Program (ISSP) National Identity Survey, a large-scale random survey of voters across North America and Europe.[32] The cross-national survey's focus on territorial identities, mobility patterns, international orientations, and demographic characteristics permitted comparisons between autonomist party voters in both countries, and other partisans in their respective party systems.

Globalization and the New Localism: The Members

The Lega members are typically young males with middling levels of education, although the proportion of individuals with a completed university degree exceeds the national average of 6 per cent.[33] They tend to work as office employees or professionals in small firms, with more than a third reporting annual household incomes above the Italian median of 36 to 50 million lire.[34] More than two-thirds live in small communities with 30,000 or fewer people. Thus far, their youth, affluence, and residential patterns confirm many of the expectations of the globalist-localist thesis (Table 12.2).

Their issue orientations reflect a concern with both domestic and international subjects. A plurality of the respondents cited the public debt as the most important problem facing Italy, while the environment was the second-ranked topic. Their

Table 12.2: Lega Nord and Bloc Québécois Membership Profile (%)

	Lega Nord (n=181)	Bloc Québécois (n=193)
Males	60.3	66.3
Mean age in years	40.0	47.4
High school	51.7	16.7
University	19.5	61.0
Office employee/sales	21.5	5.7
Professional	20.4	18.2
Owner of business with < 10 employees	5.0	6.8
Retired	8.0	25.5
Annual household income:		
> L 50 million	35.2	
>C$60,000		29.5
Workplace size: 1–10 employees	35.4	48.9
Lives in multicultural neighbourhood	35.6	12.0
Community size: < 30,001 residents	70.8	42.3
Most important issue	Debt	Unemployment
Second most important issue	Ecology	Unemployment
Territorial identification:		
town/city	35.8	2.6
province/region	32.6	96.4
continent	24.9	1.0
Supports reduced immigration	80.0	52.8
Supports immigrant assimilation	37.8	79.3
Technology use: > 3 times/week	61.1	58.9
Foreign travel:		
one or more times in last six months	60.2	40.4
High interest in local news	62.4	71.4
High interest in international news	46.6	70.5
Bilingual	65.0	86.5
Lived outside birth region (Lega):	33.1	
Lived outside birth community (BQ):		50.3
Studied outside birth region/province	33.9	24.4
Inter-generational class mobility	36.7	43.0

N=374; Source: See endnote no. 31

bifurcated territorial affinities also suggest that sub-national and continental identities are compatible within the party. Almost a quarter of the Leghisti feel closest to Europe, while two-thirds feel most attached to their towns and/or cities or Piemonte.

The Lega members exhibit considerable spatial mobility, although on some items, there is less evidence of an appreciation of foreign influences (Table 12.2). They are heavy users of the new technology, frequent travellers abroad, and at least a third have either lived or studied outside the region. However, the data on class membership and linguistic proficiency do not furnish evidence of exceptional mobility, as their levels of bilingualism mirror overall regional rates of 64 per cent.[35] Finally, their interests are generally rooted in their communities. A majority of them pay close attention to local news, but far fewer express 'a lot of interest' in international news, multicultural events (16.2 per cent), and sports broadcasts from other countries (7.3 per cent).

Their orientations towards global cultural diversity do not confirm either the convergence or globalist-localist perspectives. Only a minority favour immigrant assimilation, signifying that the Leghisti reject 'modern' preferences for cultural standardization. Nevertheless, two-thirds live in ethnically homogeneous areas, and an overwhelming majority oppose increased immigration. The latter findings recall previous research showing that Lega sympathizers in Lombardia and Veneto are more likely to oppose migration from southern Italy and the developing world than are other parties' sympathizers.[36] Subsequent studies found that supporters of centre-right parties, which include the Lega, the Movimento Sociale Italiano-Alleanza Nazionale (MSI-AN), and to a lesser extent, Forza Italia, were more likely than leftist voters to feel that immigrants increase crime rates and should return home.[37]

Overall, the Leghisti defy characterization as either 'parochial and insular' or 'cosmopolitan and global'. The evidence suggests that while their demographic profile and mobile lifestyles reflect global and post-industrial tendencies, their cultural interests and attitudes towards immigrants from the developing world cannot be considered cosmopolitan.

The sociological composition of the Bloc respondents mirrors some of the patterns detected in the Lega data. Although the Bloquistes are older and include a substantial proportion of retirees (20 per cent are over 60), their education and occupation profile conforms with the theoretical expectations. More than 60 per cent have completed a university degree, compared to about 12 per cent of the general Quebec population.[38] Those who are still in the workforce tend to work in small-scale, tertiary businesses. An additional 8 per cent are employed as educators or civil servants (data not shown). Large-scale manufacturing and processing industries do not provide fertile ground for Bloc support; rather, its membership base is drawn from the tertiary and knowledge sectors. Their household incomes tend to fall in the same category as the Quebec average ($42,229 in 1995 constant dollars).[39] Unlike the Leghisti, there is no distinctive community size pattern, as they are split between smaller (30,000 or less) and larger centres.

Their issue orientations and territorial loyalties do not confirm the expectations of the globalist-localist thesis. They are more concerned with unemployment, the debt, and social programs, rather than with transnational issues. Unlike their European counterparts, the Bloquistes do not identify closely with North America or their municipalities. The unidirectional nature of their territorial attachments may be partly explained by the comprehensiveness of the European Union project to advance the economic and political integration of its member states. The North American Free Trade Agreement has erased most barriers to trade and capital mobility and some that restrict labour mobility, but there has not been a parallel move to create an executive, assembly, bureaucracy, and judiciary with authority over continental affairs. North American political integration is less advanced than it is in Europe, and this may partially explain the relative absence of continental identification.

The Bloc respondents, as with their Lega counterparts, are frequent users of the new technology. Unlike their Italian counterparts, they report higher levels of bilingualism, a stronger interest in international current events, and greater class mobility. They are more likely than the Italians to report high levels of interest in international sports (11.5 per cent name Formula One racing or the Olympics as examples) or multicultural events staged in Quebec (39 per cent). While their linguistic skills and interests denote a greater degree of cosmopolitanism, their geographic mobility is limited in comparison to the Italians. Far fewer Bloc respondents had travelled abroad in the previous six months and only a quarter have studied outside the province. The only exception to this observation is that while Bloc members do not tend to leave the province or Canada as frequently as the Piemontesi leave their region or Italy, they are not averse to moving between communities within Quebec. Since one in two has lived in a city or town where he or she was not born, the Bloc respondants cannot be considered immobile.

Finally, their attitudes towards ethnic diversity are not consistent with postmodern tendencies. They are even more likely to live in ethnically homogeneous neighbourhoods than the Leghisti, and they overwhelmingly favour the assimilation of immigrants in Quebec society. While they are far more favourably disposed towards increased immigration than the Italians, the split on the immigration question reveals considerable ambivalence about the desirability of pluralism. When these indicators are considered together, there is less evidence to suggest internationalist orientations.

The Bloc respondents' occupational and educational profile reflects several aspects of post-industrial restructuring, and their interests and linguistic proficiency show evidence of cosmopolitanism. However, they are not as mobile as the Italian respondents and they report attitudes about assimilation that are more in keeping with modern preferences for cultural homogenization.

The Voters

The ISSP survey conducted in Italy reveals few statistically significant demographic differences between Lega voters and supporters of its main competitors.[40] This casts doubt on modernization theory expectations that regionalists or ethnic nationalists will be inherently more insular than voters for parties that do not cater to sub-state interests. While Lega voters tend to be males (59.4 per cent) in their mid-forties with a high school education or less (90.6 per cent), the differences between them and supporters of parties located across the political spectrum are statistically insignificant. When they differ from Italians supporting the MSI-AN and Forza Italia, or the leftist Democratic Party of the Left (PDS) and Communist Refoundation (RC), their characteristics reflect post-industrial affluence and residence patterns. For instance, 27 per cent of Lega voters report household incomes in the top quartile of incomes ($x^2=18.71$, df 12, p$\leq$.10), and 70 per cent live in communities with 30,000 and fewer residents ($x^2=49.38$, df 20, p$\leq$.001).

Lega voters are not significantly different from other Italians in their attachments to Europe: 72.1 per cent feel close to the continent and 82.8 per cent think Italy should unite fully with the European Union rather than try to protect its independence. However, they and RC voters are distinguished from most Italians by their rejection of state nationalism (Table 12.3). Supporters of both parties would not support Italy if it erred. Not surprisingly, the Leghisti also differ from other party sympathizers in their overwhelming support for Italy's dissolution.

Several survey items shed light on the mobility of Italian voters, their openness to foreign economic and cultural influences, and their attitudes towards supra-national governance.[41] Both the RC and Lega voters have led more mobile lifestyles than other Italians, but all the respondents (including the Leghisti) overwhelmingly favour limits on foreign imports. Although the differences between party supporters are not statistically significant, Forza Italia voters report the strongest protectionist tendencies, with 80.4 per cent supporting these limits. On another item, Lega voters and supporters of the leftist PDS and RC are more amenable to allowing foreigners to purchase land than voters for the centre-right Forza Italia and MSI-AN (Table 12.3).

Italians generally express widespread confidence in the desirability of international bodies to enforce solutions to problems like environmental pollution. More than 98 per cent of the Lega voters express support for international involvement, and all of them agree that more foreign languages should be taught in schools. (Inter-party

Table 12.3: Territorial Attachments, Mobility Patterns, and Immigration Orientations of Italian Voters (column percentages)

	MSI-AN	Forza Italia	Lega Nord	PDS	RC	x^2
How close do you feel to Italy? . . . not very close/ not close at all	3.7 (2)	14.8 (17)	21.9 (14)	8.3 (10)	21.1 (4)	12.67b
I support my country even if it is wrong . . . SA/A	60.0 (27)	52.6 (51)	36.4 (20)	33.7 (34)	37.5 (6)	13.53b
Parts of Italy should be allowed to separate . . . SA/A	9.3 (5)	16.7 (19)	58.3 (41)	6.0 (7)	21.1 (4)	96.44a
How long have you lived in other countries? . . . one or more years	3.7 (2)	1.7 (2)	9.4 (6)	5.8 (7)	15.8 (3)	9.41c
Foreigners should not be allowed to buy land . . . SA/A	37.5 (15)	44.8 (39)	27.5 (14)	23.7 (23)	28.6 (4)	10.59c
Immigrants increase crime rates . . . SA/A	87.5 (42)	82.9 (87)	88.5 (46)	60.2 (62)	50.0 (8)	30.29a
Immigrants are good for the economy . . . SA/A	27.7 (13)	8.7 (8)	17.0 (8)	38.3 (36)	33.3 (5)	24.84a
Immigrants take jobs from people . . . SA/A	52.1 (25)	55.9 (52)	46.2 (24)	26.0 (26)	23.5 (4)	22.61a
Immigration should be increased . . . SA/A	6.5 (3)	3.4 (3)	0.0 (0)	11.4 (9)	21.4 (3)	14.00b

Source: International Social Survey Program National Identity Survey (Italy); n=1094
a) p≤.001; b) p≤.01 c) p≤.05

differences were insignificant for both items.) Finally, only a minority of Lega voters (46.2 per cent) feel that television programming should give preference to Italian films and shows, indicating that they are open to the cultural products of other societies. (Party differences were insignificant.)

What the globalist-localist thesis fails to account for is the resistence on the part of many Lega voters to ethnic diversity, although their orientations often do not differ significantly from those expressed by other Italians. For example, while 65 per cent of the Lega voters believe that ethnic minorities should be given government assistance to preserve their traditions, 64 per cent feel that different racial and ethnic groups should assimilate into Italian society. Almost all supporters of the PDS and centre-right parties (including the Lega) also believe that Italy should take strong measures to deport illegal immigrants. (Party differences are insignificant for the three items.) These findings indicate two patterns: first, that Lega voters are no more or less cosmopolitan than most Italians; and second, that the traditions of the Piemontese, Friulan, South Tyrolean, and Occitanian minorities are held to be more worthy of preservation than immigrant customs.

Table 12.3 reveals that supporters of the Lega and the two centre-right parties are significantly more likely than leftist voters to feel that immigrants increase crime rates and that they offer dubious economic benefits for Italy. While few or no voters for the centre-right favoured additional immigration, between 79 and 89 per cent of leftist voters also oppose increases. As with the membership survey, Lega voters are wealthier than most and are very enthusiastic about the institutions, products, and symbols of globalization; yet, when it comes to ethnic diversity within Italian society, their attitudes confirm the predictions of the convergence theorists.

The ISSP Canadian survey revealed that Bloc voters are significantly younger, better educated and more likely to be concentrated in smaller communities than voters for the Liberal, Reform, New Democratic, and Progressive Conservative parties (data not shown). Almost two-thirds are aged 44 and under (x^2=66.05, df 20, p≤.001) and 43.4 per cent had received a university education (x^2=31.48, df 16, p≤.01). Relative to other parties, the Bloc claims the highest proportion of its support from small-town dwellers (one in five) and the lowest from city residents (x^2=63.30, df 12, p≤.001). Sociological characteristics that do not conform to the globalist-localist thesis include the fact that 63 per cent work in large organizations employing more than 100 people (x^2=37.27, df 20, p≤.01). Bloc, NDP, and Reform voters also report lower annual household incomes than Conservative or Liberal voters, with 55.8 per cent of Bloc respondents earning less than $45,000 ($x^2$=29.33, df 12, p≤.001).

Previous findings that suggested Bloc voters are not as attached to North America or as mobile as their Italian counterparts were confirmed. They are less likely to feel close to North America, and both Bloc, and Reform supporters are more likely to have spent their childhood in the same town or to remain in the country (Table 12.4).[42] Supporters of the Bloc, Reform, and Progressive Conservative parties are not as mobile as NDP and Liberal voters; between 22 and 23 per cent of the former groups have lived outside Canada for one or more years, compared to over a third of the NDP and Liberal voters. While Bloc voters tend to stay closer to home, they report significantly higher

Table 12.4: Territorial Mobility and International Orientations of Canadian Voters (column percentages)

	PC	Liberal	NDP	BQ	Reform	x^2
How close do you feel to Canada? . . . Very close/close	83.3 (125)	88.7 (519)	83.7 (128)	25.4 (35)	75.4 (92)	270.49a
How close do you feel to North America? . . . Very close/close	60.3 (88)	64.9 (362)	45.8 (65)	40.9 (54)	58.8 (70)	35.74a
Canada: one nation or separate . . . separate	8.2 (12)	7.9 (44)	19.6 (27)	93.7 (118)	23.4 (26)	474.13a
Where did you spend your childhood? . . . this town	33.1 (50)	38.1 (226)	32.1 (50)	45.2 (66)	45.8 (55)	55.41a
. . . outside country	11.3 (17)	14.3 (85)	16.7 (26)	3.4 (5)	7.5 (9)	
How long have you lived outside the country? . . . 1 or more years	23.0 (35)	34.6 (206)	35.2 (56)	23.3 (34)	22.8 (28)	17.48a
Int'l bodies enforce solutions . . . SA/A	87.6 (113)	88.1 (459)	96.2 (127)	86 (111)	80.7 (92)	14.67a
Schools should teach more foreign languages . . . SA/A	70.2 (66)	73.1 (305)	85.7 (96)	73.0 (73)	49.4 (39)	31.11a
Foreigners should not be allowed to buy land . . . SA/A	37.7 (46)	30.7 (138)	42.9 (48)	36.4 (40)	45.5 (46)	11.83c
NAFTA has brought benefits to this country	84.4 (92)	71 (284)	31.6 (37)	76.6 (72)	63 (58)	88.43a
I support my country even if it is wrong . . . SA/A	21.2 (24)	22.7 (110)	3.6 (5)	11 (14)	14.3 (15)	33.28a

Source: 1995 International Social Survey Program National Identity Survey (Canada); n=1,544

a)p≤.001; b)p≤.01; c)p≤.05

levels of linguistic mobility than voters for non-separatist parties (x^2=151.05, p≤.001, data not shown).

Bloc voters generally embrace international economic links, institutions, and cultures. Only a minority feel that foreigners should not be allowed to buy land, although a majority support limits on foreign imports. (Party differences are insignificant for the second item.) Bloc voters feel that the North American Free Trade Agreement has brought benefits to the country—a positive evaluation of international free trade that stands in sharp contrast to the negative evaluations of voters for the social democratic NDP (Table 12.4). They also agree that international bodies should enforce solutions to problems like environmental pollution, although they are not as enthusiastic about international involvement as NDP, Progressive Conservative, or Liberal voters. Similar patterns emerge with respect to foreign-language instruction in schools. Almost three-quarters of the Bloc voters favour the teaching of more

Table 12.5: Immigration Orientations of Canadian Voters (column percentages)

	PC	Liberal	NDP	BQ	Reform	x^2
Help minorities preserve their traditions . . . SA/A	10.3 (12)	21.5 (103)	27.4 (32)	42.4 (42)	3.8 (4)	57.01a
Immigrants should maintain their traditions . . . SA/A	31.0 (40)	34.6 (168)	49.6 (64)	35.2 (44)	20.9 (23)	22.69a
Immigrants increase crime rates . . . SA/A	33.7 (35)	24.2 (102)	18.8 (24)	21.6 (22)	54.8 (46)	42.56a
Immigrants are good for the economy . . . SA/A	73.6 (81)	89.8 (407)	80.7 (109)	76.2 (80)	84.1 (69)	26.48a
Immigrants take jobs away . . . SA/A	38.5 (45)	27.3 (127)	27.4 (40)	27.3 (30)	46.8 (44)	18.76a
Immigration should be increased . . . SA/A	22.2 (18)	32.4 (95)	43.9 (43)	31.3 (26)	8.4 (7)	30.78a
It should be easier for immigrants to obtain citizenship . . . SA/A	20.2 (17)	20.7 (82)	11.6 (13)	22.7 (22)	8.8 (8)	11.89c

Source: 1995 International Social Survey Program National Identity Survey (Canada); n=1,544
a)p≤.001; c)p≤.05

foreign languages in schools, although NDP voters are the most supportive of all Canadians.

Ambivalence about ethnic pluralism was noted in both parties.[43] Among Canadian voters, Bloc electors report the most support for maintaining minority traditions, yet, as with the Lega voters, 65 per cent feel that immigrants should adapt to the wider society rather than maintain their traditions (Table 12.5). While Reformers are the least receptive to the idea of immigrants maintaining their cultural traditions, only a third of the Bloc, PC, and Liberal voters support the retention of heritage cultures. Bloc and NDP voters are less likely to agree than other party supporters that immigrants increase crime and are generally positive about the contributions of foreign-born citizens to the economy. Finally, Bloc and Liberal voters share virtually identical attitudes towards immigration and naturalization. Table 12.5 shows that while there is little enthusiasm for increased ethnic diversity, Bloc voters are no more intolerant than most Canadians on these matters.

The voter data support most of the conclusions drawn from the membership survey. The sociological composition of Bloc voters is mixed, their spatial mobility comparatively limited, and their territorial affinities unidirectional. However, they are open to international economic influences, and on many of the questions about immigration, their lukewarm attitudes parallel those expressed by PC and Liberal voters.

The Globalist-Localist Perspective and
the New Localism in Northern Italy and Quebec

This study has demonstrated that our understanding of 'new localist' appeals can be advanced through an analysis of how international forces and economic restructuring are reflected in the attitudes, lifestyles, and social characteristics of citizens who support autonomist parties. It is also evident that the perspective is more applicable to the European case, meaning that domestic factors play a comparatively larger role in describing the nature of the Bloc's appeal.

Post-industrial and post-Fordist economic transformations, an interest in ecology, bifurcated territorial loyalties, a resistance to immigrant assimilation, and considerable spatial and linguistic mobility characterize the Lega membership. Three major observations can be drawn from the survey of Italian voters. For the most part, Lega voters are not sociologically distinctive. Second, they embrace foreign influences and minority rights through strong support for the European Union, foreign investment, cultural products and languages, and the preservation of minority traditions. The final observation weakens the tenets of the globalist-localist thesis: Lega voters and members strongly oppose immigration and doubt whether positive social and economic benefits accrue from it.

Bloc members are highly educated, bilingual tertiary workers who report comparatively favourable attitudes about immigration and a keen interest in the new technology and foreign cultures. However, their preferences for assimilation and preoccupation with domestic, materialist issues are more 'modern' than 'postmodern'. Their residential segregation, relatively limited geographic mobility, and rejection of North America as a source of psychological attachment weakens the applicability of the globalist-localist perspective. The picture changes slightly when the Bloc's electoral base is considered. Its voters are young and well educated, and they tend to live in smaller communities. They are open to supra-national governance and regional free trade, and they express views about immigration that are no more intolerant than those voiced by other Canadians, with the exception of NDP supporters.

The appeal of both parties can be attributed to their capacity to capture the diversity within their target electorates. While neither the convergence nor the globalist-localist perspectives completely captures the essence of these parties' supporters, predictions that sub-state loyalties could not evolve beyond the modern age are clearly premature. The Lega has demonstrated an ability to attract supporters who reflect many of the social, political, economic, and technological transformations inherent in globalization and post-industrialization. The Bloc's appeal is not as closely related to these changes, but it is clearly not insulated from them. What the supporters of both parties share is a resistence to cultural diversity, and in that respect, they also represent a reaction against some of the consequences of international interdependence.

NOTES

The field work for this study was funded by the Social Sciences and Humanities Research Council (SSHRC). I would like to thank the Department of Political Science at the University of

Calgary for providing a stimulating forum to discuss regionalism in Canada and abroad. Dr Harold Clarke, Dr Lawrence LeDuc, Professor Richard Price, and the anonymous reviewers have all provided invaluable guidance for preparing this chapter.

1. The archival research is based on the following sources: Thomas T. Mackie and Richard Rose, *The International Almanac of Electoral History* (Washington, DC: Congressional Quarterly, 1991); Giovanni Sartori, *Parties and Party Systems: A Framework for Analysis* (Cambridge: Cambridge University Press, 1976); *Western Europe, 1993* (London: Europa Publications, 1992); *The Far East and Australasia*, 20th edn (London: Europa Publications Ltd, 1994); *The Middle East and North Africa*, 41st edn (London: Europa Publications, 1994); Alan J. Day, ed. *Political Parties of the World* (Chicago and London: St James Press, 1988); Council on Foreign Relations, *Political Atlas and Handbook of the World 1945–1987* (New York: Harper, 1988); Arthur S. Banks and T. Miller, *Political Handbook of the World 1999* (Binghamton, NY: CSA Publications, 1999).

2. See Talcott Parsons, *Societies: Evolutionary and Comparative Perspectives* (Englewood Cliffs, NJ: Prentice Hall, 1966); Emile Durkheim, *The Division of Labour in Society* (New York: Free Press, 1964), 187; Seymour Lipset and Stein Rokkan, *Party Systems and Voter Alignments: An Introduction* (New York: Free Press, 1967).

3. Zygmunt Bauman, 'Modernity and Ambivalence' in Mike Featherstone, ed., *Global Culture: Nationalism, Globalization and Modernity* (London: Sage Publications, 1990), 156.

4. See Mildred A. Schwartz, *Politics and Territory: The Sociology of Regional Persistence in Canada* (Montreal: McGill-Queen's University Press, 1974); L.J. Sharpe, 'Decentralist Trends in Western Democracies' in L.J. Sharpe, ed., *Decentralist Trends in Western Democracies* (Beverly Hills, CA: Sage Publications, 1979); Derek Urwin, 'Social Cleavages and Political Parties in Belgium: Problems of Institutionalization', *Political Studies* 28, 3 (1970).

5. The definition of 'cosmopolitan' is drawn from the Canadian edition of Collins English Dictionary.

6. Raimondo Strassoldo, 'Globalism and Localism: Theoretical Reflections and Some Evidence' in Zdravko Mlinar, ed., *Globalization and Territorial Identities* (Hants, UK: Avebury Ashgate Publishing, 1992), 39–46.

7. Strassoldo, 'Globalism and Localism', 45–6.

8. Thomas Docherty, ed., *Postmodernism: A Reader* (New York: Columbia University Press, 1993), 467–8.

9. Roland Robertson, *Globalization: Social Theory and Global Culture* (London: Sage Publications, 1992), 8, 53.

10. James Rosenau, *Turbulence in World Politics* (Princeton: Princeton University Press, 1990); James Rosenau and R.B.A. DiMuccio, 'Turbulence and Sovereignty in World Politics: Explaining the Relocation of Legitimacy in the 1990s and Beyond' in Mlinar, ed., *Globalization.*

11. Lisebeth Hooghe and Gary Marks, 'Europe with the Regions: Channels of Regional Representation in the European Union', *Publius* 26, 1 (1996); John Loughlin, 'Representing

Regions in Europe: the Committee of the Regions' in Charlie Jeffery, ed., *The Regional Dimension of the European Union* (London: Frank Cass & Company, 1997); Michael Keating and John Loughlin, *The Political Economy of Regionalism* (Portland, Ore.: Frank Cass & Company, 1997), 7–11, 28; Michael Keating, *The New Regionalism in Western Europe: Territorial Restructuring and Political Change* (Cheltenham, UK: Edward Elgar, 1998), 78.

12. Lieven De Winter, 'The Volksunie and the Dilemma Between Policy Success and Electoral Survival in Flanders' in Lieven De Winter and Huri Tursan, eds, *Regionalist Parties in Western Europe* (London: Routledge, 1998), 35; Michael Keating, 'Europeanism and Regionalism' in Barry Jones and Michael Keating, eds, *The European Union and the Regions* (Oxford: Clarendon Press, 1998), 7–8; Michael Keating and John Loughlin, *Political Economy of Regionalism*, ch. 4.

13. Zdravko Mlinar, 'Individuation and Globalization: The Transformation of Territorial Social Organization' in Mlinar, ed., *Globalization*, 19–22.

14. Ibid., 28.

15. Ibid.

16. Daniel Bell, *The Coming of the Postindustrial Society* (New York: Basic Books, 1973).

17. Ron Inglehart, *Modernization and Postmodernization: Cultural, Economic and Political Change in Forty-Three Societies* (Princeton: Princeton University Press, 1997), 170.

18. Dermot McCann, 'European Integration and Explanations of Regime Change in Italy', *Mediterranean Politics* 3, 2 (1998): 79–83; Daniela Gobbetti, 'La Lega: Regularities and Innovation in Italian Politics', *Politics and Society* 24, 1 (1996): 57–82; Ilvo Diamanti, *La Lega: geografia, storia e sociologia di un nuovo soggetto politico, nuova edizione* (Rome: Donzelli Editore, 1995).

19. Carlo E. Ruzza and Oliver Schmidtke, 'The Making of the Lombard League', *Telos* 90 (1991): 60–1, 71.

20. Patrizia Messina, 'Opposition in Italy in the 1990s: Local Political Cultures and the Northern League', *Government and Opposition* 33 (1998): 474.

21. See Victor Moioli, *I nuovi razzismi* (Roma: Edizioni associate, 1990); Ilvo Diamanti, *La Lega*, 35–40.

22. François Neilson, 'Structural Conduciveness and Ethnic Mobilization: The Flemish Movement in Belgium', in Susan Olzak and Joanne Negel, eds, *Competitive Ethnic Relations* (Orlando, Florida: Academic Press, 1986); Lieven De Winter, 'The Volksunie', 35; Juan Marcet and Jordi Argelaguet, 'Nationalist Parties in Catalonia' in De Winter and Tursan, eds, *Regionalist Parties*, 79–80.

23. Jean Crête and Guy Lachapelle, 'The Bloc Québécois' in Hugh Thorburn, ed., *Party Politics in Canada*, 7th edn (Scarborough, Ont: Prentice Hall, 1996) 426.

24. Strassoldo, 'Globalism and Localism', 35–6.

25. Ibid., 37–9.

26. Rosenau, *Turbulence in World Politics*.

27. Diamanti, *La Lega*, 102.

28. Mlinar, 'Individuation and Globalization', 16.

29. Marshall McLuhan, *Understanding Media* (Toronto: McGraw-Hill, 1964).

30. Mlinar, 'Individuation and Globalization', 20–22.

31. Snowball sampling involved asking the initial respondents to identify other potential respondents, and sampling from the resulting list. The heads of five provincial sections distributed questionnaires to members in Torino, Cuneo, Varese, Verbania Cusio-Ossola, and Canavese between 27 November 1995 and 2 February 1996. In Quebec, 604 questionnaires were mailed to 73 participating riding presidents between 8 March and 15 April 1996. The riding presidents agreed to complete the survey and distribute the remainder to other party members in their ridings. The response rate was 32 per cent.

32. Karlheinz Reif and Anna Melich, *International Social Science Program National Identity Survey—Countries* (Koeln, Germany: Zentralarchiv fuer empirische Sozialforschung [producer]; Ottawa: Carleton University Survey Research Centre [distributor] 1997).

33. Selected data from 1996 Italian census available on the Web site of the Italian National Statistical Institute: http://www.istat.it/homeing.html.

34. In 1995–96, 36 to 50 million lire was the approximate equivalent of $36,000 to $50,000 Canadian.

35. The 1990 data on bilingualism are reported in James Minahan, *Nations Without States: A Historical Dictionary of Contemporary National Movements* (Westport, NY: Greenwood Press, 1996), 446.

36. Diamanti, *La Lega*, 105.

37. Roberto Biorcio, *Padania Promessa: la storia, le idee e la logica d'azione della Lega Nord* (Milan: il Saggiatore, 1997), 158.

38. Selected 1996 Canadian Census data on population characteristics can be found on the Statistics Canada Web site: http://www.statcan.ca/english/Pgdb/.

39. The 1996 census data for Quebec found that the average incomes for a single-person household was $22,028 and for a two-person household, $45,000.

40. Due to the fragmentation of the Italian Parliament, only the five parties that together won 70 per cent of popular support in the 1996 national elections were included in the analysis. They are, in order: Forza Italia, the Partito Democratico della Sinistra (PDS), the Movimento Sociale Italiano-Alleanza Nazionale (MSI-AN), the Lega Nord, and the Rifondazione Comunista (RC).

41. Each of the relationships presented in the table was controlled for by gender, age, education, income, community size, and urban-rural characteristics. The principal relationships held for respondents in the following categories:

    a) Closeness to Italy: males; respondents aged 35–50; high school education or less; household incomes below survey median of 2.7 million lire; urban residents; cities of 100,001 or more residents.

b) How long have you lived in another country? 51–65-year-olds; incomes above survey median of 2.7 million lire (per month); cities of 100,001 or more residents.

c) Foreigners should not be allowed to buy land: post-secondary education; incomes below survey median; cities of 100,001 or more.

d) One nation or separate state: holds for all statistical controls.

e) Support country even if wrong: females; respondents aged 18–34; primary school education or less; suburban.

f) Immigrants increase crime rates: males and females; respondents aged 18–50; a minimum high school education; all incomes; suburban and rural residents; communities with fewer than 10,000 residents.

g) Immigrants are good for the economy: both sexes; respondents aged 18–34 and 51–65; all education and income categories; communities with 10,001 or more residents.

h) Immigrants take jobs away: both sexes; respondents aged 18–50; all education and income categories; urban and suburban; communities with 10,001 or more residents.

i) Immigration should be increased: both sexes; respondents aged 35–65; all education and income categories; suburban and rural; communities with fewer than 10,001 residents and more than 100,000 residents.

42. The relationships reported here were controlled for by sex, age, education, income, and community type. The principal relationships held for respondents in the following categories:

a) How close do you feel to North America? females; respondents aged 45–64; high school and university graduates; family incomes less than $45,000; city residents.

b) Canada is one nation or should be separate: all gender, age, and income groups; all respondents with more than primary school education; rural, town, and city residents.

c) My country should be supported even if it is wrong: both sexes; respondents aged 35–64; some/completed high school education; incomes less than $25,000 and between $45,000–64,900; city residents.

d) Where did you spend your childhood? some/completed high school; respondents aged 18–24 and 65 and older.

e) How long have you lived in other countries? females; respondents aged 18–24 and 45 and older; some/completed high school; university graduates; family income of $25,000–44,900; city residents.

f) International bodies enforce solutions: relationship disappears with introduction of age controls.

g) Schools should teach more foreign languages: males; respondents aged 25 and older; university graduates; family incomes of less than $25,000 and $65,000 and more; city residents.

h) Foreigners should not be allowed to buy land: relationship disappears with introduction of gender controls.

i) NAFTA has brought benefits to this country: relationship disappears with income controls.

43. The significant relationships reported in this table were controlled for by gender, age, education, income, and community type. The principal relationships held for the following categories:

a) Minorities should preserve their traditions: both sexes; all respondents aged less than 65; all respondents who had a minimum of some high school education; all income groups except for those earning between $25,000 and $44,900; city residents.

b) Immigrants should maintain their traditions/adapt to wider society: both sexes; respondents aged 25 and older; respondents with a minimum of some post-secondary training; incomes between $25,000 and $64,900; city residents.

c) Immigrants increase crime rates: both sexes; respondents aged 25–34 and 45 and older; respondents with a minimum of some high school education; all income groups except those earning between $45,000 and $64,900; city residents.

d) Immigrants are good for the economy: both sexes; respondents aged 25–34 and 65 and older; respondents with a minimum of some high school education; incomes less than $65,000; city residents.

e) Immigrants take jobs away: both sexes; respondents with a minimum of some college education; respondents aged 45–64; incomes over $44,900; city residents.

f) It should be easier for immigrants to get citizenship: males; respondents aged 25 and older; some/completed university education; incomes less than $25,000 and more than $64,900; city residents.

Contributors

MILDRED A. SCHWARTZ is a native of Toronto and a graduate of the University of Toronto and Columbia University. She has also lived and worked in Ottawa, Calgary, and Chicago. After many years of teaching at the University of Illinois in Chicago, where she was a professor in the Departments of Sociology and Political Science, she is now a Visiting Scholar in the Department of Sociology at New York University. Her current interests are represented in the following articles appearing in 2001: 'Continuity Strategies among Political Challengers' in *The American Review of Canadian Studies*; 'Political Parties and NGOs in the NAFTA Debates: Creating Cross Border Ties' in *The International Journal of Political Science*; and 'Factions and the Continuity of Political Protests Movements' in *Social Movements: Identity, Culture and the State*, edited by David Meyer, Nancy Whittier, and Belinda Robnett. She is also editing *Visions of Political Sociology: A Handbook of Theory and Substance* along with Robert R. Alford, Alexander Hicks, and Thomas Janoski.

KEITH ARCHER is Professor of Political Science and Interim Vice-President (Research) at the University of Calgary. His research is in the areas of voting and elections, and the study of political parties in Canada. Recent publications include *Quasi-Democracy: Parties and Leadership Selection in Alberta* (with David Stewart); *Explorations: A Navigator's Guide to Quantitative Analysis in Canadian Political Science* (with Roger Gibbins and Loleen Youngman); *Parameters of Power: Canada's Political Institutions* (with Rainer Knopff, Roger Gibbins, and Leslie A. Pal); and *Political Activists: The NDP in Convention* (with Alan Whitehorn).

HAROLD D. CLARKE is Regents Professor and Chairperson of the Department of Political Science, University of North Texas, Denton, Texas. His research focuses on the political economy of party support and value change in Canada, Great Britain, and the United States.

BARRY COOPER, FRSC, a fourth-generation Albertan, was educated at Shawnigan Lake School, the University of British Columbia, and Duke University (Ph.D. 1969). He taught at several universities in eastern Canada before moving to the University of Calgary in 1981. He has written on Western political philosophy, both classical and contemporary, and on Canadian politics and public policy, attempting to apply the insights of political philosophers to contemporary issues. Most recently he has written *Eric Voegelin and the Foundations of Modern Political Science* (1999) and *Governing in Post-Deficit Times: Alberta during the Klein Years* (2000).

WILLIAM CROSS is Director of the Centre for Canadian Studies and a member of the Department of Political Science at Mount Allison University. He is a co-author of *Rebuilding Canadian Party Politics*. His current research project concerns changing methods of election campaigning.

MUNROE EAGLES is an Associate Professor of Political Science and an Associate Dean for Graduate Studies in the College of Arts & Sciences at the University of Buffalo—The State University of New York. His primary research interests involve the study of electoral geography and comparative politics.

SHAWN HENRY is Director of Advanced Analytics with Environics West. He has been involved in a number of research projects for clients such as TELUS, Petro-Canada, and HomeGrocer.com. He recently completed his Ph.D. in Sociology with a specialization in applied statistics at the University of Calgary, emphasizing logistic regression, clustering, and factor analysis.

HARRY H. HILLER is Professor of Sociology at the University of Calgary. He has a career-long interest in regionalism with a specific focus on Western regional movements, and particularly the Western separatist movement of the early 1980s. He has also done comparative work on regional movements elsewhere, and in particular has published explicit comparisons between Western Australia and western Canada.

DAVID LAYCOCK studied Political Science at the University of Alberta and the University of Toronto. He has taught at the University of Saskatchewan, and since 1989, at Simon Fraser University. He has written on historical and contemporary aspects of populist and third-party politics in Canada, with particular emphasis on their contributions to democratic thought. His most recent book is *The New Right and Democracy in Canada: Understanding Reform and the Canadian Alliance* (Oxford University Press, 2001).

HUDSON MEADWELL is an Associate Professor in the Department of Political Science at McGill University. He writes primarily on nations and nationalism.

JON H. PAMMETT is Professor of Political Science, Carleton University, Ottawa, Canada. His research focuses on the comparative study of voting behaviour and elections in Canada and other mature and newly emerging democracies.

ANTHONY SAYERS is an Associate Professor in the Department of Political Science at the University of Calgary. His research interests include theories of representation, political parties, and federalism. He is the author of *Parties, Candidates and Constituency Campaigns in Canadian Elections* (University of British Columbia Press, 1999) and numerous journal articles.

DAVID K. STEWART is an Associate Professor in the Department of Political Science at the University of Manitoba. His research interests focus on political parties, and he is currently working with Ian Stewart of Acadia University on a study of Maritime political parties and politics.

JENNIFER STEWART recently completed her Ph.D. in Political Science at the University of Calgary. She currently holds a post-doctoral fellowship in Canadian Studies at Mount Allison University.

MARIANNE C. STEWART is Professor of Political Science in the School of Social Sciences, University of Texas at Dallas, Richardson, Texas. Her research concerns the determinants of party support and political participation in Great Britain and other mature democracies.

LIVIANNA TOSSUTTI is an Assistant Professor of Political Science at the University of Calgary, where she teaches courses on political parties, Canadian politics, and research methods. She has published works on ethnic and regional parties in *Party Politics*, *Mediterranean Politics*, and *Italian Politics and Society*. She is currently researching political participation patterns in Britain's Muslim community, and the factors influencing the success of ethnic candidates in Canadian elections.

JOSEPH WEARING is the author of numerous books and articles on Canadian parties and elections. Since becoming professor emeritus of political studies at Trent University, he has also enjoyed the opportunity to engage in pianistic and aquatic pursuits.

LISA YOUNG is an Associate Professor of Political Science at the University of Calgary. She is the author of *Feminists and Party Politics* and co-author of *Rebuilding Canadian Political Parties*. Her current research project is a study of members of the five major Canadian political parties.

Index